Health Promotion in Action

Also by Glenn Laverack

PUBLIC HEALTH: Power, Empowerment and Professional Practice

HEALTH PROMOTION PRACTICE: Building Empowered Communities

HEALTH PROMOTION PRACTICE: Power and Empowerment

Also by Ronald Labonté

POWER, PARTICIPATION AND PARTNERSHIPS

FATAL INDIFFERENCE: The G8 and Global Health (*with T. Schrecker, D. Sanders and W. Meeus*)

HEALTH FOR SOME: Death, Disease and Disparity in a Globalizing World (*with T. Schrecker and A. Sen Gupta*)

CRITICAL PERSPECTIVE IN PUBLIC HEALTH (*co-editor with J. Green*)

Contents

Figures

Boxes

Tables

Foreword

This book presents an ideal companion volume to the 2008 Report from the World Health Organization's Commission on the Social Determinants of Health. An idea central to the Commission's report is that empowered people and communities are much healthier than those that are not. Indeed the Commission drew on the work of one of its members, the Nobel Laureate economist Prof. Amartya Sen, to argue that empowerment is a central social determinant in rich and poor countries alike, and that development goals are unlikely to be met unless empowerment is central to policies and practices. Like many buzz words, empowerment can come to lose its meaning through overuse and simply be a word added to policies and programme plans. In this book it is seen as beginning with community identification of what is needed to improve and sustain health, progressing to the extent of support from government for healthy and redistributive public policy and stretching to the rules and systems of global governance to ensure health and well-being for all. Civil society is envisioned to have a role at each level in lobbying, demanding and fighting for power for those who are disempowered. Labonté and Laverack remind us very clearly that if some people are going to be empowered, then others will be sharing their existing power and giving some of it up. Thus, far from presenting a cosy view of consensus participation happening in romanticised, well-functioning communities, devoid of economic and gender struggles, we are given a perspective on the power struggles that underpin the work of health promoters in whichever arena they work.

Often empowerment is associated primarily with working locally using community development methods. This book challenges this view and demonstrates unequivocally that health promotion does indeed involve local empowerment but is equally concerned with national and global power and that each level is intimately connected. Stories, rooted in communities, tell of the working and family lives of poor people and show the extent to which the tentacles of economic globalisation reach into everyday experience. These stories make a compelling case that effective health promoters have to understand the broad context that affects the lives of people with whom they work. This is a far cry from the early days of health promotion when the most important understanding health promoters were expected to have was of the various theories of behaviour change. The social theories woven through this book provide the twenty-first-century health promoter with a picture of the grand narrative that shapes health and well-being in our modern communities.

Acting locally and thinking globally has been an important mantra for many concerned with social justice. A step further than this is the concept of 'glocalisation' which describes how health promoters can combine action that link the two. This book provides ample tools which are designed to break the process of empowerment down into stages, build capacity and to analyse the blocks to empowerment. These tools are essential because, despite three decades of evidence about the lack of effectiveness of behaviour change methods, when they are not backed up by a strong policy framework to change the environments within which people make their lifestyle choices, many health departments and agencies still invest most resource in direct attempts to change behaviour (Baum, 2008). This is because doing so has a beguilingly simple logic: the behaviour leads to ill-health; so persuading people directly to change their behaviour must be the most efficient and effective way to reduce illness. But diseases are caused by a complex interaction of factors and behaviours, which while playing a part in many, are generally well down the list in terms of percentage contribution. By far, and by way, the most crucial list of causes are those driven by social and economic determinants. The fact that in some African countries life expectancies are in the thirties while in the best performing countries of the world they are in the eighties, or that Indigenous people in Australia live 17 years less than their non-Indigenous counterparts, owes very little to behaviours other than such behaviours being an expression of the broader structural factors driving the opportunities for health. Labonté and Laverack deftly explore the connections between life circumstances, social and economic structures and the concept of empowerment. They examine the borders and terrains that connect powerlessness to power and reveal very clearly that a more equal world will not come about without a struggle of ideologies. This examination is situated in the dynamics of our globalised twenty-first-century world and, despite its complexities, it is made to seem possible that health promotion can come to play a central role in working for a more equitable distribution of health.

The Commission on the Social Determinants of Health has, since its establishment by the World Health Organization in 2005, determined that its legacy would be more than a report (CSDH, 2008). It has recognised that a vibrant social movement involving civil society, academics, public servants and others will be required to bring about the changes it will recommend. This movement is already gaining momentum through the activities of civil society groups such as the People's Health Movement. This book is an essential handbook for that movement.

Fran Baum
Professor of Public Health
Flinders University, Adelaide Australia
Co-Chair, People's Health Movement Steering Council
Commissioner, Commission on the Social Determinants of Health

Acknowledgements

The authors would like to thank the many people with whom they have had the privilege of working and exchanging ideas during the preparation of this book. In particular, Elizabeth Vendetti and Jessica Melnik-Gavreau for assistance in the final preparation of the manuscript, Dr Tim Tenbensel for his insights into health policy and the late Dr Eberhard Wenzel for his passionate belief in the importance of health promoters confronting the global even while strengthening their work on the local.

Ronald Labonté would like to thank all participants in the Globalisation Knowledge Network for the insights they brought to global health, only some of which are reflected in this book; and his partner, Lisa Coy, for her usual long-suffering tolerance.

Glenn Laverack would like to thank his family – Elizabeth, Ben, Holly and Rebecca – for their continued support, love and understanding.

Introduction: Localising the Global

> The average plate of food eaten in western industrial food-importing nations is likely to have travelled 2,000 miles from source to plate. Each one of those miles contributes to the environmental and social crises of our times.
>
> (Bello 2002)

In a Canadian city, a ghettoising enclave of high-rise apartments holds thousands of poor families on social assistance allowances. Most are single-parent families. Most live well below the poverty line. Most cannot afford healthy food. If they could, they would first have to weave their way past convenience stores selling high fat, salt, carbohydrate and sugar processed foods offering cheap but unhealthy bursts of energy. A stalwart group of single mothers decides that they have had enough of being preached to about nutrition. They have as good an understanding of what is better and worse for themselves and their children as most non-poor households. They're clear: It's about access. It's about affordability. It's about exerting control over their environments. They start a community garden which, in turn, starts a small movement in low-income neighbourhoods across the country. The garden, though, is only minimally about the food. It is primarily about the capacity that it creates: the empowering experience of negotiating successfully, and from a position of agency, with all the authorities and individual professionals whose 'gaze' of regulatory watchfulness has been so disabling in the past.

For some in the group, the garden is an organising tool best used to mobilise more political activism against welfare retrenchment and income inadequacies. For others, the sense of control and coherence so important to the experience of health exists in the simple act of tending

1

their tomatoes. For the health promoters involved, their role is one of opening the communicative channels between the women and the state agencies that have the resources the women need, and supporting the legitimacy of the women's claims to these resources.

In a British city, a health promoter starts another community garden. It is on the outskirts of the city where the relatively poor have been pushed by the global inflation of inner-city property values. The garden is large, requires a sizeable volunteer group to maintain, and produces a harvest substantial enough to fill about half the participants' food needs during the growing season. Negotiating with state authorities for the space and resources was less of a concern than developing the farming skills of the volunteer group. With prescient foresight (this garden project took place in the early 1990s) the health promoter's concern with healthier food knowledge and access was incidental. Her primary concerns were with reducing the carbon footprint of the globalised food industry by localising production on an expanding scale, and increasing the public reservoir of food production knowledge. Growing one's own, she surmised, would soon become less of a hobby and more of a political and survival imperative.

Two gardens. Two health promotion endeavours. Two quite different frames in which very similar activities locate the contemporary health promotion challenges of local empowerment in a globalising era.

The first approach works from the inside-out, seeking healthful change one marginalised person and one harvest at a time. Its politics are local, its interest in broader social movements incidental or, at best, secondary. It embodies health promotion's aphorism of health being grounded in the environments (settings) in which 'people live, work and play'. It is successful, in part, because the local is where people meet face-to-face and the power inequalities that underpin most health inequalities can be met, eye-to-eye. Human decency is easier to honour when it is a person next to you and not an abstracted category of 'welfare recipient', 'senior bureaucrat' or 'corporate executive'. It is successful, in other part, because the local is largely irrelevant to the machinations of global commerce, market integration and the national politics that both enable and are constrained by it. Community development, described by one South American health worker, was a favoured idea promoted by the international financial institutions (the World Bank and International Monetary Fund) during the worst days of structural adjustment they imposed on that continent. Why? 'It took attention away from what our governments were being forced to do to get the loans to pay their international debts', the health worker explained, 'that they had to cut public spending, sell off their assets, de-regulate their economies and open themselves up to foreign trade and investors. The idea of community development gave the impression that communities had both the responsibility and the power to make things good for everyone. Perhaps they should have the responsibility, but they do not have the power.' (Personal communication, Pan-American Health Organisation International Conference on Health Promotion 1992).

Therein lays the seed of the second approach, one that works from the outside-in. The outside is the health promoter's analysis of contemporary globalisation and its particular impact on both local economics and local food. This analysis is well-founded. As economic globalisation continues its sweep and deepens across the planet, food insecurity is rising, food control is monopolising and diets globally are in unhealthy transition. There is also a small but growing 'glocalisation' movement ('think globally, act locally') promoting the importance of the 100-mile diet (to consume food only produced within a 100-mile radius) – something obviously much easier to achieve in environments conducive to long growing and harvest seasons.

The first approach is inherently optimistic and utopian in reach, assuming that small step-wise change can eventually build a future most people desire. The second approach is intrinsically pessimistic and dystopian in grasp, embedding within it the probability of an imminent future of economic and ecological collapse. The first forecasts how the world should be and works backwards to how we might get there. The second extends present trends into a future and creates defensive strategies to cope. Both are methods variously embraced by health promotion and public health. Neither is right nor wrong.

Where both approaches falter is in their emphasis on the local. The local remains vitally important to health and will continue to dominate health promoters' work. That is one reason why half of this book reviews approaches to local empowerment that have been tried and tested, both theoretically and empirically. But the local, whether seen as a world capable unto itself or as a small domain increasingly constrained by worldwide forces, is an insufficient terrain for health promotion work. That is why another half of this book assesses the state of knowledge about how globalisation is affecting peoples' health, and the possibilities for health promotion's engagement with it.

Where both approaches excel is in their emphasis on empowerment, the development of peoples' capacities to exercise greater control over important aspects of their environments. Power, defined simply as the capacity to create or resist change, but examined more critically in

Chapter 2, is a recurring theme in human life, from its expression in interpersonal relationships to its various practices in political and economic life. It is also one of the more important determinants of peoples' health, whether regarded as the psychological experiences of control or analysed as the social organisation of communities, societies and economies which creates and distributes risks and vulnerabilities among different population groups.

An overview of the book

Chapter 1. Health promotion: Concepts and context

In Chapter 1 we define the key concepts in health promotion including health, equity and empowerment. We discuss the different roles that health promotion practitioners have and the tensions that they face in their everyday work. We help to set this within a historical context of the development of health promotion up to the present.

Chapter 2. Health promotion practice: Power, empowerment and the social determinants of health

Chapter 2 discusses how power and empowerment are central to health promotion. We unpack the concepts of 'community' and 'community empowerment' and discuss why these remain important to the role of the health promotion practitioner. We discuss the competencies and ethics health promoters require for empowering work, and review the link between health promotion and the social determinants of health and the politics of policies affecting health equity.

Chapter 3. Pathways to local empowerment

Chapter 3 provides clarity to the theme of local empowerment and its strategic pathways. In particular, this chapter discusses the continuum of empowerment as the key pathway through which individuals, groups and communities can gain more power-over social and political influence. The discussion then goes further to examine the role of health activism as a legitimate means of local empowerment.

Chapter 4. Working to build empowerment: The local challenge

Chapter 4 maintains our focus on the local level, and introduces five key steps to build local empowerment within health promotion programmes using case study material to illustrate each area: engaging communities, establishing partnerships, building capacity, influencing health policy and evaluating empowerment.

Chapter 5. Pathways from the local to the global

Chapter 5 brings to the discussion the link between the local and the global. An explanation of globalisation within the context of health promotion is developed, noting how processes of globalisation can impinge on the health of people at the local level. We identify who are the 'winners and losers' in an increasingly globalised world and what potential roles exist for health promotion practitioners in reshaping globalisation in a healthier direction.

Chapter 6. Working to build empowerment: The global challenge

In Chapter 6 we examine five different discourses in which globalisation and health have been framed and how they compete for political influence. The five discourses are health as security, development, public good, commodity and human right. Each health discourse has both limitations and strategic use, but the greatest global challenge to each is the imperative of a more equitable global resource distribution towards health.

Chapter 7. Glocalisation: Health promotion's next grand challenge?

Chapter 7 brings together the key themes of the book in an assessment of two competing ideas on how to create better global health and sustainability: relocalising the economy and democratising global governance. We discuss the principles and policy-specific interventions that could reframe a pathological economic globalisation to one premised on promoting health, reducing poverty and preventing climate change and natural resource depletion. We conclude with a reflection on the implications for health promoters, and for their efforts to engage in an empowering practice in the context of globalisation.

1
Health Promotion: Concepts and Context

> All diseases have two causes: one pathological, the other political.
>
> (Aphorism attributed to the nineteenth-century public health activist Rudolf Virchow)

The meaning of health promotion remains dynamically ambiguous. In the words of the Ottawa Charter for Health Promotion (World Health Organization 1986), 'health promotion is the process of enabling people to increase control over, and to improve, their health.' A recent content analysis of the most influential health promotion definitions in the literature found that their major discriminating feature was indeed 'the extent to which it involves the process of enabling or empowering communities' (Rootman et al. 2001). O'Neill and Stirling (2007) usefully characterise this as health promotion's discursive meaning, its broad penumbra of 'the promotion of health' within which its more organised set of practices occurs. These organised practices, in turn, are defined by Green and Kreuter as 'any planned combination of educational, political, regulatory and organizational supports for actions and conditions of living conducive to the health of individuals, groups or communities' (Green & Kreuter 2005). If the fulminating Ottawa Charter definition is the idealised 'what', the more technocratic approach to planned change is the pragmatic 'how'.

In the 20 years since the Ottawa Charter, no health promotion declaration has as succinctly and evocatively laid out the field of practice. The Charter identified five foci of the health promoter's work:

1. Develop personal skills (whether traditional forms of lifestyle health education or working with marginalised groups to increase their level of political analysis)

2. Create supportive environments (from the esteem-building support of small groups to 'making healthy choices the easy choices' in the numerous 'settings', such as schools and workplaces, in which people spend much of their time)
3. Strengthen community action (a defining ethos of health promotion, one already captured in our introductory garden stories)
4. Build healthy public policy (the locus of intersectoral or 'whole of government' work, the target of community and professional advocacy initiatives and the lever through which health equity among groups is achieved)
5. Reorient health services (to better balance the resources for health promotion work with that of curative medicine, and to improve health systems' understanding of their roles to improve health)

These five foci, along with the Charter's three strategies of 'enable, mediate and advocate', have an almost iconic stature in health promotion work in many parts of the world. Later chapters will review some simplified models that capture the panorama of practice the Charter portrays. While these five health promotion foci are usually interpreted as local or, at best, national responsibilities, we will also see how they apply at global levels of action.

Health, equity (social justice) and empowerment

Of the many concepts that inform this book, three are basic: health, equity (and its corollary, social justice) and empowerment. Below we offer some initial thoughts on how we approach their meaning.

There is no shortage of attempts to define health, from the World Health Organization's classic, 'a state of complete physical, mental and social well-being and not merely the absence of disease and infirmity' (World Health Organization 1946); to the Ottawa Charter's emphasis on its being 'a resource for everyday life' (World Health Organization 1986); to the Bangkok Charter's qualification of it as 'a determinant of quality of life . . . encompassing mental and spiritual well-being' (World Health Organization 2005). There are also the more traditional medical definitions which emphasise normal physical functions. Astute readers will notice circularity in all of these definitions: health is well-being, but what is well-being if not also health? As for health being normal functioning, who defines normal and how? These are troubling issues for the results-based approach to 'investing in health', the title of the globally influential 1993 World Bank report on health sector reform (World Bank 1993) which championed a selective approach to health care based on narrowly prescribed cost–benefit analyses. This is also why so much of the accounting in health systems remains dominated by what can be counted: death and disease (mortality and morbidity).

The important elements of the concept of health that we might take from these definitions are (1) perception and meaning (health is as much what is experienced as what can be measured), (2) social relations (health is embedded in human networks and interactions), (3) capacities/capabilities (health is a product of many intrinsic and extrinsic resources) and (4) physical functioning (health is embodied and not simply imagined).

Equity, in turn and as applied to health, is a normative judgement of what is fair. It differs from equality, a measure of 'sameness', although the terms are often used interchangeably. This is particularly so in the UK, where health inequality has become synonymous with health inequity. In stricter terms, a health inequity is a difference (an inequality) in health (however measured) that is significant in size and number of people affected, preventable through policy or other intervention and not an effect of freely chosen risk. A major concern of health promoters is social inequities that reside in the structures of society, creating systematic differences in health outcomes between different population groups. Examples of these include gender differences that arise from patriarchal norms or discrimination; class differences that arise from inequalities in wealth, power and ownership/control of capital; and geographic differences that arise from higher exposures to risk or less access to remediable care or preventive resources.

Underpinning the concept of equity is that of social justice. There are several theories of social justice with different implications for equity. The two major theories differ in their emphasis on means or ends: equality of opportunity or equality of outcome. The first, and politically dominant, theory holds to the importance of ensuring that everyone 'plays by the same rules' – there is no discrimination. Fairness is judged by equality in process. The second, and politically challenging, theory holds to the importance of ensuring that rules work to minimise preventable differences in outcomes between the players. It discriminates positively in favour of those groups that start the 'game' of social and economic life with fewer resources, since equal rules for unequal players will always produce unequal results. While fairness in process is important, health promotion's concern with preventable differences in health outcomes aligns its ethics more closely to the second theory of justice (Labonté 2000; Laverack 2004).

Empowerment, in a related fashion, has two grammatical variants. The first variant is the term's use as a transitive verb, as in 'we shall empower this or that group'. This common use may be well intended. It also recognises that there are real differences in certain forms of power that exist between groups and that may contribute to health inequities. But there are two limitations to this use of the word. The first limitation is that it renders people as objects of the health promoter's work, rather than as people capable of acting in their own right. It also masks from view the power that people might already possess. The second limitation is that it implies a purpose: empower to do what? The 'what' is often whatever the health promoter or her agency considers an important health problem. Despite decades of acknowledging such social determinants of health as poverty, unemployment or poor housing, health problems often end up being defined as a behavioural risk: smoking, obesity, substance abuse. This is not empowerment, but subtle coercion. The second variant of empowerment's use is as an intransitive verb. In this construction, people cannot 'be empowered' by others; they can only empower themselves by acquiring more of power's different forms. This requires a careful understanding of the different forms or practices of power, especially those that health promoters and their agencies might possess and that can be made available to be taken up and used by others (Labonté 1993a, 1998; Laverack 2003). The distinction in these two meanings is subtle yet important; we return to it, with examples, in Chapter 2.

Health promotion roles

Health promotion has struggled to define itself as a discipline or profession. It continues to do so, with arguments advanced in favour (e.g., providing quality assurance, legitimacy within health systems, practice standards) and against (e.g., limiting practice scope, professionalising for self-interest). There are, certainly, skills or competencies demanded of health promotion work, and useful efforts have been made to codify some of these. But in most countries health remains more a 'field of practice' than a distinct profession (O'Neill & Stirling 2007), the boundaries of which are not static. Neither are the issues, groups or institutions within the field and with whom practitioners might engage.

This does not mean that the roles health promoters assume in this field of practice are endless or complex. Their broad nomenclatures are fairly straightforward and can be characterised as follows:

1. Educator/watchdog: A combination of increasing public awareness of health determining behavioural, social and environmental conditions, and monitoring those conditions for their effects on health status.

2. Resource broker: Making internal resources (personnel, finances, material goods) more readily available to groups working on health determinants, whether or not these actions are undertaken in the name of health.
3. Community developer: Supporting community group organisation and action on health determinants, through dedicated community development/empowerment and competent health promotion staff and programmes.
4. Partnership development: Engaging in joint programming and policy development work, locally, regionally and provincially, with those in the public, private and civil society sectors with a 'stake' in health determinants.
5. Advocate/catalyst: Developing and advocating statements on policy options that influence health determinants, especially to more senior government levels (Labonté et al. 1998).

Health promotion tensions

Each of the above-mentioned roles is also riddled with tensions. This should not be surprising if we accept health promotion as an empowering practice aimed at reducing health inequities. The reason is simple: health promoters usually work for state or state-funded agencies, a social location of presumed neutrality in a far-from-neutral set of social power struggles.

Consider, first, the modern state. There are many competing theories: libertarian or neoliberal theories of the state as intruding on individual freedoms, critical theories of the state acting on behalf of elite-class interests, pluralist theories of the state as a neutral broker between competing interest groups, institutionalism theories of the state as creating its own organisational patterns of thought and behaviour and ossifying into them and feminist theories of the state as embodying patriarchal norms and practices. We are agnostic on which of these is most revelatory for health promotion practice. All contain analytical elements of usefulness.

What remains an essential feature of the state, however rendered, is that it bridges relationships that are shaped by economic markets (producer/consumer, owner/worker, creditor/debtor) with those that are formed in day-to-day living (our identities as parents, group members, hobbyists, neighbours, churchgoers). These latter relations are often short-handed as 'community' or, when more formally organised, as civil society, which the London School of Economics (2006) usefully defines as

the arena of un-coerced collective action around shared interests, purposes and values. In theory, its institutional forms are distinct from those of the state, family and market, though in practice, the boundaries between state, civil society, family and market are often complex, blurred and negotiated. Civil society commonly embraces a diversity of spaces, actors and institutional forms, varying in their degree of formality, autonomy and power. Civil societies are often populated by organisations such as registered charities, development non-governmental organisations, community groups, women's organisations, faith-based organisations, professional associations, trade unions, self-help groups, social movements, business associations, coalitions and advocacy groups.

Markets, and the relationships they create, are inherently 'disequalising', in that they create inequalities between groups in income, power and health. States intervene in markets, in part, to reduce their level of inequalities, preserve social order and smooth economic functioning. Different countries, people and political parties hold differing beliefs over the depth of such intervention and the degree of inequalities that might still be considered 'fair', with implications for health equity, as we will see in Chapter 2. People in civil society, as citizens, in turn, often pressure states for different interventions into the market, either calling for less or more depending on their particular ideology or position of economic privilege. In sum, there are inherent tensions, or what social theorists call contradictions, in the relationships between all three of the principal domains – state, market, civil society – that condition our social lives and, in large measure, our health. The German sociologist Claus Offe (1984) usefully draws attention to the strained role these contradictions create for the state. On the one hand, the state requires the market to generate the wealth from which it derives the revenue for its functioning. On the other, the state requires the legitimacy of its citizenry in all their diverse voices and demands that cause it to grate constantly against the interests of those prospering most from the market. The citizenry itself is often contradictory: how often do we hear demands for more public services and demands for lower taxes, as if the two are unrelated? The crisis in governance that this contradiction creates has worsened in our modern era of globalisation.

For now, we explore how these inherent tensions in a more mundane fashion affect each of the five simply cast health promotion roles.

Educator/watchdog

There are two tensions in this role. First, what do we watch? We've already noted that despite years of acknowledging the importance of social determinants of health, most health promotion attention remains devoted to behavioural risk factors. Rather than change social structures, a risky endeavour for those working in state organisations, we focus on changing individuals. This is not unimportant work, merely insufficient. The 'field of practice' has improved in this respect, with increasing attention given to the contexts that shape peoples' behaviours, for example, the tobacco or food industry and not just smokers or unhealthy food choices. Health systems now also give greater attention to monitoring and commenting upon the social determinants of health. But, as this chapter concludes, health promotion's actual efforts on these determinants remain marginal.

This leads us to the second tension: what do we do with what we watch? There remains a tendency in health promotion practice to default to what we characterise as the 'education and awareness paradigm': To improve health, create a pamphlet. To really improve health, create a poster and a mobile information unit. To be digitally astute, use all the resources of the Internet to tell people what they should do to keep healthy. Even as we embrace in our work the sweep of social and environmental determinants, we complain that the real reason there is so little action on them is that 'people just don't understand'. Our role is thus to teach the poor, the unemployed, the marginalised, the discriminated or the underserved that the conditions they experience are what are making them sick. We suggest that most people know this already, even if their concern is not expressed as an overwhelming desire to reduce their higher-than-population-average burden of disease. If there is education to be done about the social determinants of health, it is more likely to be with those who dominate economic markets or manage public finances, and for whom some studies show indifference, for example, towards using public policy levers to reduce economic causes of health inequities (Lavis et al. 2003).

Resource broker

There are two key tensions that play out in the role of resource broker. The first is having resources to broker, which requires that they be ring-fenced or clearly segmented from those dealing with health care. Otherwise, the seemingly ceaseless health care cost demands driven by technology, aging, media and, in the case of drug therapies, globalised patent rules could consume all of health systems' budgets. The second tension is the need to apply an equity stratifier to who gets the resources. Even staff time constitutes a resource, inasmuch as a programme or service made available at no private cost becomes an economic subsidy to whoever receives it. The 'inverse care law' is as alive and well in health promotion work as it is in utilisation of medical care. The inverse care law, first formulated by Julian Tudor Hart (1971) to describe the UK

National Health Service, describes how those with least medical need (the affluent) tend to use a disproportionately greater amount of public health services than those with greatest medical need (the poor). In health promotion, the inverse care law functions when wellness programmes attract the more affluent or maternal/child health programmes fail to attract the poorest, or when most of our investment goes into behaviour change programmes that past research finds is much more successful with the middle- and higher-income strata (Baum & Harris 2006). This does not mean these efforts should cease. State programmes that are universally accessible (open to everyone) gain longer-term and broader cross-class support than those that are targeted only to the most needy. Neither is there a simple algorithm to determine how health promotion resources should be allocated. But if we hold to the justice norm of greater equality in outcome, the first question posed in any new resource decision should be: How will this reduce the health gap between top and bottom, by raising the bottom nearer to the top?

Community developer

Tensions in community development as an empowering health promotion practice are among the best known and most discussed in the literature. We have already identified a key one in our Introduction's gardening stories: the localisation of political and economic determinants of health inequities at a level of social organisation that lacks the power and resources to tackle these effectively. Elsewhere we have called this a form of 'community-blaming' and have been critical of the simplistic idealisation of the community sometimes found in health promotion writings (Labonté 1993b).

Another basic tension exists between community development as community-based programming, where we regard the community as a setting in which to launch our education and awareness activities aimed at usually quantifiable programme outputs. And community development as empowerment, in which we act on issues of group interest, and an increase in their generic capacities is of greatest concern. There is a sense, though, in which this is a false-practice dichotomy. A community-based programme can be an entry into a community empowerment project, and community empowerment projects often incorporate community-based programmes. Extending from the Introduction's garden stories, health promoters might start with a nutrition education programme in a low-income community, because that is where greatest initial support lies, and then find themselves working with local coalitions to change social assistance rules to make it easier for welfare recipients to afford healthier foods. They might even participate in networks dealing with inequitable aspects of the global food trade. But health promoters could as easily start with such a coalition, or with community gardens and food-buying clubs, if that is where organising momentum lies. At some point they will likely find themselves invited to offer nutrition education programmes. What remains of this practice tension is how well the health systems support health promoters in their abilities to move fluidly between these two working styles.

Partnership development

For some years health promotion has accepted the necessity of engaging with other sectors, particularly if it is to influence actions on the broader determinants of health. The legacy of Western rationalism and evolution of the modern state have left it with a bewildering, and at times multiplying, number of 'sectors'. If we add to this the divergent claims of civil society organisations and the influence of private business interest groups, the tensions in partnership development are self-apparent. A more specific complaint sometimes lodged against health promotion's efforts to engage in managing these partnership tensions has been one of 'public health imperialism': a recasting of all social and environmental concerns as health promotion issues in an effort to gather diverse partners under the umbrella of 'health'. Given the large size of the public health sector in most high-income countries, relative to education, welfare, housing, environment or justice, these colonising overtures have been viewed with distrust. The following story illustrates this point: A few years ago a lecturer of health promotion teaching in a school of social work complained that he had a hard time convincing his social work students that they were really doing health promotion. His students replied that they had an equally hard time convincing health promoters they were really doing social work. The point here is simply that health promotion is not the only practice, nor health the only sector, that has discovered the need to collaborate with others. But we all share a rather pre-Copernican view of the world in which we analyse and plan our activities by placing ourselves at the centre and then orbiting everyone else around us. The rich literature on effective partnerships identifies a simple preventive: always place the problem in the centre and circle the important sectors, disciplines and partners around it.

Advocate/catalyst

This brings us to the last and most problematic health promotion strategy: that of advocacy. It is something health promoters frequently advocate for doing more of, but not much else. For in becoming advocates around policies for health and its determinants, we run straight into the jaws of politics. While not without risk, it is still relatively safe for health promoters and their state employers to challenge a single industry such as tobacco, but not the disequalising logic of global market capitalism itself. Why has the health-promoting cause of early childhood development captured governments' agendas in ways that poverty reduction has not? There are practical reasons: clarity of the policy message and convenient and market-ready slogans. But perhaps most importantly, early childhood development represents a health inequity whose remedy is not deeply structural or challenging in the same way as reducing income inequalities might be (Lavis 2002). Indeed, programmatic interventions often consist of an outpouring of small-scale pilot projects that fail to deal with the political and economic policies that lead to the family poverty that creates unhealthy development environments in the first place. It is ironic that Canada, a country that has played such a prominent role in the rhetoric of both health promotion and early childhood development, has failed singularly to use its tax/transfer programmes to reduce significantly child poverty rates, despite resolving in its parliament repeatedly to do so.

International evidence suggests that policies known to reduce health inequities are more likely to be supported by social democratic political parties than by conservative or libertarian ones (Navarro et al. 2004). This should not be surprising since such policies hinge more on a belief in the importance of a strong, regulatory and redistributive state than on the beneficence of the market's invisible hand. The tense discomfort this can create for health promoters is obvious. On the one hand, a health promotion policy platform will only survive if it is consistently lobbied on a non-partisan, all-party basis. On the other, health promotion that ignores where partisan political support exists for its work is unlikely to win any reforms in the policies that may matter most to greater equity in health outcomes.

Setting the historical context

Given health promoters' social position straddling state and civil society, these tensions are unlikely to be resolved; they are merely being grappled with. Their grappling is what provides much of the dynamism of health promotion practice, although not always comfortably. Neither are these tensions particularly new, including even the concern with empowerment.

The concept of local empowerment as a means to improve health dates back to at least the mid-nineteenth century in the UK. The political liberalism of the Victorian period led to the creation of many pressure groups, such as the Health of Towns Association, which shared concerns of the people about equity and social justice and acted as advocacy groups. These concerns arose, in part, from the dramatic dislocations, inequalities and appalling living and working conditions that accompanied rapid industrialisation. These pressure groups, with the assistance of key reformers within state institutions, mobilised broader middle-class support, which in turn, influenced the press and the political arm of government. The result was a series of new legislation aimed at curbing the worse of these conditions and enabling, for the first time, specialised local health boards to intervene to control the spread of disease. Often referred to as the 'sanitation phase', this period marked the birth of public health. Much has been written drawing similarities between this era of 'old' public health and that of the 'new' public health of the past three decades (Baggot 2000). These parallels include a concern with the social and environmental determinants of disease, political activism on the part of health reformers, the existence of social movements pressing for economic and social reform,notably unions and women's groups, and strategic linkages between health reformers and these progressive social movements.

There is also evidence of tension. Edwin Chadwick, the 'father' of public health whose 1848 Public Health Act ushered in local health boards, was a staunch advocate of the miasma theory of illness, which held that certain decaying matters in the air – created disease. The list seems strange to us today and included corpses in water along with coffee grinds and beached whales, though no reference was made to the sickly dense fog of coal-fired industrialisation. At the time evidence favouring the 'germ' theory was mounting, but this theory was opposed by the merchant class from which Chadwick required political support and among whom his own career had placed him (Ringen 1979). Had the germ theory prevailed it would have meant more regulation, including quarantine, on the global trade in goods upon which much of the wealth of the merchant class relied. There is also evidence that some of the local health boards were dominated by industrialists and merchants, who ensured that nothing was done in the name of health that might compromise their accumulation of wealth. This is a script now being played out at a much grander scale in the politics of trade treaties and the World Trade Organisation.

Other reformers took a more radical approach to grappling with the tensions of their social position. As Chadwick was manoeuvring his

Public Health Act through British parliament, Rudolf Virchow, a passionate germ theorist, famously prescribed the 'cure' for a typhoid epidemic among Silesian coal miners: improved working conditions, free education, food cooperatives, better pay, public works programmes for temporarily unemployed miners, strengthened local government and, to pay for these reforms, a tax on the nouveaux riche whose wealth relied upon the miners' labour. Unhealthy conditions, he argued, were the breeding grounds for epidemics; he also noted that all diseases had two causes: one pathological, the other political. Dissatisfied with his proposals, the government officials dismissed him. He immediately joined in street protests, ran successfully for local government and eventually became a powerful reformer within national government (Taylor & Reiger 1985). A few years earlier, in the same tumultuous era, John Snow undertook what today would be called a rudimentary cluster analysis of a cholera outbreak in a poor London neighbourhood, deducing that it centred on a shared water pump in Broad Street. Lacking certainty of proof, Snow nonetheless one night simply banged the handle off the pump, ending the cholera outbreak. Unlike Virchow he was richly rewarded with a monetary prize for his public health risk-taking.

Reform actions by British and other European governments during the mid-nineteenth century were not simply an effect of public health and civil society activism. They were also motivated by a need to improve the efficiency of their nation's workforce. Public health reform was as much due to the demands of economic production as it was due to a discourse of empowerment and good governance. This recurs today when health promotion or the costs of strategic medical or public health interventions are defended, in part, for the economic savings or growth returns they promise.

From biomedicine to health behaviourism

The germ theory eventually triumphed over competing explanatory discourses. This triumph heralded the twentieth-century dominance of biomedicine. Its close elision with industrial capitalism (body-as-machine, medicine-as-business), the promise of cure reducing the need to attend to economically meddlesome forms of prevention, helped (Brown 1979): although it was the antibiotic era that clinched its status.

The biomedical era continued to dominate until the 1960s and 1970s, when the growing costs of publicly funded health care collided with one of capitalism's cyclical crises of too much supply, too little demand and a declining rate of profit. This led to market pressures on the state

Box 1.1   Health education or health promotion?

The debate about the overlap between health promotion and health education began in the 1980s, when the range of activities involved in promoting better health widened to overcome the narrow focus on lifestyle and behaviour approaches. These activities involved more than just giving information and aimed for strategies that achieved political action and social mobilisation. Whereas health education aims at informing people to influence their future decision making, health promotion incorporates complementary social and political actions. These include lobbying and community development that facilitate political changes in peoples' social, workplace and community settings to enhance health (Green & Kreuter 1991). Health education around obesity issues might include school-based awareness programmes or exercise classes. Health promotion around obesity extends to legislation on food advertising and restricting access to unhealthy products in school shops. While in some countries, such as the USA, health education and health promotion still tend to be used interchangeably, health promotion is generally viewed as encompassing health education as one of its many roles.

to lessen taxation and liberalise the economy, which in turn fuelled government interest to find ways to reduce the fiscal pressure of rising medical care costs. At the same time, the 'epidemiological transition' in high-income countries was complete: few infectious diseases remained as threats, and chronic degenerative illnesses (heart disease, cancer, autoimmune disorders) had become the major causes of morbidity and mortality. These chronic diseases involve the interplay of different behavioural risk factors over time such as smoking, lack of exercise and a poor diet and have become synonymous with a 'healthy lifestyle'. The search for genetic explanation had yet to commence, and few were discussing the role poverty or hazardous environments played in creating disease. Health education to modify unhealthy behaviours became the principle public health intervention, slowly expanding to a broader policy focus to influence the economic and cultural forces that pattern unhealthy behaviours. As with the biomedical approach, however, there was little room for concerns with local empowerment and social equity. Many critics of this early phase in the transition from health education to health promotion in the 1970s to 1980s (see Box 1.1) cited the tendency of practice to focus on individuals in ways that became victim-blaming (Brown & Margo 1978; Freudenberg 1978; Labonté & Penfold 1981). The confluence of state interests in medical cost containment, the rise of chronic disease with more scope for prevention and the emergence of powerful new social movements nonetheless created a fertile ground for a 'new' public health embrace of 'old' public health activism.

Health promotion on the ascendancy

The maturing of many of these progressive movements during the 1960s and 1970s played a marked role in the reconceptualisation of health promotion during the 1980s, at least in high-income countries. There are differing theories of social movements. Some emphasise their discursive role in changing how problems are framed and politics debated (Melucci 1989), while others emphasise their role in mobilising resources to become political competitors in policy change (Freeman 1983); without large organised civil society groups in these discursive fields, there would be little pressure to change state–market relations. Differences in these theories attest to new tensions: is empowerment a contest over meaning or a struggle over material resources? It is both, of course, and finding a balance between them is a central theme of this book. What is important here is recognition of the role social movements played, and continue to play, in challenging the medical and behavioural approaches to health by raising concerns for equity, justice and environmental sustainability. The most recent social movement reframing how we think about health, and one of the reasons for this book, is the one erroneously labelled 'anti-globalisation' and which might better be called the 'just globalisation' movement.

The knowledge challenges created by social movements entered public health and health promotion thinking through a process described by Ron Eyerman, a sociologist, and Andrew Jamison, an academic interested in social and political policy, as 'cognitive praxis' (Eyerman & Jamison 1991). Their argument is that the discursive reframing of societal images and identities that forms part of social movement activism shifts fields of practice via 'movement intellectuals'. These movement intellectuals, in the mode of activists like Virchow, drift from organisations to positions within the state, taking with them their new movement ideas. Others already in the state incorporate these new knowledge challenges in various policies, declarations and state documents. Some movement intellectuals shift into academia, influencing new generations of practitioners and creating new practice theories. An early reflection on how the Ottawa

Charter came to be, and why it had the impact it did, found the ideas of cognitive praxis and movement intellectuals compelling explanation (Pederson et al. 1994; Labonté 1994a). For a period of time, the mid-1980s to the mid-1990s, health promotion was on a discursive ascendancy. While practice lagged behind its preaching, there was a powerful and empowered sense of momentum and optimism.

This sense was not restricted to high-income countries alone, although these were the first to embrace the Ottawa Charter. Internationally, the World Health Assembly in 1977 set a target of 'health for all by the year 2000', a utopian quest that became operational in the following year's UNICEF/WHO conference in Alma Ata in the former USSR Kazak Republic. The much higher burden of infectious disease in many of the world's poorer nations, and the spartan condition of many of their public health systems, cast health activism at this conference under the rubric of primary health care. Like the Ottawa Charter, the 1978 Alma Ata Declaration on Primary Health Care arose in part as a response to the limitations of a biomedical and technological approach to improving health and as an affirmation of numerous experiences of community-based health care (Cueto 2004). It recognised that the gross inequalities in the health status between and within countries were ethically unacceptable and identified the practice of primary health care as key to attaining 'health for all by the year 2000'. The three essential features of Alma Ata–inspired primary health care resembled those of the Charter: a recognition that equity in health depends fundamentally on improving socio-economic conditions and alleviating poverty and underdevelopment; in this process, people in their community/citizen roles should be both major activists and the main beneficiaries; and health care systems should be restructured to support priority activities at the primary level because these respond to the most urgent health needs of the people (Werner et al. 1997; Magnussen et al. 2004). While not using the term 'empowerment' explicitly, the Declaration went on to underscore that 'people have the right and duty to participate individually and collectively in the planning and implementation of their health care' (World Health Organization 1978).

Health promotion in decline

The Ottawa Charter and the Alma Ata Declaration did not dominate global health discourse for long. Another movement was also afoot during the 1970s and 1980s, one with more powerful backers and greater political reach: neo-liberalism. This movement has its intellectual roots in eighteenth- and nineteenth-century British liberal theorists such as Adam Smith and John Stuart Mill. Smith's influential economic theories maintained that when people acted in their own economic self-interest in a free market, all would benefit. The logic of the market's 'invisible hand' was simple: when people wanted goods, other people would make and sell them. If they became too greedy, no one would buy the goods or other manufacturers would compete with lower prices. If prices fell too low, the lack of profit would end production until people were prepared to pay more. When peoples' need changed, no one would buy, profits would drop and manufacturers would shift to producing goods people really wanted. Mill buttressed this argument with philosophical writings on liberty, which contain ideas few in health promotion or the progressive social movements that buoyed its 1980s activism would disagree with: guaranteeing individual choice as long as it did not harm another person and protecting free speech even if the opinions expressed may be factually erroneous. These ideas are consistent with justice as equality of opportunity. His economic writings, though, and like Smith's, weighed in against justice as equality of outcome. He argued against all but the lightest of taxation, which he considered a form of robbery of those who saved and benefited from their own efforts.

Classic liberalism, and the writings of these two influential theorists, is of course more complex. Even Smith's 'free markets' were deemed in need of state intervention when markets failed to provide beneficial public goods, infrastructures, services or other 'public works and . . . public institutions', as Smith referred to them. How the market's invisible hand is supposed to work in an era of monopolies and cartels, mass media, manufactured need and huge inequalities in economic wealth and power between nations that did not exist at the time of Smith's theorising remains the more contentious point. As for Mill, his defence of individual choice and free speech weaken when we consider that choices are conditioned and constrained by peoples' living environments with rippling effects on others that can be subtle yet substantial, and that the boundaries between erroneous speech and hate-mongering are blurry and politicised. Even so, the revival ('neo-') of their liberal theories in the 1970s and 1980s blunted the complexity of their sources' own writings, ignored the even greater complexities of social life two centuries on and, in populist discourse, reduced the sound bite to free markets and individual choice. Some argue that neoliberalism is a carefully managed attack by elites on what they perceived as a 'nanny state' costing too much money and encroaching too much on private wealth and privilege (Coburn 2000; Teeple 2000). We would add that, unintentionally, many of the progressive social movements may have aided in this, since most of their activism was directed against the state and not the market. This helped to delegitimate state authority. What few dispute is that neo-liberalism became a direct assault on the interventionist welfare state that had characterised much of the post-World War Two period. Its story is basic to understanding how globalisation now affects health, and is discussed in later chapters.

For now, we consider how some of neo-liberalism's rolled-out ideas undermined the progressive activism of the Ottawa Charter and Alma Ata Declaration. Health systems became increasingly obsessed with new forms of private sector management theories which emphasised quantifiable results, short-term gains and 'value for money' (Baum & Sanders 1995; Barder & Birdsall 2006), rather than money for what is valued. In Canada there was a short turf war between health promotion and a reminted concept of population health. The issue was less about focus; like the Ottawa Charter, the population health approach emphasised the importance of the non-medical or social determinants of health. The issue concerned the rationale: much of the early population health literature promised reductions in public expenditures in health and welfare, characterised such spending as economically 'non-productive' and avoided the importance of socio-economic inequalities (Coburn & Poland 1996; Pindar 2007). Funding for health promotion, while not evaporating, became more confined to activities such as behaviour change and chronic disease prevention for which powerful cost-savings arguments could be made (Bernier 2007).

The Alma Ata's Declaration's comprehensive vision of primary health care similarly suffered. Policy makers, donor agencies and national leaders realised the potentially liberating nature of primary health care's emphasis on citizen participation and socio-economic determinants. Many, feeling threatened by this potential, became resistant to its implementation (Werner & Sanders 1997). Selective Primary Health Care (SPHC) arose as a competing concept, in which only interventions that contributed most to reducing child (<5 years) mortality were given priority. SPHC advocates argued that the comprehensive approach was too idealistic, expensive and unachievable in its goals; greater and more immediate gains would be made through a focus on growth monitoring, oral rehydration therapy, breastfeeding and immunisation, the so-called GOBI formula (Walsh & Warren 1979). This reasoning is true in the short term. There have also been notable successes in SPHC such as the low-cost Tanzanian Essential Health Interventions Project (TEHIP) (de Savigny et al. 2005). But decision-making power and control in most instances of SPHC rested increasingly with foreign consultants with technical expertise, rather than flowing to community members (Magnussen et al. 2004). SPHC, like lifestyle health promotion, proved attractive to many political leaders: it promised easily quantifiable and achievable results within a short time; it dealt with high-prevalence health problems; and it was a simple and less resource-demanding alternative to establishing a network of permanent and equitably accessible health services (Gangolli et al. 2005). It also shifted focus from the awkward political issues of underlying health determinants rooted invariably in pervasive poverty or inequality.

The new millennium

Practice fields and their discursive constructions are dynamic; in popular argot, pendulums swing. In more recent years the activist language and social concerns of the 'old' public health and the 'new' health promotion have been reinvigorated for an array of reasons, a few of which we list below:

- The selective approach to primary health care has yet to show sustainable long-term results. Evidence suggests that only when it is supported by a more comprehensive system do selective interventions work effectively and efficiently (Knippenberg et al. 1997; Soucat et al. 1997).
- An outpouring and systematic gathering of research on the socio-economic determinants of health began to suffuse throughout health systems, notably, but not exclusively, in high-income countries. Conventional biomedical and behavioural explanations proved increasingly inadequate to account for differences in death and disease rates between different populations, drawing attention to causes in peoples' living and working conditions.
- Civil society opposition to the neo-liberal retrenchment of the state grew in many countries and coalesced globally in campaigns against what was regarded as the unhealthy and inequitable economic practices of modern globalisation. Neo-liberalism was increasingly shown to have failed on its promises of increased growth, trickle-down poverty reduction and improved health (Labonté et al. 2007).

The activism inherent in these critiques, though, has yet to trickle down to health promotion practice. In a provocative essay on health promotion in Canada, a group of young and old health promotion scholars argue that health promotion remains a marginal practice in most health systems. Despite a decade of rhetoric on the social determinants of health, this practice continues to be dominated by health behaviour change programmes (Dupéré et al. 2007). Empowerment and social change as the 'defining elements' of health promotion remain marginal within its still marginalised field of practice.

But these defining elements still remain. They have also gained, if not practice traction, at least a rebounded legitimacy. One could even argue that health promotion as an empowering practice neither descended nor rebounded. If we dig beneath the term to what it represents, health through empowerment, justice through equity, social relations that are respectful, political mobilisations that are effective, we find in it the attempt to address the inequitable contradictions of capitalist modernity that have characterised many of the world's societies for at least two centuries.

2
Health Promotion Practice: Power, Empowerment and the Social Determinants of Health

> Failing to meet the fundamental human needs of autonomy, empowerment and human freedom is a potent cause of ill health.
>
> Sir Michael Marmot 2006

In this chapter we provide an introduction to health promotion practice, politics and ethics and link the three central themes of the book – health, equity and empowerment – in a discussion of the social determinants of health. We conclude with a reflection on what this means for practitioner competencies and ethics.

Power: The capacity to create or resist change

At its simplest, power is the capacity to create or resist change (Kuyek & Labonté 1995). But that is power's simplest. It comes in different and complex forms, some understanding of which is rudimentary to grasping the dynamics of local empowerment.

There are three basic types of power-over in which the person exercising power attempts to have others behave according to his desires: domination, exploitation and hegemony (Lukes 1974; Foucault 1980). Domination, or the direct exercise of force, is rarer in democracies but exists in institutions such as the police, the army and any legislation that empowers some people to have authority over others. In health promotion, we see this primarily in quarantine, infectious disease reporting and other legislated powers of medical health officers, or in legislative 'healthy public policies' such as those governing smoking and alcohol or environmental protection. These practices of power-over are not necessarily undesirable or wrong, although they must be recognised for the coercion they represent.

Economic exploitation, the second type of power-over, is one cause of social class, and speaks to how the neutral language of the market and the economy work to obscure that, as economist Herman Daly (Daly & Cobb 1989) expresses, the market is blind to distributive justice. Some people gain only to the extent that others lose. Where this touches health promotion practice directly is in the costs of our salaries, our institutions and our programmes. These costs represent a transfer of wealth from poorer communities to wealthier professionals. John McKnight (1987) talks of a study in a poor New York neighbourhood which found that 2/3rds of all public spending went to professional service providers and only 1/3 went in the form of direct income transfers to poor people. He argues that if all public spending had gone directly to poor persons in the neighbourhood, their lives may have been far healthier even with the relative lack of professional services. We don't entirely agree with this analysis; at the least, no one knows the proper balance between public service provision and individual or community group choice. But it is important to know that every new programme or service dollar gained by institutions represents a dollar that is not under the more direct control of less powerful individuals and groups.

It is the third type of power-over, hegemony, which may be the most insidious. It speaks to how professional powers are sometimes used to control how others come to see themselves: as powerful or as powerless. Consider two prenatal assessments (Tables 2.1 and 2.2).

The first (Table 2.1) represents a typical assessment format that purports to be objective and professional, but which presents an overwhelming burden of difficulties, many of which are actually power-over judgments. 'No apparent substance abuse' implies that Marian could still be a substance abuser; she's simply clever enough to hide it. Imagine the behaviours of the health worker who 'constructs' Marian in this way,

Table 2.1 Judgemental assessment

Marian:
- Low income, single mother.
- Inadequate protein, calcium and overall caloric intake.
- One-bedroom basement apartment.
- First child low birth weight.
- Insufficient weight gain.
- Fears labour and delivery.
- Does not speak or read English well.
- No apparent substance abuse.

and how these behaviours define Marian by her deficits and problems only; and how Marian, when confronted by such institutions and practices time-in and time-out, begins to internalise these as being true about herself. This internalisation of self-blame can create a learned helplessness (Seligman 1975) or surplus powerlessness (Lerner 1986) that accounts for part of the greater disease burden of the poor. In this hegemonic power-over, Marian, as a person capable of acting with agency, is completely absent. There is no evidence of her own capacity or power; no reflexivity indicating whether the way the professional assesses Marian resembles the way Marian sees herself.

In the second assessment (Table 2.2), a completely different way of viewing Marian emerges.

Here we see her abilities and many more opportunities for actual change, and for a health promoter's role in helping that change, e.g. obtain fridge, mediate with landlord, assist in marketing quilts, mediate with national consulate office in Guatemala over release of husband, meet with delivery room professionals in hospital over language concerns. (These assessments were first developed and used as training tools by community nutritionists working with the City of Toronto Department of Public Health. Due credit for their insightfulness belongs to those practitioners.)

If we fail to look for peoples' gifts we simply reinforce or extend the idea that people are powerless to make a difference. As another example, and one commonly experienced by new émigrés: By focussing on the presenting edges of their relative powerlessness (their poverty, their lower status and the low-paid jobs in which they lack much authority), we may not see the status and power they had in the countries they left, or even the authorities they might still enjoy within their own local

Table 2.2   Empowering assessment

- Poor appetite due to stress and isolation; child's father political prisoner in Guatemala.
- Enjoys preparing traditional vegetable soups, bean dishes and corn bread.
- Would like more milk and meat but finds these too expensive.
- Healthy 3-year old daughter born with low birth weight, no complications.
- Worried about income and childcare when child comes; refugee status claim still pending.
- Has cousins locally who can help financially, but not enough.
- Quilts and paints as hobbies; would like to sell her work.
- Spanish literacy, school-teacher in Guatemala; concerned poor English skills will be interpreted as stupidity.
- Small, tidy apartment.
- Wants fridge; afraid to ask landlord as she can't afford to be evicted.

communities. An African-born janitor in the UK may have been a university teacher in her home country, and remains a respected leader among her émigré community in her new one.

As professionals, our relationships with others always have different elements of all types of power-over. Our education or training, the higher incomes that we can earn, the types of jobs we occupy, can give us a higher social status. The positions we occupy in institutions often give us some decision-making authority or influence over resources, such as grants or social service benefits, or simply access to goods and services such as photocopiers, telephones, meeting spaces and so on. Other times our control over access to these resources is more closely linked to our social status. We have the professional 'authority' to give or withhold legitimacy to the named concerns expressed by individuals or groups with whom we work, and so affect their abilities to mobilise public resources. Our social status and authority, in turn, also gives us considerable power to influence or persuade decision-makers further up the hierarchy of power-over systems. We can help 'set' political agendas around health, and it is in how we define these agendas that we either hegemonise the relatively powerless, or transform that power-over by sharing what power we possess.

There are other forms of power besides those associated with power-over. 'Power-to' (Wartenberg 1990) or 'power-from-within' (Starhawk 1988) describe the sense of mastery or personal integrity that often derives from philosophical, religious or spiritual sources (Labonté 1996). Partly arising from this centered location is a third form: power-with. This describes the use of certain forms of power-over for the specific intent of increasing another person's experience of power-to or power-from-within. It is the transformative use of power-over. The classic examples often given are those of parents or teachers whose exercise of authority over children is often (though not always) with the intent of it disappearing as their wards assume more of their own 'power-from-within' (Wartenberg 1990).

This discussion of some of the dynamics of power and empowerment becomes the more pertinent when we consider power's relationship to health. Sir Michael Marmot, an internationally respected social epidemiologist and Chair of the World Health Organization's Commission on Social Determinants of Health (2005–08), recently reflected on the evidence of the importance of a sense of control to one's health (Marmot 2006). Numerous studies now document that low perceived control equates to greater disease risk, especially, but not exclusively, for coronary heart disease. There is also a psycho-biological pathway: the stress associated with low control creates a chronic, sub-acute response with long-term damaging effects on the circulatory and immune systems. Improving one's sense of control, which Marmot elides with the Nobel economist, Amartya Sen's, concept of 'freedom' as the ability to lead a life one has reason to value (Sen 1999), leads to better health. Even democracy, which holds a greater promise of control for more people than might other political systems, appears to equate with better average health, even when accounting for other social determinants (Besley & Kudamatsu 2006). As Marmot continues, 'power is key' to better health; and its unequal social distribution undermines many peoples' capabilities for leading healthy, valued lives.

Health promotion: Power, empowerment and the practitioner

In the previous chapter we encountered two approaches to defining health promotion: as an empowering practice aimed at social change, and as a particular approach to programming. While striving for the former, health promotion practice is most often delivered as the latter: a planned set of activities within the design of an intervention or a project. As this chapter shows, this does not prevent it from becoming empowering.

Consider, first, health promotion's intention to help people to gain more power by way of a cursory review of the five basic roles that we identified in Chapter 1.

- *Educator/watchdog*: Health communication and health education programmes can increase peoples' capacities to make informed choices about their lives and health. The greater control that they may experience over decision-making is a form of power, provided the information is timely, relevant, actionable and not the sole 'health messaging' people receive.
- *Resource broker*: Training, role-play, work experience and counselling are examples of how health promoters provide resources that can help people to develop or enhance different skills. These skills improve peoples' abilities to exercise control over many situations in their lives, which can improve their health. Health promoters also often help individuals and groups to mobilise financial and material resources to aid them in their work.
- *Community developer*: Organising new groups, increasing community members' participation in activities aimed at personal or social health change and strengthening community capacities are all forms of development work that can reduce inequalities in the distribution of

power. Health promoters can use these approaches to increase the assets and attributes which a community is able to draw upon to exercise more control over the conditions affecting its members' lives.

- *Partnership development*: Individuals and communities do not exist in isolation. Just as health promotion programming must increasingly work across sectors, local communities need to link with others to learn from shared experiences and build a broader and more powerful base for political campaigning. Health promoters often become useful conduits through which these linkages are formed.

- *Advocate/catalyst*: Policy change that affects the determinants of health inevitably requires advocacy to counter resistance by those who might oppose the change. Citizens/communities in many countries have democratic rights to influence policy decision-making through a variety of advocacy means. Even in non-democratic states, people have the right to participate in decisions that affect them under internationally ratified and legally binding human rights covenants. General Comment 25 on Article 25 of the Covenant on Civil and Political Rights, for example, states (amongst other rights) that 'Citizens also take part in the conduct of public affairs by exerting influence through public debate and dialogue with their representatives or through their capacity to organize themselves. This participation is supported by ensuring freedom of expression, assembly and association' (Office of the High Commissioner for Human Rights 1996). Health promoters can assist people in this advocacy work in many ways: through the 'inside' knowledge they have about government policy priorities, with health research to support their claims and, through their professional associations or in their own role as citizens, as fellow advocates (Labonté 1998).

These roles do not apply only to those persons specifically designated as health promoters within their state or NGO employment. Many other practitioners, such as nurses, social workers, educators, community development workers and physicians, are likely to engage in health promotion activities as part of their duties. What we say about health promotion and the health promoter can apply to any person attempting to work in an empowering way to improve peoples' abilities to control their health and the social and environmental conditions that shape it.

The 'domains' of empowerment

Empowerment in the broadest sense is seen as a process by which people work together at a 'local' or 'community' level to increase the power (control) they have over events that influence their lives. Several authors have attempted to identify empowerment's areas of influence at the local or community level in order to provide a guide to planning, implementation and evaluation of health promotion programmes (Gibbon et al. 2002; Laverack 2001). In particular, recent work (Laverack 2001) has identified a set of nine robust 'domains' of community empowerment (see Table 2.3).

Table 2.3 The empowerment domains

Domain	Description
Participation	Only by participating in small groups or larger organisations can individual community members act on issues of general concern to the broader community.
Leadership	Participation and leadership are closely connected. Leadership requires a strong participant base just as participation requires the direction and structure of strong leadership.
Organisational structures	Organisational structures in a community represent the ways in which people come together in order to socialise and to address their concerns and problems.
Problem assessment	Empowerment presumes that the identification of problems, solutions to the problems and actions to resolve the problems are carried out by the community.
Resource mobilisation	The ability of the community to mobilise resources both from within and the ability to negotiate resources from beyond itself is an important factor in its ability to achieve successes in its efforts.
'Asking why'	The ability of the community to critically assess the causes of its own inequalities.
Links with others	Links with people and organisations, including partnerships, coalitions and voluntary alliances between the community and others, can assist the community in addressing its issues.
Role of the outside agents	The outside agent increasingly transforms power relationships such that the community assumes increasing programme authority.
Programme management	Programme management that empowers the community includes the control by the primary stakeholders over decisions on planning, implementation, evaluation, finances, reporting and conflict resolution.

Source: (Laverack 2001).

These domains function as a 'parallel track' to conventional forms of health promotion programming. Whatever the health issue (health behaviour or social determinant) the basic question for health promoters is: How has the programme, from its planning through its implementation, through its evaluation, intentionally sought to enhance community empowerment through each domain? This is not simply an instrumentally important question. It may be true that a more empowered community is better able to participate in health promotion programmes, sustain efforts past the funding period and 'take ownership' of the health issue. But improvements in many of these domains can be intrinsically health promoting in their own right (Laverack 2007), as discussed in Table 2.3.

Participation

Individuals have a better chance of achieving their health goals if they can participate with other people who are affected by the same or similar circumstances to build interpersonal trust and trust in public institutions (Brehm & Rahn 1997). Trust is a key element as it helps to foster cohesive relationships and to build capacity by devolving responsibilities. Participation in groups that share interests can help individuals to compete for limited resources and to increase the sense of personal control in their lives. For example, the use of participatory learning exercises in women's groups in a poor rural population in Nepal led to a reduction in neonatal and maternal mortality (Manandhar et al. 2004). The women in the intervention clusters were found to have better antenatal care, higher rates of institutional delivery and greater trained birth attendance and more hygienic care, which together led to improved birth outcomes. By participating in groups the women were better able to define, analyse and, through the support of others, articulate and act on their concerns around childbirth. The advantage of participation was that it strengthened social networks and improved social support between the women and also between the women and the providers of health services delivery. Increases in social support and social networks can be health-enhancing in its own right, as is the decreased isolation and the experience of increased control or mastery it brings (Labonté & Laverack 2001; Marmot 2006).

Leadership

Leaders themselves often experience personal health gains from their increased sense of control/authority (positional leaders) or self/social esteem and social networks (reputational leaders). Leaders nurtured through organising efforts gain materially and psychologically from the experience, often taking advantage of the broader opportunity networks in which they find themselves. For the group itself, leaders contribute to its effective functioning both internally (relationships) and externally (mobilising resources). This improves the members' abilities to speak their voice with authority, and to influence health-determining policy debates and decisions. There are many forms of leadership, all of which need to be respected. In La Casa Dona Juana, a social space for Latin American women in Toronto, participants identify the different leadership skills or 'gifts' that individual members bring to the collective and to its activities. Women skilled in writing prepare the grant applications. Those skilled in cooking take a leadership role in the collective kitchen. Others skilled in budgeting plan the menus or purchases for the collectives, while those knowledgeable in sewing techniques take leadership in the sewing collective. In the 'outside' world, budgeting and grant-writing skills are often more highly valued, and those who have them may be given more social status and power-over others. But in La Casa Dona Juana, due partly to the feminist organising beliefs of the health promoters who provided the space and resources to start it, budgeting and grant-writing are merely one set of leadership skills no more or less important than those involved in cooking, menu-planning or sewing (Labonté 1998).

Organisational structures

Community organisations provide the opportunity for their members to gain the skills and competencies that are necessary to allow them to move towards achieving health outcomes. On an individual basis this includes self-help groups that provide knowledge, skills and social support around issues such as smoking cessation, dieting and exercise classes. On a collective and organisational basis these skills include planning and strategy development, team building, networking, negotiation, fund-raising, marketing and proposal writing. Organisational structures are the 'hardware' (infrastructure) that runs the 'software' (interactions) of good public participation (Labonté & Edwards 1995). They constitute the bedrock of social capital. Organisations can be healthy or unhealthy for their members, depending on their levels of hierarchy, decision-making styles, development of cliques and management of conflicts, i.e. on the type of interpersonal 'software' they allow to 'run'. Generally, though, areas with few or ineffective internal organisations will be less able to mobilise internal or access external resources, provide opportunities for social support or network development or otherwise influence decisions affecting health-determining conditions (Labonté & Laverack 2001).

Problem assessment

Problem assessment is an aspect of capacity that is closely related to learning. In broad terms, people with higher education enjoy better health through a variety of pathways: more affluence or material security (whether or not through more competitive labour market participation), healthier personal behaviours (though not always), better self/social esteem and efficacy, greater social network access, more experience of control and, perhaps through improved sense of coherence, less self-blame and a greater ability to influence decision-makers and mobilise personal and extrinsic resources. Internationally, investments in education, particularly for girls, are more strongly associated with improved population health than economic growth or labour market development *per se* (Labonté & Laverack 2001). Increased community capacities in problem assessment often lead to new forms of health-promoting interventions. For example, a health programme in India, working to improve the lives of rural women in Gujarat, worked with women to assess the most immediate health needs in their daily lives. The women firstly requested and then received cooking stoves that would reduce the level of smoke in their small airless huts. Their involvement in assessing and finding a solution to this initial problem led the women to go on and identify other health-related problems in their community including poor maternal and child-health facilities and the gynaecological training of health workers (Rifkin 2003).

Resource mobilisation

There is evidence to suggest that resource mobilisation, together with improved literacy and education, particularly for women, can lead to improved health outcomes in developing countries (Bratt et al. 2002; Pokhrel & Sauerborn 2004). An example of the link between resource mobilisation and improved health is the use of swimming pools in remote Aboriginal communities in Australia. These were found to reduce ear, nose and throat infections (Carapetis et al. 1995) and to provide an overall improvement in the well-being of the community (Peart & Szoeke 1998). The public swimming pools invariably operated at a loss and costs were borne or subsidised by the government because it was seen as a recreational facility which promoted the health of the population. The people living in the communities had low incomes and access to only limited resources. They were expected by the local government to raise finances to maintain the pool. The communities started to raise additional internal resources on a small scale through fund-raising and pool entrance fees and to raise external resources through other funding sources. In this way the ability of the community to mobilise resources had an effect on its health through the continued use of the swimming pool (Laverack 2005).

Asking why

Asking why is the ability of the community to be able to critically assess the contextual causes of their disempowerment and to be able to develop strategies to bring about personal, social and political change based on their heightened awareness. Asking 'why' can be described as 'the ability to reflect on the assumptions underlying our and others' ideas and actions and to contemplate alternative ways of living' (Goodman et al. 1998). This cycle of discussion, reflection and action is a process of emancipation through learning or education developed by the educationalist Paulo Freire (1973), the roots of which lie in liberation pedagogy ('freedom through education') (Carey 2000). An example of this is the work by Nina Wallerstein and Ed Bernstein (1988) and their analysis of the Alcohol and Substance Abuse Prevention (ASAP) Programme which operated through the University of New Mexico. The Programme brought small groups of high school students together in the settings of a hospital emergency centre and a county detention centre to interact with patients and detainees who had drug-related problems. Youth were able to share experiences directly with the inmates and learn through asking questions and exploring problems at different levels. Gradually the students took leadership roles and organised meetings and events to raise the issues of drug abuse and drink driving in village meetings. While an evaluation study did not track behaviours, risk perception was much higher in students participating in the Programme as compared to a control group (Wallerstein & Bernstein 1988).

Links with others

Links with others demonstrates the ability to develop relationships outside of the community, often based on mutual interests. The development of partnerships is an important step towards empowerment and can also lead to an improvement in health outcomes through the pooling of limited resources and collective action. The Asian Health Forum in Liverpool, England identified a large number of cases of depression and isolation amongst Asian women in the area. A health worker with the local Asian women held discussions with them and then approached a leisure centre to arrange swimming lessons. This arrangement would ensure privacy, for example, windows would be blacked out and the lessons run by other women. The alliance between the Asian women and the leisure centre was able to organise weekly lessons and to secure funding for a female instructor. The lessons were very popular and timings had to be reorganised to avoid conflict with other pool activities and to accommodate the young children of the Asian swimmers. The lessons had a health benefit to the women by helping to reduce weight but mostly through an improved feeling of well-being brought about by the regular exercise. Eventually the health worker was able to delegate some of the responsibility for the lessons to the alliance and slowly their interest moved to other sports activities and an increase in the choices available to Asian women (Jones & Sidell 1997).

The role of the outside agents and programme management

Health promotion programming is traditionally professionally led. It is the practitioner or her agency that chooses the individuals, groups and communities that she will work with and the methods to be used. The initiation of the empowerment process and the enthusiasm for its direction and progress in the programme is also often professionally led. Practitioners, who are in a position of relative power, work to help others who are in a less powerful position to gain more control. Individual control, in part a consequence of the position of people in structural and social hierarchies, has been shown to have an influence on their health and well-being. In a programme context the issue becomes how much control the outside agent (the practitioner or agency) allows the community to take in programme design, implementation, management, evaluation, finances and administration.

An example of this is provided by the Health Authority in Oldham, England which established a 'local voices' steering group with the purpose of involving local people in health activities. The group was made up of representatives from different departments, community trusts and government agencies in a poor housing area. The group decided to employ an independent consultant to carry out a participatory needs assessment. The community members were invited to attend meetings to express their concerns. Child care facilities and transport were arranged and meetings were held at times that would be convenient to the community. Large meetings were often followed by small group discussions to elicit further information from the community about what they felt affected their health. These initial discussions led to the development of a questionnaire which was administered on a door-to-door basis by trained interviewers. This process involved a relationship between different representatives working and living in the community to co-ordinate the activities of an outside agent, the consultants, to provide a specific technical input (Smithies & Webster 1998). The important issue is that the outside agents were able to collect information in a way that was acceptable to all representatives and that allowed the community to take the necessary action to effect change.

The concept of 'community'

If the domains above describe attributes of an empowered community, who or what do we mean by community? Much has been written about this term, which we will not belabour here. Of importance to health promoters is that they think beyond the customary view of a community as a place where people live, for example, cities or neighbourhoods, because these are often just aggregates of non-connected people. Communities have both social and geographic characteristics. In practice, geographic communities consist of heterogeneous individuals with dynamic social relations who may organise into groups to take action towards achieving shared goals. In practice a community will have the following characteristics:

1. A spatial dimension, that is, a place or locale. Even though the Internet is creating new virtual communities without bounded geographies, connections made this way often lead to desires to meet face-to-face which requires some geographic proximity.
2. Non-spatial dimensions (interests, issues, identities) that involve people who otherwise make up heterogeneous and disparate groups. A definition of community developed by one of us earlier was simply that of a group, membership in which was important enough to persons belonging to it and that it was one of the ways in which they identified themselves (Toronto Department of Public Health 1994; Labonté 1996).
3. Social interactions that are dynamic and that bind people into relationships.
4. Identification of shared needs and concerns (Laverack 2004).

Within the geographic dimensions of community, multiple non-spatial communities exist and individuals may belong to several different such communities at the same time. Interest groups, those communities that organise around issues, exist as a legitimate means by which individuals can find a 'voice', increasing their abilities to participate in more formal and effective ways to achieve their goals. Interest groups can be organised around easy-to-implement concerns such as social activities or localised issues (which is often where community organising starts); or they can target more deeply structured social, economic or environmental problems (which is where some initially local groups wind up).

The diversity of individuals and groups within a geographic community can create problems with regard to the selection of groups with whom to work (Labonté 1998) as well as representation of that group by its members (Zakus & Lysack 1998). In ideal terms, health promoters work with those in greatest need or facing greatest disadvantage (inequity), and strive to avoid the establishment of a dominant minority that might dictate community issues. This requires some judgment that people coming forward as spokespersons or representatives of a community are in fact supported by its members and that they are not simply acting out of self-interest. During health promotion's 1990s surge, community health workers in Toronto attempted to define more specifically some of the criteria for selecting and working with groups, based on empowerment and social justice principles and their own extensive experience (see Box 2.1).

Health promotion choices such as these invariably require practitioner competencies and involve ethics, two issues to which this chapter now briefly turns.

Health promotion competencies and ethics

In Chapter 1 we commented that health promotion is still struggling to define itself as a unique discipline or profession. We believe that the risks of professionalisation outweigh any benefits. Legitimacy, the primary benefit for a practitioner and an empowering practice alike, can be acquired through other means besides a claim to unique status. This does not mean that health promotion should avoid some codification of the competencies required of its practitioners. Defining requisite norms and skills is not only an incomplete claim to a unique scope of practice; it is, and should be, primarily ensuring an ethically informed and capable set of behaviours in relation to the people being served.

Competencies are a combination of attributes that enable an individual to perform a set of tasks to an appropriate standard. Core competencies for health promotion include not only practical knowledge and skills but also the values and principles that shape the professional practice. In an earlier work, Laverack (2007), drawing on the literature on

Box 2.1   Some criteria for selecting groups to organise or support

1. **The group has unmet needs**
   - the unorganised.
   - groups that are neglected by other service providers, politicians, the media.
   - groups experiencing serious disadvantages.
   - groups who don't know how to 'use' the 'system'.
2. **Our support will have an impact**
   - the group is able to identify its goals and objectives and to focus on an issue.
   - the group becomes able to organise itself and its own activities, and to act upon its issue.
   - leadership arises within the group.
   - there is a sufficient membership within the groups that some success will be likely.
   - the group is able to achieve some short-term, visible successes.
   - there is a sizeable number of people whose health will be affected positively by the group's success.
3. **A new group needs to be organised**
   - there are no other agencies better able to do the organising.
   - there is a critical mass of individuals who express interest in meeting as a group.
   - there is health institution support and clear decision-making to do the organising.
   - there is positive movement in group dynamics; the group will not become stuck in an unproductive rut.
   - the group develops a sense of responsibility for its own actions.
4. **I have knowledge or skills relevant to the group's issue**
5. **The group will grow and become autonomous**
   - the group knows or learns its rights, privileges and responsibilities.
   - the group is or can become independent of the health promoter and community agencies, able to negotiate its own terms of relationships with those workers and agencies.
   - the group learns how to look for, and use, resources from within its own community, and from government.

(Continued)

Box 2.1 *(Continued)*

6. **The group is open in membership and accountable to those it claims to represent**
   Groups might be inclusive (open to anyone who wants to join) or exclusive (closed except to those who meet its own criteria, e.g. single mothers, black youth, gay or lesbian, etc.). Being open in membership does not mean that the group is inclusive. But if it is exclusive, it must be able to clarify who it represents (its criteria for membership), and to be open to all those who meet these criteria. The group should also be able to develop some means to be accountable to those whom it claims to represent. This accountability ensures that the group does not become a small gathering of elites whose own sense of power is improved, but at the expense of a larger number of persons.

7. **The group is internally democratic**
   The group should not be authoritarian in its internal decision-making style. Authoritarianism is distinguished by:

   - unilateral decision-making.
   - censoring opposition within the group.
   - controlling information.
   - excluding others from leadership positions.
   - favouring hierarchical forms of organisation, not because they may be more efficient for certain tasks, but because they allow a few persons to control the whole group.

Source: adapted from Labonté 1998.

health promotion competencies and his own reflections on health promotion as an empowering practice, developed a reasonably short list of such competencies:

1. Programme design, management and implementation.
   This involves an understanding of programme cycles, budgeting, the planning and evaluation and how and when community members should be engaged in these different programme steps.
2. The planning and delivery of effective communication strategies.
   Communication strategies are an integral part of many health promotion programmes. A high level of competence is needed for communication strategies that differently target individuals, groups and communities, including one-to-one communication, the design of

print materials, the use of the mass media (including the Internet) and engaging with journalists.

3. Facilitating skills.

Training, usually within a workshop setting, is a key part of many health promotion programmes. Good facilitation skills are essential for health promoters and are an important part of programme design.

4. Research skills.

Health promotion programme design and evaluation is based on sound research including the use of participatory techniques, qualitative and quantitative methods and systematic reviews.

5. Community capacity building skills.

This is a process of capacity building and health promoters should be competent in a range of strategies (described in Chapter 3) that they can use to help individuals, groups and communities to gain more power.

6. Ability to influence policy and practice.

Health promoters have the opportunity to influence policy and practice in their everyday work, for example, through technical advisory groups and through helping communities to mobilise and organise themselves towards gaining power. Health promoters must develop competence in the use of strategies to influence policy, developing partnerships and sound working relationships.

But what drives the application of these competencies? Laverack (2007) speaks of values of equity and compassion. Labonté (1993a) earlier wrote of the importance of practitioners' ethical stance, based on respect (which demands efforts to learn why others have come to different opinions or judgments than ourselves), generosity (which, as the Sufi tradition defines the term, means doing justice without requiring it) and service to (caring for) others. These are all claims to ethics or moral principles. They are not dissimilar to those that traditionally have guided most other health professionals:

- Beneficence – a practitioner should act in the best interest of the person
- Non-maleficence – 'first, do no harm'
- Autonomy – the person has the right to refuse or choose their treatment
- Justice – equity in the distribution of scarce health resources
- Dignity – the person and practitioner both have to the right to be treated with dignity
- Truthfulness and honesty – informed consent

All of these have some pertinence to health promotion, most of which are obvious. Some are not; for example, health promoters who extend their practice into community organising activities (described in Chapter 3) have sometimes done so with little prior training or competency with potentially harmful effects. Do we seek the empowerment of all equally? Even equity in scarce health resources tends to become a question of who gets what and omits the issue of *why* such resources might be scarce in the first place. And scare to whom? The reason for these limitations is simply that traditional ethics, reflecting Western individualism, are based on *individual* level of ethical responsibility.

The application of ethics to health promotion has been written about more extensively, including some of its community change ideals. In a lively (and largely deserved) critical disassembling of health promotion definitions and models that suffused the 1980s and 1990s, David Seedhouse (1997), a health promoter-turned-philosopher, posits a 'foundational' theory of health promotion built on a short series of logically linked propositions:

- a core respect for the autonomy of individuals
- a focus on central conditions in people's lives that support such autonomy
- prevention of disease, illness, injury and disability as legitimate health promotion 'targets'
- prevention of obstacles in the way of achieving the previous three

His reasoning combines a blend of liberalism (provision of core resources but not a guarantee of full equality), utilitarianism (improve these core conditions for all rather than for particular 'groups') and egalitarianism (make this improvement a social priority for all). His reasoning is similar to the more elaborated arguments for a social ethic based on 'capabilities' advanced by Nobel economist, Amartya Sen (1999), and philosopher, Martha Nussbaum (2000), both of whom claim that societies have an obligation to ensure that all its members have access to the minimum resources required for them to live a valued life.

While these writers' foci on autonomy and core resources are important counter-balances to the social engineering for which health promotion has been criticised, what remains missing is recognition of the institutions that create and sustain poverty and other social inequalities, especially at a time of great global wealth. We return to this point in Chapter 7; to close this discussion for the moment, we present an intentionally provocative scenario that cuts to the quick of contemporary health promotion ethics.

The history of most civilizations, as writers Jared Diamond (2005) and Ronald Wright (2004) inform us, has been one of ruining their ecologies. This despoliation underpins their collapse, fuels population movements and, where there have been contiguous land masses or the technologies to cross oceans, gives rise to the next rising empire. This is clearly illustrated in the story of the Easter Islanders, whose ideological enslavement to a belief in the ancients led to the erection of huge stone monuments, whose movement required skids of timber which, as competition among the families for more and bigger monuments accelerated, denuded the island of every last tree. No trees, no birds, no insects, no mammals, no fresh water, no food. And by the time the Europeans bumped into the island, almost no people. The tragedy is that they likely knew what would happen even as they cut the last tree.

Just as we know what will likely happen as we continue to fish our oceans to extinction; as early as 2048, by one recent estimate, we would eliminate our carbon sinks and biodiversity, contaminate our sources of fresh water, grow our economies with toxic fossil fuels and blind ourselves to the consequences with an ideological enslavement to growth as the only marker of progress. This time, however, the collapse will not be confined to a single island. It will be global, and the toll will be in the multiple millions; if for no other reason than, a few years ago, we surpassed the brown rat in becoming the most populous mammalian species on the planet.

Therein lays the ethical affront. For promoting the physical and mental health of individuals whose well-being rests, in part, on economic practices that are today's equivalent of logging, the last Easter Island tree is, we contend, morally unacceptable and, from an intergenerational health vantage, indefensible.

Health promotion and the social determinants of health

Our discussion now turns to another of health promotion's empowering axioms: working on the underlying social determinants of health, and not merely on their more visible manifestations as disease or behaviour. The reason for this imperative is simple. While medical care has been important in prolonging life expectancy during the twentieth century, inequalities in health persist, and recently have increased globally, between people from different social classes, ethnic groups and genders. This is because the common causes of ill health are shaped by social, political and economic forces that differ by nation, region and 'community', and the effects on power these forces create. The Ottawa Charter identified these causes in its list of 'basic prerequisites for health': peace, shelter, education, food, income, stable ecosystem, sustainable resources, social justice and equity. This list has been more rigorously refined by researchers into different compilations of what are now referred to as the 'non-medical determinants of health' or, more recently, the 'social determinants of health' (SDH). These determinants encompass the economic and social conditions that influence the health of individuals, communities and whole jurisdictions. They are influences that may seem distant to an individual or community, but they nonetheless exert enormous influence over their everyday lives.

Table 2.4 provides one such listing of the SDH, based on the work of Wilkinson and Marmot (2003). The factors influencing these determinants of health often involve public policy decisions concerning the distribution of income, social security and the quality and availability of education, food and housing.

Ten years ago, the federal Canadian government established a similar list of population health determinants, using slightly different headings and categorisations. Because this list has been used as a guide for health promotion practice within Canada (albeit primarily at the local or programme level), it offers some initial insights into how health promotion practice can address the SDH for each of the list's determinants (Adapted from Labonté 2003).

Social determinants of health in health promotion practice

Income and social status

This is the single most important determinant of health. Health status improves at each step of the income and social hierarchy. Higher income levels affect living conditions such as safe housing and the ability to buy sufficient good food. But money isn't everything. How people feel about the adequacy of their income, how it compares to a broader social standard is also important. It is a measure of one's social status or rank. The psychological impacts of being low on a social hierarchy can be as health-damaging as lack of money itself. It links directly into people's sense of their own self-worth, their self/social-esteem.

Health promotion programme contributions:

- Hiring programme participants and other low-income people.
- Providing or brokering free services (e.g., free clothing, laundry facilities, office equipment or resources, transportation).
- Providing individual advocacy around welfare entitlements, subsidised housing, bank or other debts.

Table 2.4 The social determinants of health

Social Determinant of Health	Description
The social gradient	Life expectancy is shorter for people further down the social ladder and who are likely to experience twice as much disease and ill health as those nearer the top in society. This influence also affects people across society, for example, within middle-class office workers those with lower ranking jobs experience more disease.
Stress	People that are worried, anxious and unable to psychologically cope suffer from stress that over long periods of time can damage their health, for example, high blood pressure, stroke, depression, and may lead to premature death. Stress can result from many different circumstances in a person's life but the lower people are in the social gradient the more common are these problems.
Early life	Slow physical growth and poor emotional support can result in a lifetime of poor health and a reduced psychological functioning in adulthood. Poor fetal development, linked to, for example, stress, addiction and poor prenatal care, is a risk for health in later life.
Social exclusion	Poverty, discrimination and racism can all contribute to social exclusion. These processes all prevent people from participating in health and education services, are psychologically damaging and can lead to illness and premature death.
Work	While having a job is generally healthier than not having a job, stress in the workplace increases the risk of ill health, for example, back pain, sickness absence and cardio-vascular disease. This is more pronounced when people have little opportunity to use their skills and have low decision-making authority.
Unemployment	Job security increases health; unemployment or the insecurity of losing one's job causes more illness and premature death. The health effects of unemployment are linked to psychological factors such as anxiety brought on by problems of debt.
Social support	Having friends, good social relationships and supportive networks can improve health. People have better health when they feel cared for, loved, esteemed and valued. Conversely, people who do not have these factors in their lives suffer from poorer health and premature death.
Addiction	Alcohol dependence, illicit drug use and smoking are not only markers of social and economic disadvantage but are

(Continued)

Table 2.4   (Continued)

Social Determinant of Health	Description
	also important factors in worsening health. People can enter into addictive relationships to provide a temporary release from the pain of harsh social and economic conditions and stress but as a result their long-term health is damaged.
Food	A good diet and an adequate supply of food are important to health and well-being. A poor diet can cause malnutrition and a variety of deficiencies that can contribute to, for example, cancer and diabetes and can also lead to obesity. Poor diet is often associated with people who are lower on the social gradient.
Transport	The reliance on mechanised transport has resulted in people taking less exercise, increased fatal accidents and pollution. Other forms of transport such as cycling and walking increases the level of exercise and helps people to reduce obesity and diseases such as diabetes and strokes.

Source: (Wilkinson 2003).

- Assisting in community economic development initiatives.
- Anywhere programme activities generates new income for participants, or reduces the income they would otherwise have had to spend on privately provided activities.

Social support networks

Support from families, friends and communities is associated with better health. The support of family and friends who provide a caring and supportive relationship may be as important to health as risk factors such as smoking, physical activity, obesity, and high blood pressure. Social networks describe what is now more commonly called social capital, the web of relations and ties that bind people together into communities. Networks are different from friendships or relationships. They are more impersonal. People can move in and out of them with reasonable ease. They are the larger pot from which friendships and relationships might be ladled. They are also the range of groups, affiliations and loose connections through which potential opportunities and resources flow. Connecting participants to other groups, organisations and neighbourhoods are all ways in which programmes can broaden participants' social networks.

Health promotion programme contributions:

- Opportunities the programme creates for informal conversation and friendship formation.
- Peer-support initiatives.
- Intentionally created support groups for people with shared issues.
- Increase participants' access to broader social networks.

Education

Health status improves with level of education. Education increases opportunities for income and job security and gives people a sense of control over their lives. These are key factors which influence health. The content and style of education is based upon increasing all persons' understanding of how health issues and concerns arise, how these are shaped personally and socially, and what can be done about them.

Health promotion programme contributions:

- Opportunities for critical learning.
- On-site education facilities (something many children's programmes or shelters already offer).
- Opportunities for participants to improve their own reading, numeracy and other literacy skills in the context of programme work.

Employment and working conditions

Unemployment, underemployment and stressful work are associated with poorer health. Those with more control over their work and fewer stress-related demands on the job are healthier.

Health promotion programme contributions:

- Providing opportunities for employment to programme participants.
- Offering services or referrals that improve participants' employability, for example, providing skills training, interview assistance, access to information on employment opportunities.
- Providing training in health-promoting workplaces for participants who have jobs, and helping them to make sure their workplaces are healthy.
- 'Practicing what we preach' internally, by increasing income equity and control over conditions experienced by people working in our programmes, creating a flat hierarchy in decision-making levels and reducing workplace stress.

Social environments

The values and rules of a society affect the health and well-being of individuals and populations. Social stability, recognition of diversity, safety, good relationships and cohesive communities provide a supportive society which reduces or removes many risks to good health. There are, however, differing social values, some of which are more health-promoting than others. Discriminatory prejudices (the '-isms' of racism, sexism, ageism, heterosexism and so on) can be internalised by people creating poorer health.

Health promotion programme contributions:

- Advocating for health-promoting changes in the social environment.
- Helping participants increase their own policy advocacy skills.
- As staff and organisations, participating in broader coalitions or other collective efforts to influence policy.
- Increasing public understanding of the needs and capacities of people whose health is compromised by their social and economic marginalisation.
- Improving people's abilities to interact more effectively with their existing social environments.

Physical environment

Physical factors in the natural environment (e.g., air, water quality) are key influences on health. Factors in the human-built environment such as housing, workplace safety and community and road design are also important influences.

Health promotion programme contributions:

- Reducing environmental threats to human health.
- Reducing exposure to environmental tobacco smoke (ETS).
- Reducing toxics and toxins in the home environment.
- Lobbying for more equitable access to recreational green space for people in poorer neighbourhoods, reduced traffic risks and so on.
- Increasing access to healthy, affordable housing.

Personal health practices and coping skills

Social environments that enable and support healthy choices and lifestyles, as well as people's knowledge, behaviours and coping skills for dealing with life in healthy ways are key influences on health.

Health promotion programme contributions:

- Tangible supports for behaviour change, such as free food, physical fitness classes, stress reduction/management sessions, smoking cessation courses.

Healthy child development

The effect of prenatal and early childhood experiences on subsequent health, well-being, coping skills and competence is very powerful. A low weight at birth links with health and social problems throughout a person's life. Children live in families, and families live in communities. The challenge for many programmes where the primary focus is healthy child development is developing activities on other health determinants at a broader community level.

Health promotion programme contributions:

- Nutrition, home visiting and parenting programmes.
- Peer supports for parents.
- Infant stimulation programmes.
- Recreational programmes for parents and children.

Culture

Culture and ethnicity come from both personal history and wider social, political, geographic and economic factors. Culture is a determinant of health to the extent that *cultural roles* shape health-promoting (or damaging) behaviours, *cultural biases* create stereotypes that influence physical and mental well-being or access to health-promoting services, and *cultural discrimination* (racism) prevents equitable access to other health determinants (income, social status, education, employment and working conditions) on the basis of one's ancestry. Multicultural health issues demonstrate how necessary it is to consider the interrelationships of physical, mental, spiritual, social and economic well-being at the same time.

Health promotion programme contributions:

- Incorporation of concepts from non-dominant (non-European) ethnoracial cultures into programme content.
- Staff training in cultural sensitivity and anti-racism.
- Providing culturally appropriate content to newcomers (immigrants, refugees).
- Offering interpretive services when required.

- Recognising positive indigenous identity as both pluralist (there is no singular aboriginal identity) and health-promoting in its own right.

Gender

Gender refers to the many different roles, personality traits, attitudes, behaviours, values, relative powers and influences which society assigns to the two sexes. Gender is a determinant of health to the extent that *gender roles* shape health-promoting (or damaging) behaviours, *gender biases* create stereotypes that influence physical and mental well-being or access to health-promoting services and *gender discrimination* prevents equitable access to other health determinants (income, social status, education, employment and working conditions) on the basis of sex. Each gender has specific health issues or may be affected in different ways by the same issues.

Health promotion programme contributions:

- How does the programme support healthful gender roles and challenge those that are not?
- How does the programme break down damaging gender stereotypes?
- How does the programme contribute to overcoming systemic gender discrimination?
- How does the programme ensure it is gender-sensitive in its own design, content and implementation?

Health services

Health services, particularly those which are publicly funded and universally accessible, such that the rich or healthy subsidise the poor or sick, contribute to population health.

Health promotion programme contributions:

- Ensuring participants have access to required medical and primary health care.
- Educating health care providers on the issues or concerns particular to programme participants about which they may be unaware.
- Participating in community discussions on health-system reform.

Biology and genetic endowment

The basic biology and organic make-up of the human body are fundamental determinants of health. Inherited predispositions influence the ways individuals are affected by particular diseases or health problems. Few health promotion programmes are involved directly in changing biological or genetic health determinants. Indirectly, any programme that improves other health determinants in this list *is* improving a biological pathway to health. Programmes improving prenatal and post-natal health are more clearly helping to shape a healthier biological pathway for children. Other programmes aimed at reducing tobacco or drug use also affect biological pathways to health.

The politics of policies affecting the social determinants of health

Many health promoters now recognise the importance of a social determinants approach in their work, one that moves beyond the individual behavioural model. This requires, in part, an approach that moves their work towards a model that posits health as being determined by how societies themselves are structured (Mouy & Barr 2006).

There are four useful and empirically supported ways in which to model how social structures create health inequities:

- Social stratification: where people are located in a social gradient (by economic, gender, racial status), which affects . . .
- Differential exposure: to risks or hazards in the workplace, the community, the broader social and physical environments; the response to which is influenced by pre-existing . . .
- Differential vulnerability: which increases the likelihood of morbidity or mortality when exposed to risks or hazards, leading to . . .
- Differential consequences: both in terms of access to remedial health or other social services, length of time recovering from illness and the impact of illness on their position in a social gradient (Diderichsen et al. 2001).

The degree of stratification and differential exposure, vulnerability and consequences is very much a function of economic and political policies chosen by different states. Among high-income states, those favouring a more 'liberal' (or neoliberal) political economy (primarily the 'Anglo-American' nations of the UK, Ireland, USA, Canada, Australia and Aotearoa/New Zealand) have given lower priority to policies aimed at social spending than have social democratic states. As Raphael and Bryant (2006) point out:

These differences among nations help explain variations in population health. [N]ations predominantly governed from 1945–1980 by social democratic political parties show greater union density, social security expenditures, and employment levels . . . They had the largest public expenditures in health care from 1960–1990, and greatest coverage of citizens by health care. These nations had high rates of female employment, and lowest income inequalities and poverty rates. On a key indicator of population health – infant mortality – they had the lowest rates from 1960–1996. Recent work extends these findings to life expectancy with similar advantages associated with [social democratic] nations.

Until recently, much of the literature on the SDH has focussed only on specific living and working conditions that create health inequities. This has led to efforts to consider how health promotion programmes can take greater account of the SDH in their more routine programme work. But, as Raphael and others argue, unless health promotion recognises the political context of the SDH it will be largely ineffectual in reducing health inequities. This requires engagement in partisan politics. Bryant (2006), for example, found that there are particular political forces that are more likely to produce equitable health-promoting policy change:

- The presence of 'left' political parties to influence government decision-making.
- Proportional representation electoral systems that increase the likelihood of such a presence.
- High union density and effective labour powers to negotiate favourable wage and employment conditions.
- A historic state commitment to active labour policy, support for women's employment, adequate spending to support families, assistance for the unemployed and those with disabilities, provision of educational and recreational opportunities and efforts to reduce social exclusion and promote democratic participation.

To these we would add the presence of strong civil society organisations with similar commitments and the caution: modern globalisation is reducing the policy space of even the most committed governments to act on the SDH. The implication this has for health promoters concerned with an empowering practice is straightforward if discomfiting: support for those political parties, labour groups and civil society organisations that hold to these aims. This is not to the exclusion of working across political spectra. But if we hold to the new mantra of 'evidence-based' or 'evidence-informed' practice, the evidence of where support for health promoting policies lies is unambiguously clear.

3
Pathways to Local Empowerment

A small group of thoughtful people could change the
world. Indeed, it is the only thing that ever has.

Margaret Mead, Anthropologist

In this chapter we examine empowerment's strategic pathways. These
pathways are viewed as a five-point continuum that identify the
organisational characteristics by which people move from individual
experiences of power towards more collective forms of social and
political action. The end result of such action may be a change in policy, legislation or even societal norms. We focus in this chapter on
local empowerment, the identification of a community concern about
which people share their ideas and experiences and engage in bringing about some form of personal, political and social change. As we
move along the continuum of strategies, however, local empowerment's translocal links to global issues and networks start to become
apparent.

Why a continuum? A brief history

The continuum model was first introduced to explain how unequal
power relationships can be transformed as people progress from personal empowerment to more politicised forms of mobilisation. As a
model it arose from reflections on health promotion practice. Labonté
was preparing a series of training workshops for health and social service workers to be delivered in several Australian states in 1988. He developed his continuum of strategies based on community health workers'

experiences during a particularly activist phase of the Toronto public health department. His five-point continuum comprised:

1. Personal empowerment
2. Small group development
3. Community organisation
4. Coalition advocacy
5. Political action (Labonté 1990)

When presenting this model to the group of community workers in Sydney, he was surprised and delighted when they presented back to him a model they had developed independently around the same time. Their five-point continuum was based on their community development work in the Fitzroy Community Health Centre in Australia. Their five-point continuum comprised:

1. Developmental casework
2. Mutual support
3. Issues identification and campaigns
4. Participation and control of services
5. Social movements (Jackson et al. 1989)

The close parallels between the two are obvious, and were later adapted to explain how psychological empowerment relates to the process of local empowerment (Rissel 1994). The three sets of authors use slightly different terminology that essentially hold the same meaning and represent the same conceptual design: the potential of people to progress from individual to collective action. The version we present modifies somewhat earlier renditions, and comprises five elements (see Figure 3.1).

1. Personal action
2. Small groups
3. Community organisations
4. Partnerships
5. Social and political action (Laverack 2004)

The empowerment continuum

The continuum model we present has been written about extensively (e.g. Labonté 1990, 1993a, 1998; Laverack 2004, 2007; Rissel 1994). While some readers may already have encountered variations on the continuum,

Figure 3.1   The local empowerment continuum
Source: (Laverack 2004, 48).

for many it remains a new tool. It is also one that has been unchallenged in the literature for more than a decade and a half. The continuum identifies various levels of empowerment, from personal to organisational to the collective. The strength of its modelling is also its weakness: the continuum offers a simple, linear interpretation of what is actually a more fluid and complex process. There are several points here worth noting.

First, groups and organisations as they move their activism further along the continuum will have their own dynamics. They may flourish for a time and then fade away for reasons as much to do with changes in the people as with a lack of broader political or financial support, or changes in the importance of the issues they confront. Sometimes their success becomes their undoing: Local struggles over service provision and new resources for marginalised populations can lead to the creation of new service organisations with staffing and state-funding, gradually eroding the need for volunteers and leading to a decline in active citizen participation (Labonté 1998). Such is the dialectic of radicalism and reform, something practitioners need to bear in mind when they work with community groups but one that is not necessarily to be mourned. New service organisations fill a function, albeit a politically less challenging one. They also often become a local employment structure offering new locations from which practitioners can identify the next issues around which community mobilisation and empowerment might proceed. There is no endpoint to empowerment: it is a continuous feature of social organisation and change.

Second, interpreters of the continuum emphasise the importance of each of its five points. Unless all members of a group individually experience some sense of greater power or control (partly through the self/social-esteem accorded one another) the risk of cliques and unhealthy power dynamics within a group or organisation increases. Similarly, unless organisations that engage in partnerships and advocacy work have a larger community constituency to fall back upon, they risk their own marginalisation in political discourse.

Third, building the self-confidence of individuals and strengthening the skills of small groups, the first two points on the continuum, are insufficient in themselves as empowering strategies. These points embody 'power to' or 'power-from-within', the sense of control or mastery that individuals experience. Yet it is precisely these two continuum points that many health promoters emphasise (Labonté 1996) because, as Buchanan (2000) writes, the 'power to' experienced by individuals 'appears ethically unproblematic, since it does not have the connotations of domination, coercion, and manipulation'. In our experience the reason is less philosophical than pragmatic: such forms of power appear to relieve practitioners of the discomfort of engaging in organised forms of political activism aimed at gaining more power-over for some (the community) by limiting the power-over of others (elite groups). Buchanan poses a further challenging question: 'To what extent is it possible to have "power to" do something without exerting "power over" others?' (2000).

Fourth, and our reply to Buchanan, the continuum model works simultaneously from both an interpersonal and a structural perspective. The interpersonal perspective describes the network of support through which people interact to organise and mobilise themselves: personal action and participation in small groups. The structural perspective addresses more the role of the market, state, its government departments and those who hold political and economic power-over others. The continuum model addresses the structural perspective through the politically orientated activities of partnerships, alliances, coalitions and social movements. Significantly placed on the continuum between the interpersonal and structural perspectives is the role of organisations based in local communities. Community organisations are pivotal because it is the point at which groups either progress to having a wider influence or else remain focussed on issues of more local or relational concerns. The tension between inward and outward looking interests sometimes requires groups themselves to separate. In our Introduction's first garden story, some members wanted to concentrate on tending their harvest while others saw the garden as a tool for mobilising a campaign to challenge welfare and social housing reform. This eventually led to creation of two distinct groups.

Our point here is simply that more practice attention needs to go towards helping community-based organisations to build their capacities, establish sound organisational structures and increase their participation in broader coalitions or alliances. A recurring theme in this book is that local, while necessary, is insufficient; as Alan Durning (1989) of the Worldwatch Institute once opined, paraphrasing the title of economist E.F. Schumacher's popular 1973 book, 'Small may be beautiful, but it can also be insignificant'.

Personal action

All forms of social and political activism that change the conditions of peoples' lives inevitably start with the actions of discrete individuals. History doesn't just happen; it is made, and often by the efforts of people who remain invisible in the chronicles of change. In everyday life the first step onto the continuum is often a triggered response to an emotional or symbolic experience in a person's life. Experiencing a neighbourhood traffic accident, for example, can lead persons to become active in organisations dealing with road safety. There is a long history of individuals beginning to organise when confronted by a perceived threat, whether it be a new environmental risk, an unwanted neighbourhood development or the closing of local sources of employment. An entire theoretical tradition explaining collective action starts with the assumption that it is motivated first and foremost by self-interest (Olson 1965), a derivation of Adam Smith's idea that acting from self-interest via free markets works to mutual benefit. Others object to this 'rational actor model' of empowerment, noting that there are multiple motivations that cause individuals to engage in group mobilisation, including a desire to care for others, love, strong political or religious beliefs, even idealism (Knoke 1988). Just as communities are multiple in their identities, so too are people multiple in their motivations for creating them.

Participation in groups of others affected by the same or similar circumstances increases individuals' chances of achieving their goals (Brehm & Rahn 1997). This leaves unresolved whether these goals are ethically defensible in terms of a broader understanding of the conditions that create health equity. The sparks of personal action at local levels can often be reactionary and health inequitable.

For many people living in unhealthy environments, personal action often starts with mobilisation for access to useful services and resources, or simply with the existence of caring services that provide relief and compassion. Studies of effective primary health care further find that services and programmes have a better chance of achieving their purpose if they involve people in the process of problem assessment, design and decision making (Confederation of British Industry 2006). Perhaps most importantly, services cannot be segmented from other forms of intervention that drive movement along the continuum.

Small groups

Small groups provide an opportunity for individuals to progress on the continuum by meeting to share their common experiences and concerns. Generally these small groups only focus inwards on the immediate needs of their members and may not have a well-established structure; there is some evidence that self-help groups deliberately avoid contextualising their issues in broader social conditions or policies (Labonté 1998). Different variations of small groups have become popular sources of government funding, for example through

1. 'Self-help' groups organised around a specific problem (e.g. weight control, diabetes, addiction, disease recovery) or consumers wanting to find suppliers for organically grown produce. Members who usually have a shared knowledge and interest in the problem, are participatory and supportive and the groups are often set-up and managed by the participants;
2. 'Community health' groups which usually come together to campaign on a specific local health issue, for example, better facilities for socially excluded groups such as people with disabilities. People are motivated to come together usually for only short-term periods of time in regard to issues that influence the group; and
3. 'Community development health projects' such as neighbourhood-based initiatives set up to address broader issues of local concern such as poor housing, often with an appointed and paid government community worker (Jones & Sidell 1997).

This last example begins to take us to the next continuum point of building new community organisations, but before arriving there it is helpful to consider a few practitioner issues in small group development. The first is the need for a high degree of competence in group facilitation. A professional role is often integral to the success of building these support groups and moving them into a more outward-looking stance. But it can also sometimes be confounded by poor facilitation imbued with too much of the professional's own agenda. A fatal fire in a rooming house in Toronto, Canada, led to renewed efforts by many community service agencies to mobilise roomers around housing issues and tenants' rights. Early organising efforts, intent on creating tenants' unions, rent strikes and other forms of political activism, failed. Some organisers were even told to leave the groups of roomers they had attempted to mobilise. Roomers felt that their own concerns weren't being respected in the rush towards social action. Many felt pitted against landlords. At the same time, public health nurses and other direct service providers were welcomed for the less intimidating forms of individual and group support they brought. As one nurse described her work: 'We cannot expect people to do this "social action" process just because we can see a need for social change . . . But we can help people build some small base amongst themselves, and support them in going as far along an empowerment process as they are willing and able to go' (Labonté 1996).

This story captures the truism that choice, the ability to exercise control over decisions, is the simplest form of power. It also illustrates the basic ethical axiom of respect for the autonomy of individuals, provided that autonomy is not exercised in ways that denies it to others. Health promoters cannot enforce an empowering activism; the very idea is an oxymoron. But they can, and should, pay close heed to where the potentials for a broader social engagement exist within the communities with which they work. This requires identifying those groups that are ready to strike outwards to the conditions contributing to their marginalisation and poorer health. Jones and Laverack (2003) found that such groups share a number of identifiable organisational features: A membership of elected representatives, an agreed membership structure, participation by a majority of members in regular meetings and properly kept meeting and financial records. The most successful groups were those able to identify their own problems, solutions to resolve them and where resources could be found to initiate their work.

Community organisations

Community organisations occupy a pivotal point on the continuum, the junction at which groups either move towards exerting greater influence over the policies and politics that affect their lives or remain focussed on local issues and actions only. But which groups? Which policies? Which politics? These questions announced themselves in our arguments about empowerment and health from the very start of this book. We have so far offered some thoughts about criteria for selecting groups and urged a nuanced approach to non-partisan advocacy while ensuring support to those partisan interests most closely aligned with actions on the social determinants of health.

Political scientists offer another useful tool for decision-making in their distinction between 'sectional' and 'promotional' interest groups. Sectional groups are those that organise to protect primarily the economic or partisan interests of their members. This includes business groups (sometimes referred to as 'bingos' for 'business interest non-governmental organisations'); trade unions; or political parties seeking elected office. Promotional groups (sometimes referred to as 'pingos' for 'public interest non-governmental organisations') are those that are organised to promote value-based causes such as human and animal rights or environmental issues such as climate change. Membership is open to anyone interested in the particular value-based cause of the group (Tenbensel 2006). While self-interest (the 'rational actor') undoubtedly plays some role in promotional interest groups the distinction rests largely on whether the interests being pursued accrue only to group members, or are available to a larger polity.

Authors such as David Truman (1951) have long argued that interest groups promote a healthy democracy by providing viable routes for people to have direct political influence. At the same time, interest groups that 'shout the loudest' are often given the most attention. Even if such groups are urging policies that will benefit large sweeps of marginalised people, this effectively gives more advantage and power to those who are more capable at organising themselves and who are the most articulate. The dilemma this creates for the practitioner is the trade-off between efficiency and empowerment. On the one hand, a small number of loud interest groups may be better able to influence policy change than a large number of interest groups of varying volume. There may even be greater equality in outcome as a result. On the other hand, equality in opportunity suffers, since those with less voice remain comparatively voiceless and arguably burdened with fewer experiences of capabilities to control their own lives and conditions. There is no resolution to this dilemma, apart from recognising its existence and making a judgement suitable to the moment: increasing voice, or winning a policy change.

A crucial stage in the development of community organisations is an increase in members' abilities to think outwards to the environment that creates their needs in the first place. In chapter 2 we referred to this as the capacity of 'Asking "why"', which others have described as '. . . the ability to reflect critically on the assumptions underlying our and others' ideas and actions and to contemplate alternative ways of living' (Goodman et al. 1998). 'Asking why' captures a process often characterised as a ceaseless spiral of assessment, analysis, action and reflection. The key term here, though, is 'critical', wherein community members take a long, hard look at their situation to determine the social, political and economic reasons for their relative powerlessness and poorer health. Much has been written on the many techniques that health promoters can use in this process, which begins to fuse their role of facilitator in small groups with that of developer in community-based organisations (Wallerstein & Bernstein 1988; Wang et al. 1998). Most of these techniques owe their provenance to the work of Paulo Freire and his concept of conscientisation (critical consciousness) or, more popularly, 'popular education' (Freire 1968; Freire & Macedo 1987). At the local level of practice, conscientisation is unlikely to lead to major political mobilisations, but often succeeds in small-scale improvements. In a small slum in Nairobi, Kenya, for example, a project aimed at improving maternal/child health worked with resident women to assess and map their community using cooperatively designed questionnaires, photography and narratives. Results were shared in an open forum that prioritised creation of a day-care centre, working with a youth group on environmental cleanliness and employment opportunities, and increasing skills among community members. A centre was successfully built and managed by the community; funding to support the work of the youth group is being sought; and women have been trained in making toys and management skills to supply and maintain the day care centre (Metzler et al. 2007).

Partnerships

Partnerships are an increasingly invoked strategy in health promotion; we thus take some time discussing two examples of partnership forms for what advice they hold for this strategic point.

Our first example is the Voluntary Health Association of India (VHAI), an alliance of over 4000 health and development agencies. Fifteen years ago, VHAI, with the financial support of a German foundation, initiated a linked series of projects to improve community health-related problems in remote areas. This required creating partnerships between local health officials, development organisations, the private sector and community members. One hundred and sixty villages were involved in 17 different projects. One project linked together 20 particularly remote villages. Based on their expressed interests, village members were trained in numerous income-generating areas. Particular emphasis was placed on gender empowerment, through such activities as kitchen gardening, livestock farming and women's savings clubs. With support from existing government and NGO resources and infrastructures, access to most forms of primary care, notably prenatal care, improved, as did local sanitation systems. Some 64 self-help groups were created, and each village established its own women's saving club and development committee. Over a ten-year period of study (1993–2003) school attendance increased, housing improved, environmental conditions were cleaned up, infant mortality rates dropped from 124/1000 to 50/1000, and annual maternal mortality deaths decreased from 15 to 0 (Metzler et al. 2007). These successes are attributed to themes already encountered: working on community-identified issues and increasing relevant capacities amongst community members. But equally important was drawing in the partnership support (both financial/material resources and knowledge resources) of local NGOs and government.

Similar examples emanate from high-income countries, often as efforts to create partnerships across different sectors. Referred to by the Ottawa Charter as building 'healthy public policy', these more bureaucratic partnerships generally seek to make the broader array of government policies and programmes more supportive of health equity goals (Public Health Agency of Canada 2007). Often a response to outside pressures from interest groups or coalitions, these 'intersectoral' partnerships can be horizontal (different jurisdictions, same level), vertical (same jurisdiction, different levels) or both.

Our second example comes from the Canadian province of Saskatchewan which since 1999 has maintained a 'Human Services Integration Forum' (HSIF) comprising the highest level civil servants from seven government ministries. Like the VHAI example, the HSIF goal is to create more responsive and better-integrated services to communities in need. This horizontal partnership is linked vertically through a number of 'Regional Intersectoral Committees' (RICS). These local partnerships ensure that resolution of integration problems at the level of direct contact with communities is either enabled, or at least not constrained by, policies at the higher governance level. Local partnerships also involve polyphonies of NGOs and community groups, and work to broker new resources for new initiatives identified by partnership participants. The HSIF in turn is explicitly committed to a community development approach to new service delivery. While no formal evaluation of the impacts of this combined horizontal and vertical partnership has been undertaken, it is credited with changing how government workers and NGO service providers plan their future activities. The first question posed when any of them confront a new problem is: What other sectors, including community organisations, need to be present to help take new action on it? (Chomik 2007).

The constellation of health promotion partnerships that have been created over the past 20 years is sizable: it includes Healthy Cities/Healthy Communities projects; initiatives built around different settings such as schools, workplaces, prisons; and scores of local pilot projects such as the UK's and Aotearoa/New Zealand's Health Action Zones. The literature on these partnerships is almost as large, and will not be recounted here. A few generic lessons, though, seem to recur. Based on the authors' experiences and a recent synthesis of published literature on intersectoral action on health determinants (Public Health Agency of Canada 2007), these can be summarised as:

- *A problem that can't be fixed by any one group or sector.* This should seem obvious, but it often is not. Many partnership forums are simply information exchanging networks which, while helpful in a limited way, are a questionable use of both government and community resources. The financial, logistical and time costs of effective partnerships can be quite large; engaging across sectors should be done with careful forethought and clarity of purpose.
- *Partners with compatible motives for action.* Ensuring that partners have overlapping interests in the problem is basic to establishing some principled action. While an argument can be made that fundamental values must also be shared, extending even to those partisan social democratic policies that cohere most with empowerment and health equity, partnerships can sometimes be narrowly strategic. This brings together groups that may not hold to the same core social vision. Susan George, a political scientist and longstanding campaigner for a just globalisation, writes of the importance of building alliances with small business people. She defends this as an important strategy in efforts to restrain the incursion of global retail chains, such as anti-union, human rights offending Wal-Mart (George 2004); although for different reasons, there is a confluence of shared interest in the single-issue campaign. Similarly, anti-poverty activists involved in a campaign to improve welfare benefits in a Canadian province successfully sought the support of some small businesses by commenting on how many of these 'ma and pa' shops relied upon poorer families for their customer base. Improving income transfers would also improve their local business. Interestingly, the personal values of individuals may be more important to well-functioning partnerships than the stated values of the organisations they represent. When people meet to plan new partnership activities the innate dynamics of small groups and interpersonal relations begin to intersect with any formal negotiations or agreements that might be driven by the goals espoused by their respective groups.
- *Partners with the resources necessary to resolve the problem.* Resources do not always have to be financial; for many community participants in partnerships that involve state sectors and NGOs, the resources they

bring to the table are primarily intimate knowledge of the causes and consequences of the 'problem' the partnership formed to resolve. But money matters. Indeed, for some, a defining feature of partnerships is the willingness of members to pool resources for new initiatives that no longer bear the imprimatur of any one of them: its identity becomes that of the partnership.

Such is the case with the 'Vancouver Agreement', a partnership involving three government levels, a regional health authority and several community organisations that has been working with some success since 2000 to improve housing, health and quality of life in four inner city neighbourhoods facing urban decay. The partnership began with a focus on harm reduction for the large population of IV drug users in the area who were 'sleeping rough' or in exploitative single-occupancy room hotels; and whose drug-related petty crimes had created a loss of safety for other residents. The health authority diverted funds from its tertiary care budget and challenged other government levels to match them. The intent was to develop cooperative housing for IV drug users, along with needle-exchange programmes and a safe-injection site. This would not only reduce the health risks faced by such persons; it would also reduce the risk of crime. A parallel project helped to revitalise the arts in the neighbourhoods, essentially reclaiming them as desirable and safe places in which to live. While the continued existence of the safe-injection house is precarious, given Canada's current 'tough on drugs' rather than a harm reduction approach, three levels of government have each committed $10 million to continue the partnership activities over the next five years (Labonté 2006; Chomik 2007).

- *Strong champions within each partnering group/sector.* The resource costs of partnership work can cause organisational leaders to balk at the commitments. Pooling resources can be risky and face internal opposition. In the early days of the Vancouver Agreement the reallocation of tertiary care funds to housing and programmes for IV drug users was not met kindly by medical specialists, some of whom mounted a counter-campaign. Committed and forceful leaders within the partnering groups helped to deflect this campaign. The role played by community groups representing citizens (rather than professionals or government agencies) was pivotal since they were 'pingos' (public-interest NGOs) and not 'bingos' (business-interest NGOs).

How do partnerships become empowering for community groups themselves? The answer depends partly on a reflection on what groups are being asked to partner for. There is a risk in many partnership activities, especially those where new service provision is one of the driving outcomes, of unintentionally transforming community/citizen activists into volunteer bureaucrats. A stylised tale illustrating this point concerns a health promoter's desire to work with community groups on their self-identified issue of inadequate housing. A committee was formed. Research syntheses were undertaken. The groups, seduced by the expectation of local government action, even participated in a new survey of residents to document the health consequences of poor housing. A report was written and moved slowly up the health promoter's bureaucratic ladder. Twice it was rejected because the recommendations were too strident, too much in the tone of the community groups. Twice it was rewritten to become more acceptable to a system whose principle role is to maintain a peaceful status quo and manage any required change in ways that absolutely avoid conflict. The community groups drifted away from the partnership, feeling slightly cynical and used; while the health promoter felt dejected and wondered what had gone wrong. In simple terms, the mistake was to involve community groups in a bureaucratic planning process. Instead, partnerships with community organisations need to be thought of more as strategic alliances than merged identities. Community groups pursue their own interests using their rights as citizens to make claims upon the state; health promoters buttress their claims 'inside the system' in the politically neutral style of statistical reports and policy analyses (Labonté 1993b).

We might extract two other points from these examples. First, and attested to by the available literature, partnerships around the determinants of health have so far worked best at local levels. To some observers this is because policy decision-making at higher levels of governance is much more complex (Public Health Agency of Canada 2007). Second, the likelihood of successfully 'winning' policy gains at the local level, and certainly at any higher governance level, usually demands some form of direct action. While our discussion of the empowerment continuum so far has offered reasons why each point is important in itself, creating or supporting different forms of social and political action must be taken as a requisite outcome.

Social and political action and beyond

Addressing inequalities in the distribution of power requires collective action; but such action must also be of sufficient force if those with power-over decision-making in the markets or government that determine the allocation of wealth, resources and legitimacy are to take notice. A key difference between local empowerment and the types of actions envisioned by this continuum point is that efforts here are aimed explicitly at changing deeper structural practices of our politics and economics. Table 3.1 provides examples of the types of indirect and direct actions that people can use and have used to influence policy. Essentially, people use their own decision-making power to create or resist change in political or economic policies in two ways:

1. Indirectly, such as registering a complaint to government authorities, writing a letter to their elected representatives about their concerns or mobilising what is now called 'shareholder activism';
2. Directly, such as taking legal action, funding an aggressive publicity campaign or actively lobbying people in positions of power. For example, the environment movement, to gain a seat in the corporate-government boardrooms where environmental policies were being formed, engaged in 'direct action' campaigns that blocked effluent pipes, stopped polluting activities or prevented whaling, logging or other forms of unsustainable resource extraction (Gray 1989).

Stated simply, social action means that people use their collective capacity to cause trouble. The 'anti-globalisation' protests at the World Trade Organisation meeting in 1999 is partly credited with that meeting's collapse and heightened international attention on the negative effects of economic globalisation. The disruption such protests create and the level of subsequent public participation in these groups becomes the basis for their social and political influence. But once invited to the 'roundtables' of policy discussion with more elite group members such as the World Economic Forum's annual global meeting, their radicalism and legitimacy stays current only so long as part of their allied groups maintain the pressures of direct action.

An interesting example of recent indirect 'shareholder' activism, a strategy that targets the market rather than the state, was launched by an American nun over 30 years ago. Recognising that faith-based organisations in the metro New York area had stock investments worth over US$110 billion, Sister Patricia Daly formed the Tri-State Coalition for Responsible Investment to pressure multinationals to decrease pollution, improve working conditions and practice more ethical forms of global sourcing. Her coalition puts forward hundreds of shareholder motions each year, while she meets and cajoles senior executives around the issues of social justice and environmental sustainability. The economic

Table 3.1   Direct and indirect actions towards empowerment

Indirect Actions	Attend a local planning meeting.
	Vote at a local or national election.
	Lobby, such as sign a petition.
	Assuming a moral superiority.
	Send a letter, email or text to a local MP or newspaper.
	Deliver promotional campaign material house to house.
Non-Violent actions	Peaceful civil protests and demonstrations such as 'sit-ins'.
	Refusal to pay taxes or bills.
	Infiltrate a meeting such as one being held by shareholders.
	Take part in a boycott or strike action.
Direct Actions	Create a media event such as climbing a public building to deploy a banner.
	Engage in an aggressive publicity campaign.
	Instigate legal action against someone else.
	Hack into another computer ('Hacktivism') to obtain information or to insert a virus package.
Violent actions (physical action against people or property)	Physically alter something to prevent action such as 'spiking' trees with metal pins.
	Place oneself in a position of manufactured vulnerability to prevent action such as building and occupying a tunnel under a road or a tree house, squatting in a house detailed for demolition.
	Take part in a riot or revolt with the intention to carry out physical damage on property or persons.

weight of the faith-based portfolios her Coalition pools is her empowering entrance key. It has also been effective in forcing major US automakers to require better working conditions in the developing world factories from which they source many of their parts. Shareholder activism, of course, can work regardless of ideology or belief systems. Conservative evangelists have created investment funds for their faithful that carefully exclude companies or groups supporting gay/lesbian rights, sex education, abortion rights or any other issue they find religiously repugnant (Wray 2007). Empowerment strategies discussed in this chapter are ethically neutral; only when they are linked to explicit goals of justice and health equity do they become health-promoting strategies.

The list of representative actions in Table 3.1 helps to convey the importance of persistence in social action. A former federal Canadian cabinet minister once noted that during all her time in government, the only groups that won their policy point, when such point was not consistent with the government's own platform, were those that came back again, and again, and again. This does not mean that persistence is a guarantee of success. One of the more durable social action campaigns of recent decades that arose from community need and health promotion activism monitors compliance with the World Health Organization's 'International Code of Marketing of Breast-milk Substitutes'. Introduced at the World Health Assembly in 1981, this voluntary Code restricts a number of marketing mechanisms used by infant formula manufacturers to persuade mothers not to breastfeed and to purchase their products instead. Some countries have since written provisions of the Code into their own legislation (though few developing nations have), and abuses of the Code are not as widespread as they were in the 1980s. Violations do continue, however, as does the 'naming and shaming' work of the Infant Baby Formula Action Network (IBFAN), a global organisation of national and local groups that tracks the actions of formula manufacturers (IBFAN 2007). Our point here is that the work to constrain the practices of power-over, especially those instantiated in economic interests, is a lifelong commitment.

Health activism

Sister Daly's work, and that of the hundreds of anonymous staff and members of IBFAN, embodies such a commitment. They are health activists, engaged in intentional acts to bring about social or political change. Such change can be slow and gradual so that it is barely noticeable, the incrementalism of reform. But change can also be radical, sudden and revolutionary. The term 'popular activism' is often associated with direct and fast actions, both violent and non-violent, such as civil protests (Jordan 2002).

For many health activists, their concern is principally the policy development cycle. We discuss the policy cycle in more detail in Chapter 4 and conclude this chapter with two examples of such activism, both of which employed a range of empowerment strategies leading up to social and political action. Box 3.1 describes how women who were concerned by the lack of access to Herceptin®, a drug used to treat breast cancer, used both indirect and direct actions to influence government policy. Box 3.2 tells the story of the Treatment Action Campaign in South Africa, which challenged the drug patent rules of pharmaceutical multinational companies that were restricting access to antiretroviral drugs.

The high cost of Herceptin® owes partly to the expense of research leading to its development, but also to the recent extension of intellectual property rights under international trade treaties that prevents the

Box 3.1   The case for and against Herceptin® in the UK

Herceptin® is one of a new group of cancer drugs called monoclonal antibodies. Herceptin® works by interfering with the way breast cancer cells divide and grow when a protein that naturally occurs in the body, known as human epidermal growth factor, attaches itself to another protein, known as HER2. Herceptin® blocks this process by attaching itself to the HER2 protein so that the epidermal growth factor cannot reach the breast cancer cells. This stops the cells from dividing and growing. Only about one in five women with breast cancer have tumours that are sensitive to Herceptin®.

Women's groups campaigned for NHS trusts in the UK to fund the use of Herceptin® more widely to treat breast cancer. The minimum cost to pay for the treatment is well beyond the means of most women who have breast cancer. However, the trusts refused to fund the drug until it was licensed for use in the early stages of the condition because of safety concerns and the absence of a product licence for the drug's use. The trusts indicated that they would wait for a published decision from the National Institute of Health and Clinical Excellence (NICE).

This decision outraged many women who established local groups to organise and mobilise themselves to try and bring about a change in the decision made by local trusts. The groups consisting of ordinary people such as mothers and housewives organised indirect and direct actions such as local demonstrations outside hospitals, petitions, sit-in protests and wrote to their MP. At a national level the women established a website to support others and embarked on an aggressive publicity campaign against the government.

As a result the NICE was put under pressure to make a quick decision on the use of the drug and the government and local trusts were put under intense pressure to provide Herceptin®. Eventually, the success of a high-profile court case ensured that Herceptin® was approved for use on the National Health Service. This was largely because of the determined action of women to individually and collectively take action. This action started at a local level but soon developed collectively at the national level in order to have a wider influence on the redistribution of resources and decisions (power) regarding Herceptin®. The other side to this case is that thousands of patients could be denied medicines if hospitals have to pay for the few women who need Herceptin®. Their treatment will be borne by other patients whose own cancer treatment will be withheld to balance the account books (Boseley 2006).

Box 3.2   Treatment Action Campaign

The South African Treatment Action Campaign (TAC) first mobilised around HIV treatment access in 1998, building from a number of self-help groups to become a national organisation with branches in all South African provinces and most major cities. It was started by two individuals who were angered by their countries' lack of response to the HIV pandemic and who realised that few self-help groups existed for blacks, or brought both blacks and whites together around the issue of AIDS treatment. As it grew from a small group to a formal organisation, it included services to its members: health care, education about HIV and treatment. Through services, it also sought to broaden a base of local community activism and, through its educational work, to increase the number of people working on its multiple advocacy strategies, some of which were polite and indirect, others of which were polite and direct, and still others of which included deliberate acts of civil disobedience (Friedmann & Motiar 2005).

Being involved in the TAC has given activists a feeling of purpose and direction, which they use not only in their private personal lives but also in public. Thuli, who never had the courage to speak up in school, described how her involvement in the TAC has 'taught me how to talk in front of people. I attend meetings, I hold workshops'. This new confidence was evident when she addressed a meeting of about 500 people very articulately. How did she learn this? 'Another comrade showed me how to do this and I followed him around all the time while I was new to TAC' (Endresen & von Kotze 2005).

While TAC is only one of several popular social movements that arose in post-apartheid South Africa, it is credited with being the first 'to enjoy huge popular support' (Endresen & van Kotze 2005). It is also credited with galvanising opposition to the court challenge brought by multinational drug firms against the South African government's attempts to import cheaper versions of antiretroviral treatments (ARTs) (a challenge later dropped due to mobilised global outrage galvanised by TAC's globally broadcast protests in South Africa); and with prodding its own government to move away from HIV-denialism to a belated (though still inadequate) ART roll-out. TAC consistently framed its advocacy as:

- A matter of human rights (the right to health is part of the South African Constitution, and was used by TAC in a successful court case

(Continued)

Box 3.2   *(Continued)*

that forced the government to dispense mother-to-child HIV transmission treatment).

- Part of a larger struggle for redistribution of wealth and resources (many of TAC's member organisations are involved in labour unions, anti-poverty movements and groups seeking to prevent poor people being cut off from access to water or electricity).
- A member of the 'anti-globalisation' global movement.

In 2005 TAC commissioned an extensive independent evaluation of its work (Boulle & Avafia 2005). It recommended a number of strategies that, if acted upon, would see TAC shift from being a social movement with fluid organisation and a campaign-driven focus to a bureaucratic civil society organisation with specified projects and outputs. This type of transition in 'grassroots' community health-organising is well known and documented in the health promotion literature, along with the potential loss of advocacy edge it might bring. However, unlike many social movement groups in Africa, TAC has attracted significant external funding and operates with a multi-million dollar budget and over 40 full time staff (Friedmann & Motiar 2005). Its attributed successes include the treatment court challenges in which it participated, the destigmatisation of HIV in South Africa (and beyond), and becoming a model for other movements defending socio-economic rights and monitoring government accountability. On this last account, however, there is some disagreement. A non-commissioned evaluation of TAC (Friedmann & Motiar 2005) added a theoretical analysis of new social movement theory. TAC's reluctance to engage actively in a critique of the neoliberal economic contexts accepted by South Africa's government, and its willingness to use legal challenges to win single-issue campaigns, *de facto* legitimised what other activist groups perceived as an illegitimate political order.

manufacture of cheaper 'generic' equivalents. It was this ironic form of increased protectionism wrapped up in trade deals promoting liberalisation that created the South African Treatment Action Campaign.

There are three limiting implications that can also be drawn from both the Herceptin® and TAC experiences. First, it is often easier to mobilise action around single, simple issues than around multiple, complex problems. Second, it is often easier to win policy change on medically defined problems than on those residing in the social determinants of health. Third, despite the powerful vested interests represented by pharmaceutical multinationals, moral and political challenges to one sector of neoliberal globalisation does not necessarily question the basic structure or rules by which it works. The same lesson can be drawn from the quarter-century experience of, first national and now global, campaigns against tobacco. Fourth, the numbers of active campaigners in both organised actions is relatively small; TAC has a membership roster of just over 10,000 out of 5 million HIV-infected South Africans. A broader base is important when there are particular mobilising moments, but the strength of social action groups lies less in their numbers than in other assets: strong leaders, evidence-backed positions, good media contacts, links with multiple other groups willing to support their positions, ability to use multiple campaign strategies, a capable organisation and sufficient financial resources to 'stay in business'.

These limitations do not preclude a health activism that is more challenging of state/market conditions and social structures that impede the goal of greater health equity. They do give us pause, however, to consider how such health-determining conditions, and campaigns to change them, have slipped beyond national borders to become inherently global.

4
Working to Build Empowerment: The Local Challenge

Before examining how the global now suffuses the local, Chapter 4 discusses the empowerment challenges that are faced at a local level. Many of these challenges apply to global mobilising as much as they do local empowerment. Five key steps that health promotion programmes should take into consideration are addressed: (1) engaging with people to address local concerns; (2) building local partnerships; (3) building community capacity; (4) influencing health policy; and (5) evaluating local empowerment.

The local empowerment challenge is to initially create sufficient support for a particular concern in order to form a 'community of interest' or 'interest group'. This community and its members then embark on a process (referred to as an empowerment continuum in Chapter 3) towards gaining more control over the decisions that influence their concern. This may be in regard to resource allocation such as the award of a grant, or to decision-making such as the development of policy or legislation.

Engaging with people to address local concerns

Engaging with people is a collaborative process, often between an outside agency and a 'community', a term we use in quotes to remind readers of its plural meanings and dimensions discussed in Chapter 2. This is not a straightforward process. For example, research in the UK has shown that of 55 per cent of local residents who wanted to be involved in a programme, only 2 per cent actually participated; and of 80 per cent of people who claimed to want to get involved in public services, only 25 per cent were actually prepared to give up their time when further questioned (Confederation of British Industry 2006). Successfully engaging with the community is often a crucial first step towards local empowerment; but it is one that requires careful attention to the barriers to and enablers of engagement. Barriers, such as time, financial costs, meeting on agency terms rather than in a community space and tokenism, are well known. Below we focus on a few key enablers: effective communication, participation opportunities and needs assessment.

Effective communication

Community engagement begins with people becoming better informed of issues that meet their own concerns and how they can become personally involved in addressing them. A lack of understanding can be addressed by having clearer and more accurately targeted information. Effective communication, however, is more than just informing community members about issues. Within a context of gaining people's participation in health-promotion programming, communication advice that aids the process of their engagement include

1. A single point of communication or person as a reference;
2. Clear information especially about the planning process of a programme;
3. Opportunities to consult with and provide feedback to the outside agency;
4. Opportunities to have an influence on the programme, for example, to be involved in the decision-making processes regarding policy change;
5. Systems that ensure that all stakeholders are accountable to a constituency (Confederation of British Industry 2006).

A common problem facing health promotion (and other social) programming, however, is the assumption that knowledge in itself is sufficient to change practice. Instead there is substantial evidence of a gap between what people know and what they do. Recent work in Viet Nam, for example, found that the knowledge of school pupils about the proper use of latrines (98%), safe water supplies (98%) and the prevention of worm infection (95%) was very high (Trinh et al. 1999). However, a study of worm infection in adults and children found rates for round-worm, thread-worm and hook-worm to be 83%, 94% and 59% respectively (Needham et al. 1998). Worm infection rates are felt to be a reliable indicator of hygiene practice and sanitary conditions.

This gap between knowledge and practice can be exacerbated by health promotion programmes that tend towards

- Reliance on top-down programming using largely didactic styles of communication;
- Communicators lacking the knowledge and skills to effectively use participatory methods and materials;
- Communication interventions lacking adequate research;
- Proper audience segmentation not being included in programme design, resulting in inappropriate message content and the exclusion of specific groups;
- Demand generated by the message content not being matched by supply, for example, the supply of condoms, latrines or hand-washing facilities (UNICEF 2001).

To bridge this 'know-do' gap, as it is now short-handed, requires that health promoters be very skilled communicators. They must know who else it may be important for community members to speak with about their concerns; and be able to facilitate effective intracommunity communication from the outset. Here it is useful to consider the theoretical arguments for communication put forward by the German social philosopher, Jurgen Habermas (1984). Habermas identifies two types of rationality that co-exist and frame every act of communication: a strategic or purposive rationality, in which we try to maximise self- or even collective material gain, that is, it is tied to the material world; and a communicative rationality, in which we try to maximise our understandings with one another. He argues that strategic rationality, by itself, is irrational, since in the absence of understanding what one's strategic behaviours mean to others, something only accomplished through communicative rationality, one cannot ensure that they will accomplish the desired results. Where this arises in groups, especially in their initial forming periods, is the balance between task (strategic rationality) and process (communicative rationality). But the more specific contribution Habermas makes to those trying to create empowering (or what Habermas would call 'emancipating') forms of community engagement is his four norms of 'ideal' communication:

1. What people speak is comprehensible; others understand its meaning because speakers have mastered logical argument and have expressive and interactive competence.

2. The propositional content (what people are proposing) is true; it is not logically or rationally false. This means that it can be defended by argument or evidence, a point we make later in our discussion of evaluating empowerment.
3. The propositional content is appropriate; it is justifiable on the basis of moral or ethical argument or theory. That is why this book opened with a brief discussion of equity, justice and ethics.
4. It is spoken with sincerity; the speaker more or less 'walks the talk'.

Remembering these basic norms can help to improve all forms of communication which, in turn, can help to build local trust, community participation and community confidence.

Participation opportunities

Ensuring opportunities for participation is also important to community engagement; it allows people to become collectively involved in activities which influence their lives and health. Participation has both instrumental and constitutive health effects. Instrumentally, it allows for greater programme effectiveness; constitutively, communities with greater rates of citizen participation also have comparatively better health, likely for the psychological sense of empowerment and control it creates (Labonté & Laverack 2001). Participation is a process that continuously changes and unfolds as individual actors and their varying group or organisational constituencies negotiate the terms of their relationships. In simplest terms, participation describes the attempts to bring different stakeholders together around problem-posing, problem-solving and decision-making. By stakeholder we mean:

1. someone with decision-making authority over the programme or policy;
2. someone significantly affected by the decision (this requires a judgement call over what 'significantly' means, but this should serve as a screen to limit the size of the eventual group);
3. someone who can make a key contribution to decision resolution (they may possess knowledge resources or material resources, and knowledge in this case is both the formal knowledge of researchers and academics and the informal knowledge of community members);
4. someone otherwise able to prevent or enable decision-making (such as a specific lobby or interest group).

It is also important to distinguish participation from other forms of engagement between governments, institutions and communities to avoid the constant threat of tokenism (public involvement without authority). We can do this by defining three terms, often and incorrectly used synonymously: consult, involve and participate. Consultation is straightforward: We ask, but do not dialogue. Involve and participate are more complex. Their dictionary meanings are quite revealing. Involve means to 'wrap (a thing in another) wind spirally, entangle (person, thing, in difficulties, mystery, etc.); implicate (person in charge, in crime, etc.).make complicated in thought or form'. Participate means to 'have share, take part (in thing, with person); have something of . . . entitling to share . . . taking part.' The essential and significant difference between involvement and participation is the moment when others (individuals, groups) are invited to join in the problem-posing, problem-solving process. Involvement invites others after the problem has been named in quite specific ways; participation invites others to name problems in the specific ways most useful to the largest number. Involvement, like community-based programming, is often a useful and healthful action. The conundrum arises when the problem-naming (language, frames of reference) of the institution does not cohere with that of the community group and the latter attempts to respond on the terms set by the expert, becoming 'involved' in (wrapped up in, made more complicated by) these terms. This is sometimes the case when communities are asked to become 'involved' in health coalitions where the outcomes (e.g., CVD or cancer rates) have already been defined by the health agency, often accompanied by epidemiological data and arguments that use concepts and language foreign to citizens' day-to-day experiences. At the same time, an institutional demand for constant participation can be just as disempowering as involvement that masquerades as participation. It may represent a wasteful expenditure of citizen time, and excuse the failure of politicians to make difficult policy decisions. For public participation also carries opportunity costs (time, energy) and may not even represent *how* citizens wish to engage with institutions and professionals (Labonté 1997). Table 4.1 provides a simple *aide mémoire* for these different types of engagement.

One essential opportunity for people to participate is through meetings or forums to discuss concerns that are important to them. Such meetings typically begin with a brief introduction to the purpose followed by an introduction of the participants. The meeting is a facilitated group discussion to focus on a particular local concern such as public transport, unemployment and sub-standard housing. The meeting can be supported by audio-visual materials such as a poster or a

Table 4.1 Fundamental characteristics of participation, involvement and consultation

Participation:
• Negotiated, formalised relationships
• Open frame of 'problem-naming'
• Shared decision-making authority
• Full stakeholder identification
• Resources for stakeholder participation ('levelling the playing field')
• Stakeholder accountability to a larger constituency (the group they represent)
Involvement:
• Citizens treated as individuals rather than as organised constituencies
• Terms of engagement are ultimately in control of the agency sponsor
• Structure is advisory; it may have some, but very limited, decision-making autonomy
• Tendency to non-formalised agreements in which agency sponsor retains more invisible power
Consultation:
• Information from citizens sought on specific plans or projects
• Little or no structures for ongoing engagement between agency sponsors and its publics

Source: (Labonté 1997).

video to generate discussion, and can also be used to plan for actions, identify resources, identify potential partners and for people to openly express their views.

Susan George, an activist scholar associated with many local and international organisations, considers meetings the lifeblood of citizen and community empowerment. Many of us take for granted meetings and so use them less effectively and efficiently than we might. Over years of experience, George distils the important essence of such meetings to seven 'commandments' (George 2004), which we have embellished with some of our own insights:

1. Create a single page handout with a clearly written analysis, goals, strategies, accomplishments so far. Earlier meetings may be needed to develop this. The handout will need to be revisited from time to time, but amounts to a 'mission statement' for the group.
2. Welcome everyone at the start, asking for newcomers to identify themselves. Others at the meeting should be prepared to talk to newcomers at breaks or afterwards, to elicit their input in a more personalised way and to encourage them to return.

3. Set up a table where other information around the goals of the group is available. Someone should staff the table. This is where people can sign up to participate again in future meetings or activities.
4. Set up another table where other literature on related issues or community struggles can be placed. This allows people attending to make links between their concerns and those of other groups.
5. Make sure to plan, or announce an already planned, activity. There is a cliché: Communities thrive in action but die in committee. Meetings may be the lifeblood of empowerment, but empowerment is for a purpose and that purpose is fulfilled in actions besides simply meetings.
6. Ask for resources, financial or human (volunteer time). This is the test of relevance of the issues to people in communities. If it is sufficiently important, community members, even in the poorest of circumstances, will often be willing and able to give money, time or other in-kind support. Some progressive community funding agencies actually use a requirement of in-kind contribution as a way of ensuring that the activities they support have a reasonably broad base of community 'buy-in'.
7. Do all of this at the start of the meeting, not at the end when the noisy break-up begins and everyone is more interested in getting ready to leave than committing to new activities.

Needs assessment

Needs assessment provides another specific opportunity for community engagement. The question of who identifies the concerns to be addressed and how this will be taken forward is basic to empowerment. For practitioners, a key step is the identification of, support for and commitment to those concerns 'close to the heart' of communities. If practitioners are not willing to address the local concerns of communities the programmes they then help to implement are much less likely to succeed.

In practice, a compromise often has to be met between what the local concerns are and what the implementing agency wants to achieve. Health promotion is most often delivered through top-down programmes controlled by government agencies or government-funded NGOs. It is government policy (and resources) that sets the health promotion agenda, and the difficulty begins when this does not meet local concerns. Health promotion practitioners are employed to design and deliver programmes that promote health within the parameters set by government policy. So even when those in the 'top' structures agree with those at the local level about the main concerns, the way in which the agenda is determined can still result in these issues not being addressed.

However, there are many practitioners who remain passionate about using empowering approaches even within the context of bureaucratic, top-down styles of health-promotion programming. These practitioners are adept at merging the boundary between local concerns and government agendas and have become imaginative at how to accommodate empowering approaches within top-down programmes – though, as Chapter 1 cautioned, their abilities to do so rest partly on the understanding and support they receive from their employing agency.

Engaging people to address local concerns can be facilitated by the practitioner through building partnerships and alliances with community members. The purpose is to facilitate the sharing of his/her power in a way that involves the provision of both services and resources, at the request of the community. Box 4.1 provides an example of how one local council engaged with communities to improve the delivery of public services.

Box 4.1   Improving the delivery of local services

Slough Borough Council in the UK set up a citizen's jury to decide how to improve their 'street-scene' services in response to concerns primarily from local residents. This included road maintenance and street cleaning. This was a new initiative to create a partnership between the Council and local residents and other stakeholders. A new delivery strategy was devised to bring refuse collection and disposal, recycling, street cleaning, grounds and highways maintenance into a single partnership. At that time these contracts were split between different contractors. The Slough Borough council was given a mandate to increase Council Tax to improve the service, so long as the benefits could be guaranteed.

A consultative board met every six months to help set service priorities, solve delivery problems and take forward campaigning and educational work. As a consequence local services improved rapidly and Slough is now one of the cleanest towns in the South of England. The 'Keep Slough green and tidy' campaign motivates the public to be actively engaged in the effort to increase recycling and decrease litter. The partnership has given local residents more of a 'voice' and has included them in the decision-making process to improve the environment in Slough.

(Confederation of British Industry 2006)

Building local partnerships

In a health promotion programme, one practitioner role is to provide leadership, enthusiasm and the resources necessary to move participation forward. However, this role expectation can soon change to one of more 'equal' partnership between the practitioner and the community. Partnerships demonstrate the ability of the community to develop relationships with outside agents such as local authorities based on the recognition of mutual interests and respect. The partnership may involve an exchange of services, the pursuit of a joint venture based on a shared goal or an initiative to take action to the benefit of all parties.

Local empowerment is about the redistribution of power (control of resources and decisions) often through devolution. Central bodies devolve, and support, local authorities who in turn devolve responsibility to, and support, other organisations and local people. We cautioned earlier that devolution without access to and authority over necessary resources is a form of 'community-blaming' rather than empowerment, and a strategy often used by conservative governments rolling back public entitlements to health, education or welfare benefits. As well, without strengthening community management capacities and ensuring that devolved services and programmes are not captured by local elites, decentralisation can actually work against the aim of improving health equity (Collins & Green 1994).

But even when devolution includes both resources and authority, many practitioners find it difficult to relinquish the control that they have over the design and implementation of a programme. Accepting the expertise offered by local people and sharing professional expertise so that the members can build their own empowering capacities can be difficult for some outside agents (a term we use to describe both individual practitioners and the government agency or NGO for which they work). Partnerships offer a framework in which the relationship between the practitioner and their clients can become more equal. Box 4.2 provides an example of engaging a community to take responsibility on some of the tough questions in regard to a local road maintenance project.

Health promotion practitioners have an important role in providing information, resources and technical assistance, but this role must support the concerns that have been identified by the community as being relevant and important to them. The provision of resources and technical support often provides the basis for partnerships to develop between the outside agent and the community.

Box 4.2   Improving local involvement in road maintenance

A private company was asked by the Oxfordshire County Council to develop a solution to increase the life of a major road in Oxford, UK including junctions, access and traffic calming. The work was planned to interfere as little as possible with local businesses and residents, by avoiding busy seasons and working when premises were closed. Road-user groups, local businesses and the police were involved from the design phase through regular public meetings. Residents were asked to choose from a series of options for the difficult decisions, such as when to work at busy junctions. The work itself was broken down into sections covering 200m of road and residents were told dates in advance and businesses were allowed to continue deliveries. The road maintenance was planned around the convenience of local residents and businesses who were also involved in making decisions on an ongoing basis. This type of an arrangement can become formalised as a 'neighbourhood charter' or a two-way partnership between communities and a service provider such as a construction contractor.

Maintenance of this sort does not usually involve such intensive and continuous public consultation, but it helped to ensure that the work started and finished on time by helping to identify problems in advance, and resulted in a higher level of local participation and client satisfaction. Other projects have employed a watchman-in-chief who engages with business, service users, parish councils, the Highways Agency and local representatives. Other watchmen identify issues across the area and provide feedback to the watchman-in-chief. The watch-keeper role provides a non-bureaucratic, informal method through which the outside agency can keep in touch with a range of stakeholders when appropriate, enabling a feedback and communication. The information provided is realistic and accurate and always allows local residents to provide their opinions and, if necessary, to be involved with the decision-making processes (Confederation of British Industry 2006).

Building community capacity

Sometimes communities know what they want but do not know how to achieve it. In other instances, communities may not know what they want; express concerns more influenced by local media than critical reflection; or are constrained in identifying their concerns by internal conflict. The practitioner has an important role to play, especially at the early stages of a programme when community capacity has yet to be strengthened or developed, to support communities in identifying and/or addressing their concerns. This is often a temporary role and over the longer term the practitioner will be working towards reducing her initial leadership in the programme.

The programme design should clearly define how it will build the capacity of the community from planning, through implementation and management, to evaluation. Without this focus, the community can become dependent on the outside agent to provide support during the lifecycle of the programme without themselves building the necessary capacities.

Addressing community capacity is an important issue that is often overlooked in programming. Capacity building includes two key areas:

1. Firstly, the capacity of the community is strengthened so that members can better resolve their own concerns. This involves the development of specific skills and competencies which contribute to their overall capacity, and which are captured in the empowerment domains described in Chapter 2. These skills may be used later in a variety of circumstances; for example, the organisational skills that are developed to address a local concern such as flooding may be used again to address the siting of child-care facilities. Building community capacity therefore has a generic characteristic and is not limited to one issue only.
2. Secondly, the capacity of the community to take more control of the programme is enhanced. This often involves skills development based on programme management such as financial control, report writing and evaluation. These are skills that the community can use when it is involved in managing the programme.

The key practitioner point here is to provide the appropriate level of support at the request of the community. This means that the outside agent should not commit all the resources at the programme planning stage as new resource inputs will be identified as the strategic plan of the community is implemented. To meet this demand the outside agent should be flexible in the type and timing of resources that he is prepared to provide to support the community. In a programme, context resources are often designated to a specific budget category, for example, travel costs, training and equipment. However, the resources requested by the community may not fit neatly into one of these categories. There are activities that may be difficult to justify as being strictly health promotion but that nonetheless build the social dimension of communities through a sense of belonging, connectedness and personal relationships. Examples of these types of activities include

- Organising a community event such as a sports or arts festival;
- Providing food and drink to encourage people in the community to meet;
- Providing transport to allow people to travel and take part in an event;
- Arranging child-care facilities to allow mothers to meet;
- Providing a 'petty cash' account to cover incidentals such as refreshments at meetings, gift vouchers and refunding individual travel costs.

In these instances, the practitioner's role is one of lobbying the funding body (which may even be her own employing organisation) to amend its budgetary or accountability requirements to be more conducive to programmes working from a community empowerment/capacity-building approach.

Influencing health policy

Having a policy in place does not guarantee that it will be followed, or that a community's health conditions will improve. But failing to have a policy in place that incorporates community health concerns and solutions will guarantee little or no change. Influencing public health policy remains fundamental to empowering health promotion work.

The public health policy process, however, is complex because it is difficult to sometimes define the causal links between a policy intervention and an improvement in health. There are powerful interests at stake such as the tobacco industry, pharmaceutical industry and the medical professions. There are shifting ideas about how best to deliver public health's ever-changing demands, and challenges posed by demographic changes and emergent health concerns such as obesity, SARS, multiple/extreme drug resistant infections (such as TB) and the persisting threat of a global influenza pandemic. The causes of many public health problems are due to poor nutrition, poverty, smoking and the environment; and there can be large differences in policy-relevant health concerns between different social and ethnic groups, often within the same community. Developing policy solutions therefore involves the use of a range of intersectoral strategies (Gauld 2006), and a sensitivity to its intrinsic political nature. (Yeatman 1998). The people who control the political process (governments and governmental stakeholders at the national, municipal, regional and local levels) may or may not involve those who are influenced by the policy outcome in its development. The policy process can therefore be used as a 'power tool' to further exert control-over people resources and decision-making, or to shape policies in the interests of elite social groups with greater access to, and influence over, the political decision-making process.

People influenced by the policy, however, may not necessarily agree with it and may want to change its formulation or stop its delivery. Communities can influence the policy process by persuading or forcing those who control its development to change its design or delivery. Public participation in policy change can take the form of 'direct democracy' such as a referendum that can be prospective and government initiated, or more rarely, reactive and citizen initiated. This is large-scale voting on specific questions most commonly regarding constitutional issues about how people should live together and be governed, such as compulsory military service and changes in legislation (Parkinson 2006). Evidence suggests that people are reluctant to take direct forms of participation. For example, in New Zealand a study showed that of the 89 per cent of respondents to a petition only 19 per cent attended a demonstration, 17 per cent joined a boycott, 4 per cent joined in a strike and only 1 per cent were willing to occupy a building (Perry & Webster 1999) to try and influence a policy issue. There is also a pattern to poor public participation that includes young people, members of ethnic and other minorities and those with the lowest level of education and income who are the least likely to be involved; although some of these groups may be opting to use other forms of participation such as the Internet forums (Hayward 2006). Ironically, it is these groups who are most likely to be affected by policy decisions because they have less of an economic or social 'buffer' to protect them from changes in, for example, employment, housing or welfare policies.

Influencing policy is an important form of participation that can be a direct expression of local empowerment. But more often, public participation takes a passive form such as voting, signing a petition or writing a letter to someone in the political system. Marginalised groups often lack the resources or level of organisation necessary to have a strong 'voice' through, for example, a boycott or legal action. It is therefore essential that they are assisted to become more active in influencing the policy process at its different stages of development. This is possible because, far from being predictable, the policy process is reliant on the ability of the different stakeholders in civil society and in government to negotiate a compromise.

Models of the policy process

Several useful frameworks have been developed to conceptualise how people can act to change the 'prevailing paradigm' of policy development. In particular Lindquist (2001) offers an interesting view, provided in Table 4.2, of a framework to influence policy.

In addition, to Lindquist's framework a number of models have been developed that can guide the analysis of influence in the policy process. It should be noted that these models primarily reflect processes in the developed world and assume a democratic political system. The models provide in-depth conceptualisations about how this process works within two broad paradigms: rationalist and political (Neilson 2001). The rationalist paradigm includes linear, incrementalist and interactive models as representations of the policy process. It originates from classical economic theory which presumes that actors have full information and are then able to establish priorities to achieve a desired and largely uncontested goal. It is driven by the production and consideration of different forms of evidence such as public health research, and the input

Table 4.2   A framework to influence policy

Types of Policy Influence:

1. Expanding Policy Capacities
   - Improving the knowledge/data of certain actors
   - Supporting recipients to develop innovative ideas
   - Improving capabilities to communicate idea
   - Developing new talent for research and analysis

2. Broadening Policy Horizons
   - Providing opportunities for networking/learning within the jurisdiction or with colleagues elsewhere
   - Introducing new concepts to frame debates, putting ideas on the agenda, or stimulating public debate
   - Educating researchers and others who take up new positions with broader understanding of issues
   - Stimulating quiet dialogue among decision-makers

3. Affecting Policy Regimes
   - Modification of existing programmes or policies
   - Fundamental redesign of programmes or policies

from experts and academics is a valued part of the process. Tim Tenbensel and Peter Davis (in press) provide as an example of the rationalist model, government decisions on the purchase of pharmaceutical products for health service delivery. In developed countries these are rational decisions made on the basis of a 'cost-benefit' analysis and available information. If, however, insufficient or incorrect information is available or the policy goal is highly contested, the rationalist paradigm offers limited guidance to how policy can be planned or influenced.

The political paradigm generates policy models adapted from political economy theory and derived from comparative politics and international relations. These theories stress the important of agenda setting, policy networks, policy narratives and the policy transfer in shaping final decisions (Neilson 2001). Policy decisions, in turn, are made on the basis of bargaining and negotiation between the many different stakeholders who employ a range of approaches to have an influence on each stage of the policy process, discussed below. From the vantage of health policymakers, the most effective approach to policy combines elements from both the rational and political paradigms. For example, the introduction of policy to ban smoking in public places was initially based on strong epidemiological evidence regarding second hand smoke. However, the best strategy to reduce death and illness from second hand smoke would be a total ban on smoking, including in homes. Obviously such a policy would be very difficult to police as well as would create opposition from civil libertarian groups. The policy decision was therefore a compromise based on the available evidence and the opposing interests of different stakeholders to reach an achievable goal rather than an optimal goal (Tenbensel & Davis in press). From the vantage of those aiming to influence the policymaking process, similar compromises may be necessary, with each stage in the process, offering opportunity for input or advocacy.

The steps to influencing health policy

At a practice level, the policy process can be defined as a framework that has six steps: (1) Identify issues, (2) Policy analysis, (3) Undertake consultation, (4) Move towards decisions, (5) Implementation and (6) Evaluation (Edwards et al. 2001). All these steps are subject to internal politics as well as to the politics of the state and the apparatus of administration and management that it employs. What follows is an explanation of how the policy development cycle can be influenced by people in civil society, community groups and advocacy groups often assisted by health promotion practitioners.

Identify issues

Initially the problem has to be defined and articulated before it can be properly considered and a decision be made as to whether to include it on the policy agenda. Government policy agendas are often crowded and so issues that are to be selected are in competition with one another. It is useful if those people proposing the problem can demonstrate that it is an undesirable situation and one that is getting worse. In particular, they need to show that some public harm will result unless action is taken and that this harm is able to be expressed in terms of social and economic aggregates or health outcomes. For example, policy actions on obesity or smoking are more likely to be considered when the longer-term social and economic effects, such as increased health expenditure and loss in worker productivity, can be shown. Similarly, the threat of litigation for economic costs, a strategy frequently used in the USA, has been used effectively to change the production, marketing and retail practices of tobacco companies (smoking-related damages) and food oligopolies involved in the processed/fast food industry (obesity-related damages). Finally, as we noted in Chapter 3, the problem has a greater chance of being recognised as a policy issue if there is a simple solution to resolve the situation and if government intervention is justified (Tenbensel & Davis in press); for example, to promote an increase in physical activity and smoking cessation in the population, or to provide access to essential medicines.

The responsibility to place a policy issue on the government agenda usually rests with the appropriate minister. The minister has to ensure that there is a broad enough understanding and acceptance of the issue so that it has a good chance of moving forward in the policy cycle. This provides an opportunity to influence the policy cycle through indirect actions such as lobbying the responsible minister, for example, by sending a letter, email or text message, signing a petition or meeting with the minister and other politicians. It is also an opportunity to influence the policy cycle through non-violent direct actions, for example, by taking part in peaceful demonstrations and public protests. The media can also play a significant role and people can engage in a publicity campaign to try and influence the decisions made by the minister in selecting the policy agenda, for example, an issue that is obviously widely unpopular with the public may have less chance of being selected.

But to what extent can public action have an effect on defining the policy concerns of government? Government action on policy can be seen as a democratic enterprise that, in theory, reflects the needs or wants of a significant proportion of the public. The public can express what they want through indirect and direct actions discussed earlier, and can challenge the government arguments put forward for defining a particular policy 'problem'. The basis of these counter-arguments may be supported by science and research which in turn can be contested on the value basis of the problem definition. For example, activists in the USA have successfully reframed the obesity problem from one of health to one of 'the right to be fat' based on the role of diversity and acceptance in society (Tenbensel & Davis in press). Inevitably, the success of one group's argument over another group's counter argument may be based more on access to the resources that enable them to put forward a more aggressive and convincing campaign than the positioning of the issue in relation to the value of matters of public health and safety or individual rights. An important element of such a campaign is the media as it has the potential to widely influence public opinion. An advocacy truism is that having media coverage of an issue does not guarantee it will receive political attention; but a lack of media coverage does not guarantee it political attention. If governments are shown to be unresponsive to public demands for action this can create the opportunity for others who do support the issue to step in and to carry the issue forward.

Policy analysis

Policy analysis commonly involves at least three elements: collecting the relevant data; clarifying the objectives and resolving the key questions that have been raised, and identifying the options and proposals that will form basis of the policy reform. An important factor is the level of investment made at this stage to ensure a thorough analysis of the issues and to provide sufficient clarity so that decisions can be quickly made to devise solutions to problems. But even when a policy solution exists it may have to wait for a correct political climate such as in the case of passive smoking. The scientific evidence against the causal link of passive smoking and ill health had existed for some time before it became a policy priority that was motivated from a position of moral and personal rights. This is when the 'window of opportunity' presented itself to act to introduce policy with the support of the public (Berridge 1999).

Public health advocates, researchers and academics can play an important role in helping to identify and provide the evidence necessary to resolve any issues arising during the analysis. This can be an opportunity to use lobbying tactics to try and influence staff working in government 'policy shops' who are often looking for evidence to support one or more

Box 4.3   The role of media: Advocacy that changes the frame

There are several truisms about health advocacy:

1. Without advocacy we cannot improve health. This attests to the importance of social determinants in influencing health, and the need to use policy levers to affect these determinants.
2. Health advocacy often conflicts with market liberalism. This speaks to the fact that these policies (regulatory and redistributive) often challenge elite interests vested in 'free market' ideology.
3. Advocacy requires taking a position where there is controversy. This simply notes that, when there are no competing interests in a policy area, there is no need for advocacy.
4. Advocacy involves risk-taking. This reminds us of Virchow's advocacy experience recounted in Chapter 1.

One key strategy frequently used by health advocates has been dubbed 'media advocacy', using mass media to shift the frame in which policy issues are defined. Media advocacy differs from social marketing, which attempts to persuade changes in personal behaviours. Media advocacy targets policies, policymakers and the ways in which issues come to be regarded as newsworthy or important. As Lawrence Wallack, one of media advocacy's founding scholars, comments, [T]he media agenda determines the public agenda: what's on people's minds reflects what is in the media (Wallack, 2005). Most mass media continue to frame health issues as medical cure or treatment, difficulties in getting access to treatment (waiting lists, uninsured new treatments) or the need to change unhealthy behaviours (most recently, fitness, nutrition and obesity). Since medical and behavioural health issues dominate news coverage (Gasher et al. 2007), this is what gets most attention by policymakers. Media advocacy attempts to challenge this dominance by changing the frame. This is easier to do with individual-level stories or issues than with broader social determinants. Media advocates, for example, successfully shifted tobacco control policy away from targeting smokers to targeting the tobacco and advertising industries. Similar media-targeted campaigns, increasingly with global reach, have been used to focus attention on access to antiretroviral drugs in developing countries. But social determinants 'stories' are inevitably policy analyses

(Continued)

Box 4.3 *(Continued)*

pieces, which require more depth and detail, and are less frequently covered by mass media than so-called 'hard news' stories (Gasher et al. 2007). A perennial challenge to media advocates concerned with the social determinants of health is how to capture media attention and reframe the health debate. Some examples culled from our own experiences: Staging a public event where an actual over-sized pie was sliced according to quintiles to show the increasing inequalities in wealth distribution over time; countering stories of surgery wait-times with tales of waiting lists for subsidised housing for low-income families; organising large-scale demonstrations or marches that drew attention to deepening poverty rates and the need for welfare reforms. While media coverage of these more profound health determinants, and the policy changes needed to address them, remains a distant third to medicine and lifestyles, it appears to be growing. With its slow rise comes another challenge: framing the policy debate in ways that do not stigmatise the poor or rob them of dignity or agency. The increasing role of the Internet in political campaigning, and the opportunities it presents for multiple creative ways of framing and reframing issues, is rapidly changing the entire frontier for media advocacy and policy engagement.

of the range of policy options they are exploring. But as the policy analysis is mostly undertaken internally and in confidence, the level of public influence may be difficult.

Undertake consultation

Consultation can be formal or informal and may occur at any stage of the policy process. Consultation is often facilitated by the issue of a discussion paper which outlines the policy intentions and allows feedback from individuals, groups and civil society. People may be formally asked for a response to the discussion paper or it may be placed in the public arena to stimulate an open debate on the issues. The purpose is that the consultation stage will lead to a refinement of the policy and a wider public acceptance of its intentions.

It is at this stage that there is the greatest opportunity for 'legitimate' public engagement in the policy process. A number of indirect actions can be taken to influence the policy process such as local meetings to discuss the draft policy paper, signing a petition for or against the policy paper, sending an email, fax, text or letter to a minister or local government officer or delivering promotional material to other people. A number of direct actions can also be taken to influence the policy process such as participating in public protests or by supporting a publicity campaign. The purpose of these actions is to ensure that the people involved in making the decisions are aware of their opinions and support for or against the policy, especially important when policy choices are strongly contested. Since health promoters are often in a position to help draft policy, and to convene consultations, they must also be critically reflective on when such consultation (or a fuller form of participation, as we distinguished earlier in this chapter) is appropriate. While the move to community participation by many governments is a potentially healthy step towards a more civil society, it is not always clear whose interests are being served most. Participation may have become a ritual, devoid of critical reflection on how it might be more or less empowering for the communities affected. In the end, bureaucrats become more empowered because they can say, 'I've consulted with the community, and therefore my conclusions have more politically correct weight.' If these conclusions truly do benefit local community groups, this is not necessarily a bad outcome. But that may not always be the case; and unless health promoters are clear on the reasons why they are engaging with communities on policy issues, they risk draining the energies of community groups in meetings or discussions of more importance to their institution than to the community.

Move towards decisions

Following analysis, debate and policy refinement the necessary decisions can begin to emerge. Firstly, the decision will be made by the appropriate person and then the policy proposal will be put forward for approval by the government or the necessary body with authority. In spite of the earlier analysis and consultation the final decision will have to consider issues of economy, efficiency and equity. A compromise may have to be reached, for example, one in which the policy is phased-in over a period of time to allow sufficient funds to be made available. Alternatively, the policy reforms may be introduced as a package alongside other measures, assistance and benefits. The purpose is to publicly introduce the policy reform with a minimum of opposition and criticism.

At this stage of the policy process if people are opposed to the decisions, they can continue to use a range of direct and indirect actions: the threat of collectively withdrawing their votes for those making the decision, engaging in an aggressive publicity campaign against the policy decision or instigating legal action against those making the policy decision. The purpose of these actions is to try and force those making the decision to agree upon a compromise in favour of the opinions of those against it.

Implementation

Once the decisions have been made and approved, the policy enters a period of implementation towards the desired outcomes. If the policy reform is clearly defined, has general support and is well resourced then the implementation should be successful. However, the implementation of new policy invariably entails some modification to the existing policies (Burris 1997). Unless the implementation is delivered well and sensitively, it can result in problems and even failures.

Evidence from policy implementation has found a number of causes for a failure at the implementation stage including ambiguity in the policy itself, conflict with other policies, having low political priority or engendering conflict with significant stakeholders (Edwards et al. 2001). In particular, 'bad publicity' can have a detrimental affect on the implementation of the policy especially as decision makers often lose interest at this stage and insufficient resources are given to promote the reforms. On the other hand, the greatest likelihood of implementation success is when the policy is technically simple, necessitates only marginal changes in existing policy, is delivered by one agency, has clear objectives and a short duration (Walt 1994).

Policies can actually be reformulated at the implementation stage and this provides the opportunity to interfere with and possibly stall the process of implementation by opposing stakeholders. The best chance of success they have is if the effect of 'bad publicity' can be harnessed against the policy reform. To do this they may have to use radical actions such as staging protests with the intention of attracting publicity or creating an outrageous media stunt such as climbing a public building to deploy a banner advertising a message against the policy reform. Another tactic is by placing oneself in a position of 'manufactured vulnerability' to prevent implementation such as squatting in a building to be demolished or living in a tree to be cut down. Some people may decide to take violent and illegal forms of direct action such as 'hacktivism' by accessing a computer to obtain information or placing a virus to sabotage a database or by physically altering something to prevent implementation such as 'spiking' tress with metal pins or blocking vehicles by 'sit-ins' on roads.

Evaluation

The monitoring and evaluation of the policy can lead to incremental revisions if reforms are not being met, or met efficiently. For example, if the purpose of the reform was to increase equity and participation in child support but this was shown not to have happened, the policy may be changed and reimplemented. The evaluation can be influenced by a broader political agenda which may also have changed since the original policy decision had been made. It may then be more difficult to justify a continuation of the policy if, for example, it now has a lower priority in the political agenda. Policy evaluation gives further hope to those who, if their actions and tactics to influence it have been unsuccessful, can use the revision process as a means to reintroduce changes to, or to stop, the reforms. Ultimately, the evaluation, influenced by the actions of others, can recommend that the policy reform be revised or cancelled, although evidence of this is rare. Unfortunately, the evaluation of policy is invariably never attempted except for small-scale programmes or initiatives. This could be because policy is 'owned' and implemented by more than one stakeholder and objectives may be too diverse or ambiguous to allow a clear evaluation (Tenbensel & Davis in press).

Evaluating local empowerment

Evaluation is important in health-promotion programmes, as well as in the policies that shape them. Evaluation in a health-promotion programme context has many purposes. These include providing inputs to ongoing activities, information for future programme design, evidence of effectiveness (have I met my targets?) and efficiency (the outputs in relation to the inputs), accountability to funders and participants, and the potential for sustainability over time. But evaluation that empowers also ensures that it addresses people's local concerns and provides the information that they need to make better-informed decisions that go beyond the programme's own goals. Evaluation that empowers, further emphasises the participation by people actively involved in the programme in the evaluation process. The evaluation itself ideally becomes an empowering experience by building skills and competencies of community members.

The key characteristics of an empowering evaluation

Certain commitments have been identified by Labonté and Robertson (1996) and Wadsworth & McGuiness (1992) as good ideals for an 'evaluation that empowers':

1. Respect for all parties as equal yet possessing different values, concerns and meanings, all of which are all equally important.

2. A determination to seek all parties' perceptions.
3. An opportunity for all to discuss and interpret the findings in order to reach a consensus on the best explanation.

The key characteristics for the evaluation of local empowerment also include considerations for the design and implementation of the approach:

Design

- Applies principles of rigour that are technically sound, theoretically underpinned and field-tested.
- Uses appropriate methods.
- Addresses programme effectiveness and efficiency.
- Addresses programme achievements and inputs.
- Addresses ethical concerns.

Implementation

- Clearly defines the roles and responsibilities of all stakeholders.
- Use participatory, self-evaluation approaches.
- Information provided can be interpreted by all stakeholders.

Outcomes

- Provides information that is accurate and feasible.
- Ensures that the stakeholders can use the information to make decisions and to take actions.
- Findings use a mix of interpretation, for example, textual and visual (Laverack 2007).

Measurable indicators of local empowerment

Apart from evaluation of specific health-promotion programme goals or objectives, on which much has been written that will not be recounted here, there is the matter of tracking change in empowerment itself. Empowerment is a complex concept. While empowerment approaches have an explicit purpose to bring about social and political change embodied in their sense of action and political activism (Laverack 2007), other approaches provide a focus on the individual (Zimmerman & Rappaport 1988), the organisation (Israel et al. 1994), the family (Haynes & Singh 1993) and the community (Wallerstein & Bernstein 1994). But of the different levels of empowerment it has been the psychological level and the use of predetermined outcome indicators which have received the most attention in terms of measurement (Rissel et al. 1996; Zimmerman & Rappaport 1988; Labonté 1994b).

At a psychological level, people experience an immediate and personal form of empowerment, such as an increase in self-esteem or self-confidence (Labonté 1998). Though partially measured as self-esteem or self-efficacy, psychological empowerment is a construct which incorporates the person's perceptions and actions within their social context (Zimmerman 1990). Empowerment can therefore mean different things to different people as a personal experience and it is likely to be incremental and often relative to the interpersonal relationships of the person concerned as the subjective elements of empowerment.

Empowerment can also be viewed as both a process and an outcome. Outcome indicators cover the level of control gained over a range of social, political and economic factors. Empowerment has a long time frame, at least in terms of significant social and political change, for example, a change in government policy or legislation. Health promotion programmes typically have a shorter time frame and the measurement of outcome might not take into account processes such as capacity building and the development of new competencies and skills. It may not therefore be possible to measure empowerment outcomes during a programme period. However, by measuring empowerment as a process, it is possible to monitor the interaction between capacities, skills and resources during the timeframe of a programme.

The process of local empowerment can be measured by reference to the nine distinct 'domains' discussed in Chapter 2, that is, tracking how a health promotion programme (1) Improves participation, (2) Develops local leadership, (3) Builds empowering organisational structures, (4) Increases problem-assessment capacities, (5) Improves resource mobilisation, (6) Enhances the ability of the community to 'ask why' (critical awareness), (7) Strengthens links to other organisations and people, (8) Creates an equitable relationship with the outside agents and (9) Increases control over programme management. There are many potential ways in which local empowerment, and changes in the nine empowerment domains, might be evaluated. The approach outlined below is one that has been applied in different programme and cultural contexts. The approach is robust and reliable and the experiences of its application are discussed in detail elsewhere (Laverack 2003).

Measuring local empowerment

The approach uses a 'workshop' style setting. The workshop design should be flexible and needs to consider some basic elements such as the homogeneity of the group, its dynamics, size and the time frame for the exercises. It typically takes one day to complete the baseline assessment. The participants of the workshop are representatives of a 'local community' that share the same interests and needs.

Setting the baseline

The community representatives firstly make an assessment of each domain. To do this they are provided with five statements for each 'empowerment domain', each written on a separate sheet of paper. The five statements for each domain have been published elsewhere (Laverack 2005, 2007) and are summarised in Table 4.3. The five statements represent a description of the various levels of empowerment related to that domain. Taking one domain at a time the participants are asked to select the statement which most closely describes the present situation in their community. The statements are not numbered or marked in any way and each is read out loud by the participants to encourage group discussion. The descriptions may be amended by the participants or a new description may be provided to describe the situation for a particular domain. In this way the participants make their own assessment for each domain by comparing their experiences and opinions.

Recording the reasons why

Recording the reasons why the assessment has been made for each 'domain' is important so that this information can be taken into account during subsequent assessments. It also provides some defensible or empirically observable criteria for the selection. This overcomes one of the weaknesses in the use of qualitative statements, that of reliability over time or across different participants making the assessment (Uphoff 1991). The justification needs to include verifiable examples of the actual experiences of the participants taken from their community to illustrate in more detail the reasoning behind the selection of the statement; recall that this is one of Habermas' norms for 'ideal' communication.

The visual representation of local empowerment

Finally, the measurement of local empowerment can be visually represented to provide a means by which to share the analysis and interpretation of the evaluation with all the stakeholders. Visual representation allows information to be compared over a specific time frame, between the different components within a programme and between programmes. Visual representations do not have to use text and are therefore useful in a cross-cultural context or when stakeholders are not

Table 4.3 Five representative statements for each empowerment domain

Domain	1	2	3	4	5
Community participation	Not all community members and groups are participating in community activities and meetings, such as women, youth, men.	Community members are attending meetings but not involved in discussion and helping.	Community members involved in discussions but not in decisions on planning and implementation. Limited to activities such as voluntary labour and financial donations.	Community members involved in decisions on planning and implementation. Mechanism exists to share information between members.	Participation in decision-making has been maintained. Community members involved in activities outside the community.
Problem assessment capacities	No problem assessment undertaken by the community.	Community lacks skills and awareness to carry out an assessment.	Community has skills. Problems and priorities identified by the community. Did not involve participation of all sectors of the community.	Community identified problems, solutions and actions. Assessment used to strengthen community planning.	Community continues to identify and is the owner of problems, solutions and actions.
Local leadership	Some community organisations without a leader.	Leaders exist for all community organisations. Some organisations not functioning under their leaders.	Community organisations functioning under leaders. Some Organisations do not have the support of leaders outside the community.	Leaders are taking initiative with support from their organisations. Leaders require skills training.	Leaders taking full initiative. Organisations in full support. Leaders work with outside groups to gain resources.
Organisational structures	Community has no	Organisations have been established	More than one organisation which are active.	Many organisations have established links	Organisations actively involved in and outside

	organisational structures such as committees.	by the community but are not active.	Organisations have mechanism to allow its members to provide meaningful participation.	with each other within the community.	the community. Community committed to its own and to other organisations.
Resource mobilisation	Resources are not being mobilised by the community.	Only rich and influential people mobilise resources raised by community. Community members are made to give resources.	Community has increasingly supplied resources, but no collective decision about distribution. Resources raised have had limited benefits.	Resources raised are also used for activities outside the community. Discussion by community on distribution but not fairly distributed.	Considerable resources raised and community decides on distribution. Resources fairly distributed.
Links to others	None.	Community has informal links with other organisations and people. Does not have a well-defined purpose.	Community has agreed links but not involved in community activities and development.	Links inter dependant, defined and involved in community development. Based on mutual respect.	Links generating resources, finances and recruiting new members. Decisions resulting in improvements for the community.
Ability to 'ask why'	No group discussions held to ask why about community issues.	Small group discussions are being held to ask 'why' about community issues and to challenge received wisdom.	Groups held to listen about community issues. These have the ability to reflect on assumptions underlying their ideas and actions. Are able to challenge received wisdom.	Dialogue between community groups to identify solutions, self-test and analyse. Some experience of testing solutions.	Community groups have ability to self-analyse and improve its efforts overtime. This is leading towards collective change.

(Continued)

Table 4.3   *(Continued)*

Domain	1	2	3	4	5
Programme management	By agent.	By agent in discussion with community.	By community supervised by agent. Decision-making mechanisms mutually agreed. Roles and responsibility clearly defined. Community has not received skills training in programme management.	By community in planning, policy and evaluation with limited assistance from agent. Developing sense of community ownership.	Community self-manages independent of agent. Management is accountable.
Relationship with outside agent	Agents in control of policy, finances, resources and evaluation of the programme.	Agents in control but discuss with community. No decision-making by community. Agent acting on behalf of agency to produce outputs.	Agents and community make joint decisions. Role of agent mutually agreed.	Community makes decisions with support from agents. Agent facilitates change by training and support.	Agents facilitate change at request of community which makes the decisions. Agent acts on behalf of the community to build capacity.

Source: Laverack 1999.

literate (Laverack 2005). Graphing differences over time allows conclusions to be drawn about the effectiveness of building community empowerment in a programme context. The community members and the outside agent can provide a textual analysis to accompany the visual representation to explain why some domains are strong and others are not. The visual and textual analysis can be used to develop strategies to build community empowerment during a specific period such as between programme reporting cycles. The visual representation provides a 'snapshot' of the strengths and weaknesses of community empowerment as a whole.

Not surprisingly, several authors have used visual representations as a tool to compare changes that can influence the process of community empowerment. For example, John Roughan (1986), a community development practitioner, developed a wheel configuration and used rating scales to measure three areas – personal growth, material growth and social growth – for village development in the Solomon Islands. The rating scale had ten points that radiated outwards like the spokes of a wheel for each indicator of the three growth areas. Each scale was plotted following an evaluation by the village members to provide a visual representation of growth and development. The approach used a total of 18 complex, interrelated indicators such as equity and solidarity to evaluate village development. Rifkin et al. (1988) in Nepal and later Bjaras et al. (1991) in Sweden, were the first commentators on the use of the 'spider web' configuration for the visual representation of community participation. Their approach identifies five factors: leadership, needs evaluation, management, organisation and resource mobilisation and uses a similar simple rating scale. Marion Gibbon (1999), a community development practitioner, in her measurement of community capacity in Nepal utilised a set of eight factors and a set of indicators with a rank assigned from 1 (low) to 4 (high). The rankings were then plotted onto a spider web configuration similar to the approach used by Rifkin et al. (1988).

Evaluation information, however presented, is especially important to compare progress within a community and between communities in the same programme. It is a useful means to promote the free flow of information and allow all stakeholders to visualise, to better articulate and share their ideas on the building of community capacity towards local empowerment. Importantly, evaluation provides link between measurement and tangible community actions through participation and strategic planning (Laverack 2006).

As important as meeting these local challenges, and measuring progress towards community empowerment goals remains, our health and what determines it is increasingly embedded in global economic, political and social processes. Globalisation is no longer an abstract idea that health promoters, in their measured pursuit of local empowerment, can ignore.

5

Pathways from the Local to the Global

> We no longer inhabit, if we ever did, a world of discrete national communities. [T]he very nature of everyday living – of work and money and beliefs, as well as of trade, communications and finance . . . connects us all in multiple ways with increasing intensity.
>
> (Held 2004)

This chapter focusses the discussion on the link between the local and the global. An explanation of globalisation within the context of health promotion is developed, noting how processes of globalisation can impinge on the health of people. We identify who are the 'winners and losers' in an increasingly globalised world and what the implications are for health-promotion practitioners in reshaping globalisation in a healthier direction.

Unhealthy contradictions: The emergence of global production chains

How is the local inherently global? And how did it become so? To begin answering these questions the following fictionalised accounts, based on published research and testimony, are given:

Bangladesh: The high cost of cheap clothes
In Bangladesh, Bilkis considers herself lucky to have work in one of that country's many export clothing factories. In her conservative Muslim village, she would not have been allowed work at all. Having a job in Dhaka, in one of the factories, is a small yet important improvement for her. But she wonders how long she will be able to

last. She works 10 to 14 hours a day, 7 days a week; more if there is a sudden rush order from a large chain store in the USA or UK. Many of these companies have signed a voluntary agreement for ethical trade. Workers are not supposed to work more than 48 hours a week, with no more than 12 hours of compulsory overtime. But pressures from the buyers force her factory to push aside even the 60-hour work week rules. They are told that if they can't produce so much for a set price, the buyers will move to China where things are even cheaper. If she refuses the overtime, she risks being beaten or fired. She is owed a lot in back wages, too, and hopes that if she keeps quiet she will eventually get paid. She cannot live on the 8 cents an hour she does receive. But she is afraid to ask for her money. One of her co-workers did and was promptly dismissed. Bilkis is especially concerned for the young girls who are appearing again in the factory. Child labour disappeared in the factories after global campaigns in the 1990s, and is against the law. But when the pressures to produce so cheaply are so strong, and so many families are still too poor to feed or educate properly their children, laws, too, have a way of disappearing.

(Alam & Hearson 2006; Hearson & Morser 2007;
Kabeer & Mahmud 2004a, 2004b; Kernaghan 2007)

China: Toys may be fun, making them is not
In China, Jia is one of the millions of rural young women migrating each year to the coastal cities from the poverty and the collapse of health and social infrastructures following that country's embrace of market reforms in the 1970s. She works in a toy factory in one of the many 'free trade' export-processing zones that produce manufactured goods for much of the world. The toys she decorates using cheap lead-based paints that make her nauseous are for the world's best-known brands, for which she feels proud. But the work is tedious and never-ending. Her day starts at 8 am. She gets a 90-minute break mid-day, but then works continuously until 6 pm. After an hour for dinner, she works until 10:30 pm or later before going to the company-supplied barracks where she sleeps in a tiny room with fifteen other women. She doesn't work Sunday nights, and gets one day off a month. But that isn't enough time to visit her family or plan a life outside the factory walls. She isn't paid the minimum wage the law guarantees her, must give most of it back to the factory owners for her dormitory bunk and the cafeteria food, and has no health or social benefits. She feels trapped: she cannot return to the countryside, she cannot work much longer in the factory before she will collapse

and she cannot afford to move into the city where she wishes she could be.

(Labonté et al. 2005; China Labor Watch 2007)

Bilkis and Jia are but two of the hundreds of millions of new workers now employed in an economy that trade and financial market liberalisation has rendered global. Many of these (over 66 million in 2006) work in special 'Export Processing Zones' (EPZs) located in low-income Asian, Latin American, Caribbean and African countries. Described as the 'vehicles of globalization' by the International Labour Organization (Labonté et al. 2005), EPZs are often credited for offering women in poorer, less emancipated countries a step up on the ladder of employment and financial autonomy. As Bilkis' and Jia's stories reveal, and they are far from unique, the step is not a big one. It is also one riddled with risk and insecurity.

To reduce costs, EPZs favour the employment of women because they are seen as more compliant and cheaper to hire. Because such factories are located in countries with a large, and largely, unemployed labour force, wages and working conditions are rarely improved (International Confederation of Free Trade Unions 2003). Some countries explicitly forbid unions from EPZs and require wages to be lower than the outside minimum, causing a downward pressure on all wages. To attract foreign investment in EPZs, countries often offer extensive tax holidays (International Labour Organization 1998). By definition, these special zones do not levy tariffs on imported materials, further limiting the tax benefits a country might receive for redistribution as health, education and other development investments. Few locally produced goods are used in the EPZs. In 30 years of *maquiladoras* (as EPZs are called in Mexico), only 2 per cent of the raw materials processed into manufactured goods by EPZs came from within the country (International Labour Organization 1998). Apart from the jobs created, some of which have since departed to China, the EPZs have had little impact on Mexico's development (Wade 2002).

EPZs and similar 'sweatshops' could help provide a lift out of poverty for many workers, but only if they sourced their materials domestically and transferred technology back to local firms. They do not. Instead, most have simply become part of a globalising economy in which private manufacturers 'slice up the value chain' (Krugman 1995), locating each step of production where it contributes most to overall returns. Instead of transnational companies setting up branch plants in other nations, as they once did, liberalised global capitalism now allows them to carry out product design and development in wealthier countries where they have high levels of publicly funded education and research investment; where they can obtain raw materials from whichever nation sells them at the lowest price; sub-contract factories in countries where the labour, environmental, taxation and other regulatory standards are low and workers are plentiful and cheap; and move their profits through low- or no-tax-haven nations to minimise the contributions their profits might make to the public good (Grunberg 1998; Wade 2003). Indeed, much of the world's trade (between 1/3rd and 2/3rds) takes place between different branches of the same company; the estimates would be higher if the out-sourced and nominally independent sweatshops were taken into account (World Commission on the Social Dimension of Globalization 2004). All of this so that consumers can buy at 'unbelievably low prices!' products, which advertising tells them they want, a world away from the exploitative environments in which these products were created.

The benefits for poorer consumers in high and even middle-income countries are obvious. The costs are less visible, unless one happens to live in, for example, China where the country's explosive industrial growth has created the world's most polluted air and waterways, causing upwards of 750,000 environmental deaths annually (Kahn & Yardley 2007). China complains that the world is partner in its headlong rush to free market modernity; most of its dangerous and polluting factories produce for foreign investors bent on making products for consumers that are 'cheap as chips', as one Australian discount chain is called. We are all implicated in this as producers, consumers and even as citizens, since the environmental damage emanating from China's factories is slowly sprawling across all of Asia, and is now the major source of health-damaging air particulates as far away as Los Angeles (Kahn & Yardley 2007). Market failures, in this instance the lack of internalising the high cost of pollution and poor working conditions into the low price of goods, is an inherently global problem.

This can place the globally aware health promoter in a difficult place: making life more affordably healthier for their local poor but realising that this affordability is based on outsourcing its health and social costs to other people elsewhere. It also means that health promoters, ethically and pragmatically, can no longer avoid engaging with struggles to make globalisation healthier and more sustainable.

Explaining globalisation

The first step health promoters can take in doing so is to understand better what is meant by globalisation. Globalisation, at its simplest, describes a constellation of processes by which nations, businesses and people are becoming more connected and interdependent through increased economic integration and communication exchange, cultural diffusion and travel. It is not a new phenomenon. The history of humankind has been one of continuous pushing against borders, exploring, trading, expanding, conquering and assimilating, generally driven by an economic pursuit of resources or wealth (Diamond 1997). Disease has inevitably followed its path as trade and travel have long been vectors for epidemics. Nor is this the first time in more recent history that capital, and capitalists, have had greater interest in foreign markets than in those in their home jurisdictions. The period of rapidly increased integration of global markets that began in the 1980s continues a longer historical arc. The percentage of global economic output accounted for by international trade has only recently returned to the levels characteristic of the late nineteenth and early twentieth century (Cameron & Stein 2000), before growing income inequalities and a global economic recession helped fuel renewed protectionism and, eventually, two 'world' wars (Nye Jr. 2002). But contemporary globalisation also differs from previous eras in significant ways, including

- The speed and scale of private, often speculative financial flows. The flow of these 'hedged' or other derivative portfolio funds (over $2 trillion exchanges currencies daily) dwarfs the money reserves of all of the world's countries and have precipitated several financial crises. Each of these crises led to increased poverty and inequality and decreased health and social spending (O'Brien 2002; Cobham 2002; Hopkins 2006) with women and children disproportionately bearing the burden (Gyebi et al. 2002).
- The existence of enforceable trade and investment liberalisation agreements. The best known are the global agreements under the remit of the World Trade Organisation (WTO), or which exist regionally (such as the North American Free Trade Agreement or the South American Mercosur). But many more are bilateral. As the WTO's Doha Development Round of negotiations, intended to benefit disproportionately poorer countries, sputters to an inconclusive end due to rich world mercantilism, bilateral agreements have multiplied where the economic might of the larger countries eclipses the nominal democracy of the WTO. Regardless of geographic scope, trade agreements by definition limit the policy flexibilities of national governments, often in ways that could imperil public health (Labonté & Sanger 2006a/b).

- The size of transnational corporations, many of which are economically larger than most of the world's countries. These companies exert
  enormous influence in the free trade and investment rules to which
  most governments have agreed (Jawara & Kwa 2003).
- The crisis of climate change. For over 20 years health promotion has
  recognized the centrality, if not primacy, of the physical environment as a prerequisite to health (Labonté 1991a/b). Virtually all environmental markers show deterioration in our life support. Climate
  change is undoubtedly the most urgent health promotion issue and
  its linkage to global market integration is straightforward: Moving
  goods around the world consumes fossil fuel and exhausts greenhouse gases. In the UK, increases in trade-related shipping are now
  cited as the principle reason why that country will not meet its Kyoto
  commitment.

Globalisation is not without health benefits: the potential rapid diffusion of new health technologies; the digitally linked global network of
health and social activists working to create better social and environmental conditions; the increasing adoption of multilateral agreements
affecting health and the environment or supporting human rights-
based approaches to development. But its economic aspects also carry
many health risks that demand critical appraisal.

From the international to the global

The first critical point, and one of particular relevance to health promoters whose stock-in-trade is programme development and implementation,
is the distinction between international and global health. Until recently,
most health promoters, development agencies and non-governmental
organisations (NGOs) mobilised around 'international health' issues: the
greater burden of disease faced by poor groups in poor countries. Health
promoters working to reduce HIV prevalence in Africa, or to improve
maternal/child health programmes in Latin America, or to create gender
empowerment projects in South Asia are engaging in international health
promotion work. Their programmes and projects, and the empowerment
approach discussed in previous chapters, are simply international exten-
sions, into other countries, of the work they might have done within
their own borders. The only 'global' component is that funding for this
work is often provided through the rich world's modest efforts, whether
official or funnelled through NGOs, to aid in the health development of
countries lagging behind.

But no longer can health issues and their social determinants in one country be divorced from health issues in another. Sweatshop factories and pollution tell us that. Even the HIV pandemic in sub-Saharan Africa (SSA) has part of its roots in contemporary globalisation. Consider another stylised story of a Zambian woman named Chileshe.

> Chileshe waits painfully to die from AIDS. Antiretroviral programmes are too little and too late for her. She was infected by her now dead husband who once worked in a textile plant along with thousands of others but lost his job when Zambia opened its borders to cheap, second-hand clothing. He moved to the city as a street vendor, selling the cast-offs of donations from wealthier countries. He would get drunk and trade money for sex, often with women whose own husbands were somewhere else working, or dead, and who themselves desperately needed money for their children. Desperation, she thought, is what makes this disease move so swiftly; she recalls that a woman passing through her village once said that the true meaning of SIDA, the French acronym for AIDS, was 'Salaire Insuffisant Depuis des Années' – too little money for too many years.
>
> (Labonté et al. 2005)

The globalisation facts behind Chileshe's disease lie in the global debt crisis of the 1980s and the imposition of structural adjustment programmes by the International Monetary Fund (IMF) and World Bank that indebted countries had to follow to qualify for new loans. We detail this history in the section that follows; for now the salient feature is that, in 1992, an IMF loan required Zambia to open its borders to textile imports including cheap, second-hand clothing. Its domestic state-run clothing manufacturers, inefficient in both technology and management by wealthier nation standards, produced more expensive and lower quality goods. They could not compete, especially when the importers of second-hand clothes had the advantage of no production costs and no import duties. Within eight years, 132 of 140 clothing and textile mills closed operations and 30,000 jobs disappeared, which the World Bank later acknowledged as 'unintended and regrettable consequences' of the adjustment process (Jeter 2002). Many of the second-hand clothes that flooded Zambia and many other SSA countries ironically began as donations to charities in Europe, the USA and Canada. Surpluses not needed for their countries' own poor were sold to wholesalers who exported them in bulk to Africa, earning up to 300 per cent or more on their costs.

For conventional economists, this was a textbook example of how and why trade liberalisation works, even in poorer countries: Consumers got better and cheaper goods and inefficient producers were driven out of business. However Chileshe's husband, and then Chileshe herself, paid a heavy price. It was a price that cascaded throughout other sectors of Zambia's limited manufacturing base, with some 40 per cent of manufacturing jobs disappearing during the 1990s (Jeter 2002; UN Habitat). Large numbers of previously employed Zambian workers came to rely on the informal, ill-paid and untaxed underground economy.

Other facets of structural adjustment also played a role. Part of the standard adjustment package is privatisation of state industries, partly to raise short-term revenue to continue servicing overseas debts. This robs a country of the ability to use revenues from state-run commercial sectors to cross-subsidise the costs of social spending in areas such as education and health. Liberalised financial markets, in turn, make it easier for foreign-owned firms to move their profits offshore and avoid having it taxed for public spending. The theoretical assumption that growth would inevitably follow the economists' shock treatment remedies, leading to new forms of employment and taxation to replace the sources lost by unemployment and tariff revenues, was not borne out in fact. The result: a dramatic drop in the monies available to Zambia to invest in health or education. This was buttressed by other adjustment requirements: a decrease in public spending to reign in inflation, a cut in public sector wages and the introduction of cost-recovery (user-fee) programmes in health, education and other social services. This led to a rapid rise in school drop-out and illiteracy rates and to fewer people seeking health care or following through with treatment (UN Habitat; Atkinson et al. 1999). All these changes were imposed just when the AIDS pandemic was starting to surge; and to varying degrees, this story recurred throughout Southern Africa (Labonté et al. 2005; Commission for Africa 2005).

Blaming Chileshe's HIV infection on globalisation is an oversimplification. There are other important causes that explain why rates are high in some African countries but not in others. These include cultural differences (acceptance of multiple concurrent sex partners) (Halperin & Epstein 2004)), political differences (some countries accept the need to 'scale up' prevention and intervention programmes while others still question the HIV – AIDS link) and religious differences (fundamentalists of most persuasions take a dim view on promoting condom use and traditionalists in countries where male circumcision is uncommon balk at the surgery, despite both interventions showing definitive health promoting gains). Gender politics are also important: former UN Special Envoy for HIV in Africa, Stephen Lewis, writes of the feminisation of AIDS on that continent (Lewis 2005), a result of women's comparative disempowerment, their lack of political participation, unequal access to resources and property, restrictions on mobility and cultural codes that accept sexual violence against them (Commission on Social Determinants of Health 2007).

But globalisation's role in AIDS cannot be excused away; even its gendered impact is rooted in the backwash of globalisation's neoliberal policies. De Vogli and Birbeck (2005), for example, identified five multistep pathways that lead from globalisation to increased HIV vulnerability among women and children: currency devaluations, privatisation, financial and trade liberalisation, implementation of user charges for health services and implementation of user charges for education. The first two pathways reduce women's access to basic needs due to rising prices or reduced opportunities for waged employment. The third increases migration to urban areas, which simultaneously may reduce women's access to basic needs and increase their exposure to risky consensual sex. The fourth pathway (health user fees) reduces access to HIV-related services, and the fifth (education user fees) increases vulnerability to risky consensual sex, commercial sex and sexual abuse by reducing access to education. Education is one of the strongest predictors of women's empowerment.

In effect, African people, and especially African women, not responsible for the debts that precipitated the adjustment process were required to sacrifice their health to ensure the debts would be repaid. As Sanjay Basu, in an essay critical of the behaviour change emphasis in HIV prevention programmes in Africa, succinctly summarises: 'the background for increasing HIV transmission is a background of neoliberalism – a context where the movement of capital is privileged above the ability of persons to secure their own livelihoods' (Basu 2003).

Of debts, structural adjustment and neoliberal globalisation

The dawn of neoliberal globalisation broke in 1973, the year of the first world oil supply crisis and the start of what would become the developing world debt crisis. While the specific aetiology of debt crises varies from country to country, there are shared common causes:

- The oil price shocks of 1973 and 1979–80 had a severe impact on all of the world's economies, but especially those of oil-importing developing nations. To continue their economic growth, they were forced to borrow heavily from international markets to pay for the higher oil costs.

- Rich world banks, awash in new 'petrodollar' deposits, needed to lend huge amounts of this new wealth to maximise their own profit-making. Much of this lending was indiscrete, going to corrupt rulers; or to rich world contractors hired to build damns, roads or other infrastructures at inflated costs that primarily benefited the well-off in poorer, borrowing countries. Some argue that indebting poorer countries in this way was a deliberate strategy to seize control of their economy and their polity at much lower cost than occupying them by colonial force (Perkins 2006). In an infamous speech to the US Chamber of Commerce in 1983, then US Treasurer, Robert McNamara outlined the sanctions that would be used against a defaulting indebted country: 'The foreign assets of a country would be attacked by creditors throughout the world: its exports would be seized by creditors at each dock where they landed, its national airlines unable to operate and its sources of desperately needed capital goods and spare parts virtually eliminated . . . in many countries even food imports would be curtailed' (Canak 1989).

- A rapid rise in real interest rates during the early 1980s resulting from the US Federal Reserve policy of using high interest rates to drive down inflation ('fiscal monetarism', still very much a part of global economic policy). Debtor countries often had to roll over existing debt at much higher interest rates, effectively doubling the amount they owed without borrowing anything new.

- A fall in world prices for the primary commodities such as coffee that were indebted countries' major export and source of the 'hard' foreign currency that they required to pay their debts.

- Capital flight, both outright theft or, with more legality, the shifting of assets abroad by elites worried about inflation, stability, taxation and currency devaluations at home (Labonté & Schrecker 2007). During the time that sub-Saharan Africa, home to most of the world's 'heavily indebted poor countries' as they have come to be known, became mired in debt, more money left these countries as capital flight than that went into them as loans, foreign direct investment or development assistance (Ndikumana & Boyce 2003).

While the debt crisis was the necessary precursor to neoliberal globalisation, structural adjustment was its first instrument. The term entered the international lexicon when the World Bank, usually in conjunction with the IMF, initiated loans to help indebted countries reorganise their economies to increase their ability to repay foreign creditors. The Mexican debt crisis of 1982, the first of many around the world, saw both international financial institutions change from their original post-World War Two mandates of development funding and helping countries with balance of payment problems into 'watchdogs for developing countries. This to keep them on a policy track that would help them repay most of their debts and to open their markets for international investors' (Junne 2001). This policy track was steeped in neoliberal economic ideas that first surfaced in the 1950s and 1960s in the so-called 'Chicago School of Economics', which included such famous free-market economists as Milton Friedman and Friedrich Hayek, an early testament to another of modern globalisation's features, its cultural reach through what is sometimes called 'epistemic communities' (Haas 1992; Labonté et al. 2007), a sort of social movement of academic ideas. This economic orthodoxy was carried by the School's graduates to multilateral institutions such as the Organisation for Economic Cooperation and Development (OECD), the World Bank and the IMF, as well as to the finance ministries of governments around the world. The result was '[a]n alliance of the international financial institutions, the private banks, and the [conservative] Thatcher-Reagan-Kohl governments willing to use its political and economic power to back its ideological predilections' (Przeworski et al. 1995). This alliance also resulted from the voting dominance that the world's richest countries hold at the World Bank and IMF. The G7 countries alone (Canada, France, Italy, Japan, Germany, the USA, the UK) hold a near majority, and the USA has an effective veto over any major reforms to the two institutions' present lack of transparency or good governance (Lee et al. 2007).

The ideologically driven neoliberal predilections of the conservative 1980s UK, USA and German governments, when applied to indebted poor countries, distilled to

- reduced subsidies for basic items of consumption;
- removal of barriers to imports and foreign direct investment;
- reductions in state expenditures, particularly on social programmes such as health, education, water/sanitation and housing, with recommended and usually ineffective targeting of special supports to the poor; and
- rapid privatisation of state-owned enterprises, on the presumption that private service provision was inherently more efficient, and that proceeds from privatisation could be used to ensure debt repayment (Milward 2000).

The economic outcomes of structural adjustment remain equivocal; some countries weathered the changes better than others, usually by not fully implementing them. The World Bank and the IMF continue to argue that things would likely have been worse for these countries without these structural changes. The recently established IMF Independent Evaluation Office, however, found that over half the countries undertaking structural adjustment underperformed relative to theoretical expectations; the assumed private sector recovery rarely occurred, or did so much more slowly than anticipated; and the IMF's emphasis on taxing consumption, rather than income, fuelled domestic inequalities (IMF 2004). None of these outcomes are good for health, generally, or for health equity in particular. In Africa the outcomes of structural adjustment were overwhelmingly negative and, in the case of health impacts, singularly destructive (Breman & Shelton 2001). Part of that destruction was due to the globalisation of a market-driven model of health sector reform (Lister 2007). If health promotion is a practice embedded primarily within health systems, these systems need to be sufficiently comprehensive, equitable and supportive of actions on the social determinants of health if that practice is to be empowering. The 'selective primary health care' approach was actively promoted by the World Bank from the mid-1980s until very recently. In its influential 1993 *'Investing in Health'* report, the World Bank further argued that health sector reform should be based on increased competition among providers, use of cost-effective norms and greater reliance upon private financing and private provision, unless the public system could prove that it was more efficient.

Despite its lack of democratic accountability and allegations of direct US government interference in its work that led to the resignation of its Chief Economist and latter-day globalisation critic, Joseph Stiglitz, in 1999 (Hall 2007), the World Bank is a large institution with diverse voices and programmes. Prior to the mid-1980s it promoted and funded social insurance schemes in developing countries to help make health and education more available to the poor on the assumption that social spending in these areas would lead to better economic growth. After almost two decades of promoting market solutions, the World Bank has returned to its past practice of financing such programmes (Hall 2007). It now recognises, albeit unapologetically, that markets inevitably fail to care for the health of the poor, and that the high prevalence of poverty in many developing countries continues to constrain their economic growth. From a health-promotion vantage, problems with this social insurance approach nonetheless persist: the emphasis of these insurance schemes continues to be cost-effective and selective, leaving little room for anything but behavioural health promotion. The programmes target the poor rather than building universal systems, reducing the cross-class solidarity needed for sustainability over time, while opening up private markets for service provision to the non-poor. And another branch of the World Bank that makes commercial loans (the International Finance Corporation), and whose share of total World Bank loans has jumped from 3.3 per cent to over 25 per cent in the two decades of rapid globalisation (1980–2000) (Khoon 2006), is aggressively promoting private investments in private health care around the developing world on the unsupported assumption that there is no conflict between profit maximisation and equity in access (Nah & Osifo-Dawodu 2007). In 2007, for example, the International Finance Corporation announced $1 billion in new loans to finance private sector health provision in Sub-Saharan Africa (Bretton Woods Project 2008a), a region that is home to the world's poorest families facing greatest health need.

This contrariness in World Bank and IMF policies – on the one hand, some public care for the poor; on the other, continued integration into global markets – persists in the successor to these institutions' now discredited structural adjustment programmes. Since 1999, in order to qualify for debt relief, indebted poor countries have had to prepare Poverty Reduction Strategy Papers (PRSPs) and to provide periodic updates and progress reports for approval by the World Bank and the IMF. These Papers embody some health-positive elements: they are supposed to show how funds freed up by debt relief will be used in a 'pro-poor' manner; and citizens are supposed to be involved in the process of selecting these policies. However, participation by civil society groups in many instances remains more nominal than authentic. Fundamentally, the neoliberal nostrums of structural adjustment remain firmly ensconced within PRSPs: privatisation, liberalisation in trade and services (sometimes calling for greater cuts in tariffs than those agreed to during WTO negotiations) and caps on public sector salary spending which, while not targeting health or education sectors per se, have prevented several SSA countries from expanding public spending in these areas (World Commission on the Social Dimension of Globalization 2004; Brock & McGee 2004; Wood 2006).

Alongside the explicit conditionality of the international financial institutions is the increased ease and speed with which money can move around the world, creating an 'implicit conditionality' (Griffith-Jones & Stallings 1995). The recurrent financial crises discussed earlier in this chapter have seen national currencies lose half their value or more with serious economic and health fallouts. Anticipation of such a crisis means that even governments with strong commitments to equity oriented domestic policy sometimes temper these promises to maintain their credibility with international creditors. Development policy scholar Peter Evans points out that 'the major banks' aversion to the possibility of redistributive developmentalism' led to a 40 per cent decline in the value of Brazil's currency in the run-up to elections that brought the Workers' Party to power. After the elections, the Workers' Party 'chose to suffer low growth, high unemployment and flat levels of social expenditure rather than risk retribution from the global financial actors who constitute "the markets"' (Evans 2005).

Maybe yes, maybe no, mostly no: Interrogating globalisation's dominant health 'story'

The proponents of neoliberal globalisation have a powerful and sound-biting story for why liberalisation and global market integration is good for everyone, including their health. Disentangling its assumptions by examining its more sceptical critiques provides health promoters with a solid, evidence-informed set of arguments with which to engage their communities and politicians.

The main issue starts from the dominant 'story', as economists describe their theories, that increased trade and foreign investment improve economic growth, which increases wealth and reduces poverty, leading to improved health. Increased wealth can be taxed to sustain public provision of health care, education and water/sanitation, further improving health. A more literate and healthy population, in turn, accelerates economic growth: the globalisation-is-good-for-us circle closes virtuously upon itself.

The last set of claims, while hardly novel, is nonetheless important because it underscores the positive contribution of improved population health to economic growth. The relationship between health and economic growth informed the work of the 1998–2001 World Health Organization's Commission on Macroeconomics and Health, chaired by the well-known economist, Jeffrey Sachs (Commission on Macroeconomics and Health 2001). Its research findings suggest that at least one-third of the economic growth of the so-called Asian Tiger countries (South Korea, Singapore, Hong Kong, Taiwan, Thailand and Malaysia) in the 1980s and 1990s was a result of their population's improved health. Economist Amartya Sen (2000) similarly attributes China's more rapid growth, as compared to India's, to its pre-market reform emphases on public education and health care which created a healthy, literate, cheap labour force that became that country's source of comparative advantage.

There remains an ethical issue with this formulation, of course: it assumes that the goal is economic growth, not health, and that if investments in health do not yield such growth then they are not worth making.

But more to the present point, how true is the rest of the story?

Liberalisation and economic growth

This derives from research that shows a positive relation between liberalisation, economic growth and poverty reduction (Dollar 2001; Dollar 2002; Dollar & Kraay 2002). These oft-cited studies concluded that during the 1980s and 1990s, 'globalisers' grew faster than 'non-globalisers', potentially expanding the resources at their disposal to 'trickle down' to improve health and its social determinants. This conclusion, however, has been severely criticised. Model high-performing globalisers such as China, India, Malaysia, Thailand and Viet Nam, for example, actually started out as more closed economies than those non-globalisers whose economies stalled or declined during this period, mostly in Africa and Latin America. The problem is one of definition. Globalisers in these studies are those countries that saw their trade/GDP ratio increase since 1977; non-globalisers are those that saw their ratio drop. Yet the non-globalisers started out more highly integrated into the world economy and traded globally as much as, if not more than, the globaliser group (Birdsall 2006). The growth difference, then, is clearly not one due to globalisation.

But the key contention remains: would developing countries be better off (growth-wise) if they liberalised their trade policies? The evidence here is so mixed that, according to one recent review, liberalisation on average may lead to better growth but this is 'neither automatically guaranteed nor universally observable' (Thorbecke & Nissanke 2006). It all depends on how and when countries integrate into the global economy, and on what terms. It is now commonly accepted that the model Asian globalisers did not, in fact, follow the standard package of market-oriented reforms that the laggard African and Latin American globalisers had imposed on them via structural adjustment programmes. They exercised a trial-and-error flexibility in the timing and depth of liberalisation and domestic market reforms. This unorthodox approach to economic reform is no longer available to countries struggling up the development ladder; trade treaties have removed the necessary policy flexibilities (Chang 2002) and the insertion of a billion low-wage workers from China and India into the global labour market prevents them from having any comparative advantage in terms of lower labour costs. The result: global unemployment in 2006 is at an all time high (Employment Conditions Knowledge Network 2007).

Growth and poverty reduction

Much is also made of liberalisation's 'rising tide lifting all boats' and it is now widely accepted that world poverty, at least in its most extreme form, is decreasing. Between 1981 and 2003 the number of people living on $1/day or less declined by 414 million. (See Box 5.1) Most of this reduction, however, occurred before 1987 and the annual rate of decline has since slowed by a full order of magnitude (Chen & Ravallion 2004; Nah & Osifo-Dawodu 2007). Neither did the rising tide lift people very far. The number of people living on $2/day or less rose by 285 million over the same period (Chen & Ravallion 2004). Excluding China, where the accuracy of poverty data has been questioned (Reddy & Minoiu 2005) and where half of the poverty reduction occurred before that country embraced market reforms (Chen & Ravallion 2004), the number of global poor actually rose by 30 million at the $1/day level and by 567 million at the $2/day level. As one World Bank development economist concluded: 'It is hard to maintain the view that expanding external trade is . . . a powerful force for poverty reduction in developing countries' (Ravallion 2006).

Growth and income inequalities

Another contention is that globalisation's past quarter century of growth has not worsened income inequalities. Whether, or how, income inequalities affect population health remains a disputed point among health researchers. Poverty, which is higher in high income-inequality countries, may be the bigger problem. But greater income inequality makes it harder for economic growth to lift people out of poverty. Income inequalities also continue to be associated with declines in social cohesion, public support for state redistributive social policies (Deaton 2001; Gough 2001) and even political engagement (Solt 2004); as well as with higher rates of infant mortality, homicide, suicide and generalised conflict (Deaton 2001). Cross-national studies further find that income inequalities actually dampen longer-term economic growth (Easterly 2002) delaying the health gains such growth might bring or sustain. So inequalities are bad for health and for the economy. But are they rising?

There are conflicting answers that depend on what measures are used and what units are measured (Dollar 2002; Wade 2002; Deaton 2004).

Box 5.1 Measuring poverty?

One of the most important of the Millennium Development Goals (MDGs) agreed to by the world's nations in 2000 and discussed in Chapter 6 is to reduce by half the number of people living in extreme poverty ($1/day) by 2015. But what does poverty at $1/day actually mean?

In 1985, the World Bank converted a number of country-level poverty lines into 'purchasing power parities' (PPP) based on what $1 in the USA could buy in that country. These statistical manipulations led to creation of the international poverty levels of $1/day and $2/day. The methodology has been heavily challenged for being arbitrary; using a PPP equivalence that is not well defined; and extrapolating estimates on very limited data without acknowledging their high probability of errors (Reddy & Pogge 2005). Consider, too, that in 1993 the World Bank changed slightly its calculus for the $1/day level, leading it to conclude by this new measure that extreme poverty had declined by 58 million from 1987–98. The old measure would have indicated a decline of only 8 million. Who asked the statistically richer 50 million what they thought? To make the probability of errors even worse: Some countries' poverty levels are based on surveys of household income; others, mostly in Asia, survey household consumption instead. The consumption measure includes out-of-pocket health spending. This leads to an ironic conclusion that large numbers of Asian households have 'escaped' poverty because of catastrophic medical expenses (van Doorslaer et al. 2006) that are known to be major causes of income-measured poverty, affecting over 100 million people annually (Norton et al. 2001; Wagstaff et al. 2001). Using consumption, rather than income, to measure poverty not only provides a false picture; it also substantially underestimates resulting inequalities (Asian Development Bank 2007).

Even accepting this flawed measure, the MDG poverty reduction goal if achieved (it likely will not be) would leave almost 1 billion people living below the $1/day level, causing at least 18 million preventable poverty deaths annually (Pogge 2008).

Income inequalities within many countries are rising. On most measures, income inequalities between countries are also increasing (Milanovic 2003). Poverty reduction in China and India, with their large populations, means that income inequalities between individuals across the world may be declining slightly, although there is disagreement even here. Inequalities within both countries, though, have skyrocketed since they started down globalisation's neoliberal path. Since inequality is strongly tied to social comparison and geographic propinquity it is 'within-country inequalities' that should concern us most (Marmot 2006). The important question here is globalisation's impact on these trends. Some economists claim that, because there is no consistent relationship between globalisation and within-country inequalities, we shouldn't worry; on average, the rising tide lifts all boats more or less equally (Dollar & Kraay 2002; Dollar 2002). But simple arithmetic tells a different story. Consider three people, one earning the equivalent of $5,000,000/year, another earning $50,000/year and another earning $500/year, a not atypical situation in countries like India or China. If each person's income rises by an equal 10 per cent, the effect is to increase absolute inequality between the first two persons by an astounding $495,000 and between the last two by a still substantial $4,950. To the extent that one's income or wealth corresponds to political influence and power, which we argue it does, these absolute differences should deeply concern us.

Growth and investing in health

The final part of the 'globalisation-is-good-for-health' story is one we have already encountered: the assumption that the loss of a country's tariff or border tax revenues will be made up by increased growth, wealth and new forms of taxation. This has not been the experience with most low-income countries, even those whose economies have grown (Glenday 2006). For a majority of these countries there has been a net decline in overall public revenues with obvious implications for reduced public expenditures on health, water, social services and other health-promoting initiatives. The reasons include the informal nature of their economies, with large subsistence sectors making income taxation difficult; and the lack of institutional capacity for effective revenue collection when taxation is more administratively complex than collecting tariffs at the border. High-income countries, with already well-established taxation systems and existing public infrastructures, have been able to move away from tariffs as a source of revenue with minimal loss in fiscal capacity.

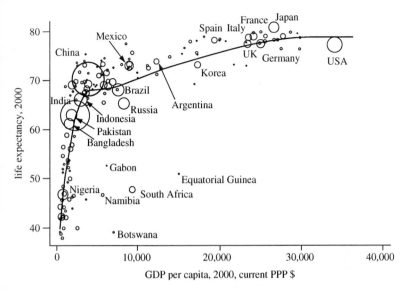

Figure 5.1 Life expectancy and per capita income (adjusted for purchasing parity)
Source: Angus Deaton, *Journal of Economic Literature*, 41, 2003, 113–58; reproduced with permission.

Growth and improvements in health

Finally, the relationship between economic growth and health improvement is not at all straightforward. First, life expectancy at birth (LEB) rises with GDP/capita in most countries, up to a level of around $5000 (Edward 2006; Deaton 2006). At this point, as Figure 5.1 shows, there is a 'kink' in the curve, with declining margins of health improvement as economies continue to grow. While there are methodological issues with establishing the certainty of this 'kink,' it's long-noted presence This has led some analysts to suggest the establishment of an 'ethical poverty line' of between $3–$4/day, an amount that correlates with an average LEB of around 70 years (Edward 2006). (Because the ethical poverty line is based on household consumption rather than national income, which no country distributes equally to its households, to achieve this $3–$4/day level actually requires a GDP/capita averaging around $5000.) Second, there are several countries with fairly low GDP/capita and growth levels that experience high levels of and continuing improvements in LEB, attributed in part to social program spending on health, education and gender empowerment and fairly low levels of income inequality. A nation's health may be prerequisite to its wealth, but it takes little wealth to provide for its health if the resources that health requires are equitably shared.

An unhealthy tale of winners and losers

But equitable sharing has not been contemporary globalisation's strong suit. Rather, and ineluctably, globalisation generates winners and losers through the logic of what economist Nancy Birdsall, of the US-based Center for Global Development, describes as the inevitable effect of globalisation's inherent asymmetries (Birdsall 2006). The reasons, she argues, is that the global marketplace rewards countries already rich in productive assets; disproportionately burdens the poor when market failures lead to financial or other crises; and is run by rules largely developed by, and for the, rich in high-income countries.

Winners from globalisation, most in high, but also some in, middle- and low-income countries, comprise a global elite that sociologist Zygmut Bauman (1998) calls 'tourists'. They have the money and status to 'move through the world' motivated only by their dreams and desires. 'Vagabonds', on the other hand, are those less privileged hundreds of millions whose migrations to escape war, famine or poverty, or to pursue opportunity and a better life are not welcome: Africans crossing the Mediterranean or Atlantic, Chinese hiding in Canadian-bound cargo ships and more than a million Mexicans each year who try unsuccessfully to enter the United States illegally. National borders are increasingly closed to them. Not all of globalisation's losers become vagabonds; some are even welcome temporarily to tend the gardens, clean the offices and houses, take out the trash and mind the kids of the 'winners'. But their numbers are continuing to rise as losers outpace winners, because of how winners have set the global rules. In the words of the World Commission on the Social Dimensions of Globalization (WCSDG), a high-level tri-partite (government, corporation, labour) group organised under the auspices of the International Labour Organisation: globalisation's 'rules and institutions are unfair to poor countries, both in the ways they were drawn up and in their impact' (World Commission on the Social Dimension of Globalization 2004).

A recent scorecard provides evidence of this (Weisbrot et al. 2001). It compares health, economic and development indicators for the pre-globalisation (1960–80) and rapidly globalising (1980–2000) periods. During the globalising period, economic growth per capita declined in all countries, but declined most rapidly for the poorest 20 per cent of nations. The rate of improvement in life expectancy declined for all but the wealthiest 20 per cent of nations, indicating increasing global disparity. Infant and child mortality improvements slowed, particularly for the poorest 40 per cent. The rate of growth of public spending on education also slowed for all countries, and the rate of growth for school enrolment, literacy rates and other educational attainment measures slowed for most of the poorest 40 per cent of nations.

How much of this was due to globalisation policies? In partial answer, a special study commissioned by the Globalisation Knowledge Network of the WHO Commission on Social Determinants of Health asked: What would have happened to life expectancy at birth (LEB) if the trends of the less globalised 1960s–1970s had continued, and how much of the difference could be explained by the globalisation-driven effects of the 1980s and 1990s (Cornia et al. 2007)? The study first reviewed evidence of pathways linking globalisation to poorer health such as material deprivation, psycho-social stress, lifestyles, social stratification, loss of social cohesion, and 'shocks' such as disasters, wars and epidemics. The research team, lead by Andrea Giovanni Cornea, one of the first researchers to study the health effects of structural adjustment, selected key variables for the most important pathways and performed a number of regression analyses against the 'counterfactual' of continued trends from the pre-globalising decades. They found that the past 25 years of intensified global market integration have indeed witnessed a slowdown or reversal in health improvements and growing health inequalities. Globalisation policy-driven changes reduced potential LEB gains by 1.52 years, due primarily to increases in income inequalities. Sub-Saharan African and Latin American countries, the former USSR and countries in economic transition suffered the greatest LEB losses. Much of the reversal in LEB in sub-Saharan Africa is a result of HIV/AIDS, the high prevalence of which, as we have already seen, is attributable in part to globalisation policies associated with debt crises, capital flight and structural adjustment programmes. In the former USSR, much of the reversal in LEB is due to the collapse of public institutions and social safety nets.

Who wins with globalisation? According to World Bank economist Branko Milanovic, who has studied this question relentlessly: the original Asian Tigers (Singapore, Hong Kong, Taiwan and South Korea) and immediately after them, the high-income countries of Western Europe, North America and Oceania (Australia and Aotearoa/New Zealand). His pithy conclusion: 'Maintaining that globalization as we know it is the way to go and that, if [its policies] have not borne fruit so far, they will surely do so, is to replace empiricism with ideology' (Milanovic 2003).

The globalising work of health promotion

The health sector and health promotion in particular entered the globalisation ideology debate somewhat late in the game and is still in its infancy in coming to terms with its implications. Environmentalists, feminists, social justice activists and civil society mobilisations in poorer developing countries were there years before. The 'just globalisation' movement is notable not only for it being the first universal social movement in human history, it is also one led as much by those in poorer as in richer countries and circumstances.

The *Bangkok Charter for Health Promotion in a Globalised World* (World Health Organization 2005) is only the second health promotion 'Charter' that the World Health Organization has seen fit to issue. Others of its various international health promotion gatherings have put out Declarations which have lacked the same imperative of a Charter. Responding to the surge of health concern with globalisation, the *Bangkok Charter* posits that health promotion must become 'central to the global development agenda'. While a reasonable claim it does not, unfortunately, provide a clear role for practitioners or a plan of action indicating who, how and when this commitment will be achieved, apart from developing the role of partnerships

> to close the health gap between rich and poor ... This requires actions to promote dialogue and cooperation among nation states, civil society, and the private sector.
>
> (World Health Organization 2005)

An interesting comparative discourse analysis with the *Ottawa Charter* finds the *Bangkok Charter* significantly lacking in action terms (Porter 2006), reading more like a lukewarm multilateral text than a manifesto. The international People's Health Movement, a global network of health activists, is particularly critical of the *Bangkok Charter*'s avoidance of the political economy and global power differentials that create the 'health gap between rich and poor' on which we must act, and of its assumption that the interests of different governments, private sector actors and civil society are free of conflict or contradiction.

Whatever the *Bangkok Charter*'s strengths or weaknesses, health promotion does not need a new Charter or a new Declaration to begin its work tackling what is unhealthy with globalisation's present form. We need to only apply the skills and strategies we already have to problems of a different order, in new settings and with a changed set of allies and a larger cast of opponents.

Before turning to this task in the next two chapters, we close with a reprise of the two stories of Bilkis and Jia to offer a few notes of cautious optimism for health promotion's globalising work.

Bilkis expressed concern that child labour, which began to disappear from Bangladeshi sweatshops in the 1990s, was making a comeback. What caused its initial disappearance was the pressure exerted on retailers and producers by a melange of unions, women's groups, new internationalists, fair trade advocates and more powerful multilateral institutions such as the tripartite International Labour Organisation. Some of this pressure was directly political, some discursive and some as consumer boycotts. New forms of pressure are now being considered to end the hazardous labour affecting over 125 million children aged 5–17 years, worldwide (UNICEF 2007). The US government, for example, is debating legislation that would 'prohibit the import, export, or sale of goods made in factories or workshops that violate core labour standards, and prohibit the procurement of sweatshop goods by the United States Government'.

There is, of course, something richly ironic about globalisation's hegemon considering such a law, especially since it is one of a handful of countries that has not itself ratified the conventions covering the ILO's four core labour standards (of six conventions, the USA has ratified only two) (International Labour Organisation 2007). Some developing nations regard such American actions more as back door protectionism for its own producers than as serious regard for the health and welfare of its outsourced factories. But support for the proposed America law is growing in Bangladesh, as well in the USA; and it is hard to argue that the core labour standards, which most countries have ratified, are unfair: freedom of association and the right to collective bargaining, the elimination of all forms of forced or compulsory labour, the abolition of the most hazardous forms of child labour and the elimination of discrimination in respect of employment and occupation. In the UK, meanwhile, a government inquiry has been launched into allegations that its big retail chains are forcing their suppliers to break their ethical codes and labour laws. What the state might do if it finds this to be the case is unknown. One might hope that the companies' voluntary ethical code becomes a national law with regular inspection and enforcement.

Jia's hopes for a healthier, better paid and more secure workplace may yet start to be fulfilled. China, under domestic and international pressure, is making some effort to improve the lot of its export workers. In June 2007, it passed a new labour law, drawing on advice from Europe's social democratic and labour-friendly governments. China's present labour laws are based on individual contracts between employees and employers. The new labour law still will not allow independent unions. Nonetheless, it will increase the rights of workers to enjoy greater security and benefits, decrease the chances of them being abused by third-party labour contractors, provide for termination with just cause only and empower the state-run central union to intercede with individual contracts to strengthen negotiations in favour of workers, including better health and safety provisions. China's modest initiative, however, was fiercely opposed by the American Chamber of Commerce in Shanghai, whose 1300 members have benefited in the past by having to pay little heed to workers' rights, health or safety (Elfstrom 2006). Foreign company lobbyists succeeded in weakening some, though not all, of the labour law amendments to their advantage (Cha 2007). In every opportunity to reform globalisation for a public health good, one can expect opposition from those who have gained from its present architecture.

The *Bangkok Charter* may be right in emphasising that without building bigger, better partnerships there will be little hope for 'health promotion in a globalized world'. But, as with local health-promoting empowerment, global health-promoting empowerment means choosing one's partners carefully. It also means taking care of how the health challenge of globalisation is framed. While most of these discourses have something strategic to offer a global health promotion, the ethical imperative is one of creating more equitable global resource distributions towards health.

6
Working to Build Empowerment: The Global Challenge

> Ultimately, the question should not be whether a human being is better off in a sweatshop working 100 hours a week or unemployed ... The question needs to be: can we come up with a better version of globalization?
>
> (Heymann & Kidman 2007)

In this chapter we begin to answer the question posed by Heymann and Kidman by examining a number of different discourses in which globalisation and health have been framed. These discourses compete for political influence and hold differing potential for what remains the single most important global health imperative: a dramatic shift in the distribution (and redistribution) of global resources essential to health.

While there are many ways in which the relationship between health and globalisation can be viewed, the immediately discernable and more dominant discourses are as follows:

- Health as security
- Health as development
- Health as global public good
- Health as commodity
- Health as human right

Some, notably health as security, are recent or recently reformulated. The preambular nod to 'health' as 'fundamental to the attainment of peace and security' in the World Health Organization's 1946 constitution gathered dust until the destabilising effects of the HIV pandemic and fears over bioterrorism re-wed the two terms in the early 2000s

(Szreter 2003; Fidler 2007). Health as a human right emerged immediately after World War II in the text of the Universal Declaration on Human Rights, but languished as a global discourse until the collapse of the Soviet Union left a vacuum in normative alternatives to market capitalism. Health as development has a more continuous, if episodic, lineage, first gaining international notice with the 1978 Alma-Ata Declaration on Primary Health and then rising and falling almost year-to-year as an aid priority of high-income countries. Health as global public good is decidedly new and owes itself to UN agency efforts to harness one economic theory to soften the harsh edges of another. Health as commodity, and the inevitable market failures in its equitable provision, has long jostled with multiple corrective state interventions. Only with the advent of global trade rules has health's commodification become a global, rather than simply national, concern.

Which elements of any or all of these discourses offer the most emancipating potential for promoting global health equity? Which framings should health promotion incorporate into its practice, philosophy and strategy?

Health as security

The most dominant discourse of recent years has been that of national security. At its extreme it finds such expression as the 'risk of infection by American citizens [and] US military personnel abroad . . . [and] increased political and economic instability in strategically important countries because of failures by their government to control the [HIV] pandemic' (US National Intelligence Council 2000). Health as national security is consistent with nation-states' often explicit duties to protect their citizens from foreign risk by guarding their borders, whether the 'invaders' are pathogens or people. It has also, post SARS, given long-neglected public health measures more political clout and fiscal resources, at least in many high-income countries. (Public health systems in many low-income countries continue to languish.) But it has also led to a distortion in global health risk and response and elides dangerously with repressive political measures in the 'war on terror'.

On the first: The securitisation of health, while now 'a permanent feature of public health governance in the twenty-first century' (Fidler 2007), disproportionately directs funding to those ills deemed politically to be security risks: HIV, twice addressed by the UN Security Council; and Avian flu as the present exemplar of feared modern pandemics. Such designation is not based upon global risk, since easily preventable maternal and childhood illnesses and a number of so-called 'neglected diseases' exact a higher toll in poorer countries than does HIV, to say nothing of the pandemic of chronic diseases sweeping developing nations alongside the globalisation of Western lifestyles, food products and consumption. Rather, and in ethically troubling ways, the securitisation of health privileges those diseases most likely to inconvenience global trade and finance or to travel to high-income nations, reversing 'international health responses' from their historic 'people-centred values to a narrower understanding of health as a national security risk' (Thieren 2007).

On the second: Health, in sharing national security with terrorism, may inadvertently lend credence to what UN human rights observers concluded is a national security that 'is reductionist . . . essentially militaristic and manifestly retrogressive . . . with reliance placed on the superiority of military firepower and the curtailment of civil liberties (United Nations Economic and Social Council, Commission on Human Rights 2003). Fear of infection can morph into a fear of (bio)terrorism, and then into a fear of the terrorist-Other itself. The continuous and heightened expression of possible risks routinised in airport screenings and building security checks, intersects with a saturated Western individualism to create a pervasive sense of helplessness. Helplessness without check becomes fear, transforming the possible into the probable (Durodié 2005). As public health historian, Simon Szreter, warns, this creates a base for, and apathy towards, political actions that abuse human rights and which can slip slowly towards fascism (Szreter 2003). Economic interests also underlie the security frame. Worry over Avian flu created windfall profits for Roche, the patent holder of Tamiflu®, in 2006 and 2007 (Cage 2007). While some of this profit might be taxed back for useful health promotion purposes, Roche (like many transnational firms) reportedly operates through two offshore financial centres to minimise or avoid tax payments (Transnationale 2007). The broader terrorist-security frame has created a massive 'security industry'; in 2003 over US$550 billion was estimated to have been spent on domestic (not military) security, ten times the amount of total foreign aid that year (Labonté et al. 2004).

The *realpolitik* of international relations, however, assures durability to the security discourse. If the resource scarcities in such life basics as food and water anticipated by environmental researchers emerge as rapidly as some climatologists now caution, one can expect national security's reductionism and militarism to deepen. This places health-promotion activists' concerned with global health equity in an awkward place. To dismiss security is to remove one from potentially useful policy engagements. To accept it risks a tacit strengthening of its worst forms.

From national to human security?

A mitigating strategy exists in national security's less commonly voiced sibling: human security. Human security, which has its own multilateral policy texts (Chen et al. 2004a, 2004b), bases itself upon a person's 'physical safety, their economic and social well-being, respect for their dignity and worth as human beings, protection of their human rights and fundamental freedoms' (Helsinki Process 2001). It emphasises attending to the needs of vulnerable peoples, representing an approach to security more consonant with the idealised principles of health promotion. It specifically stresses core capabilities, including income security, health care, housing, education, environmental security among other essentials for life. It also recognises that national security is no guarantee of human security within borders, and that the 'core moral value of people's security' may actually be in potential conflict with it (Coupland 2007). Framing security in human, and not simply national, terms thus forces open debates on policy measures beyond rich country efforts to create a *cordon sanitaire* (whether for unwanted pathogens or unwanted aliens) to consideration of a larger set of international responsibilities. In doing so, it creates an argumentative path into other, potentially more empowering, global health discourses.

Health as development

One of these – development – is perhaps the second most prominent in global health debate. Health has long been one of the desired outcomes of development. This is best expressed in the Millennium Development Goals (MDGs) (see Table 6.1). Agreed to by all the world's nations in 2000, the MDGs represent the most concentrated and collective global statement of development intent in human history. Significantly, they are all directly or indirectly health goals. While these goals have galvanised global attention on issues of health and disparity, there are at least five problems with their present iteration:

1. They lack equity stratifiers, meaning that countries can achieve them by improving the health of the better-off while worsening that of the poor.
2. They ignore any statement on the causes of the problems they seek to redress.
3. Emphasis on targets reinforces a bias towards short-term interventions that are selective, fail to be empowering and lack sustainability. Moreover, most countries lack the data to accurately track progress.

Table 6.1   Millennium development goals and targets

Goal 1: Eradicate extreme poverty and hunger
  Target 1: Halve, between 1990 and 2015, the proportion of people whose income is less than one dollar a day
  Target 2: Halve, between 1990 and 2015, the proportion of people who suffer from hunger

Goal 2: Achieve universal primary education
  Target 3: Ensure that by 2015 children everywhere, boys and girls alike, will be able to complete a full course of primary schooling

Goal 3: Promote gender equality and empower women
  Target 4: Eliminate gender disparity in primary and secondary education preferably by 2005 and to all levels of education no later than 2015

Goal 4: Reduce child mortality
  Target 5: Reduce by two-thirds, between 1990 and 2015, the under-five mortality rate

Goal 5: Improve maternal health
  Target 6: Reduce by three-quarters, between 1990 and 2015, the maternal mortality ratio

Goal 6: Combat HIV/AIDS, malaria and other diseases
  Target 7: Have halted by 2015 and begun to reverse the spread of HIV/AIDS
  Target 8: Have halted by 2015 and begun to reverse the incidence of malaria and other major diseases

Goal 7: Ensure environmental sustainability
  Target 9: Integrate the principles of sustainable development into country policies and programmes and reverse the loss of environmental resources
  Target 10: Halve, by 2015, the proportion of people without sustainable access to safe drinking water and basic sanitation
  Target 11: By 2020, to have achieved a significant improvement in the lives of at least 100 million slum dwellers

Goal 8: Develop a global partnership for development
  Target 12: Develop further an open, rule-based, predictable, non-discriminatory trading and financial system
  Target 13: Address the special needs of the least developed countries
  Target 14: Address the special needs of landlocked countries and small island developing states (through the Programme of Action for the Sustainable Development of Small Island Developing States and the outcome of the twenty-second special session of the General Assembly)
  Target 15: Deal comprehensively with the debt problems of developing countries through national and international measures in order to make the debt sustainable in the long term

(Continued)

Table 6.1 (Continued)

Target 16: In co-operation with developing countries, develop and implement strategies for decent and productive work for youth
Target 17: In co-operation with pharmaceutical companies, provide access to affordable, essential drugs in developing countries
Target 18: In co-operation with the private sector, make available the benefits of new technologies, especially information and communications

Source: (United Nations Millennium Development Goals)

4. As global targets, they do not address what is do-able country by country. It is now widely accepted that most African countries will not meet these targets.
5. Past global declarations have a long history of never being matched by the rich country resources required by poor country efforts to achieve them (Anon. 2005).

The poverty goal also warrants some elaboration as it uses the narrowly defined and ethically non-ambitious $1/day level. As the Chapter 5 recounted, modelling studies suggest a minimum 'ethical' poverty line of $3–$4/day as sufficient to allow consumption that would permit a life expectancy of 70 years. Using this ethical poverty line triples the current estimate of world poverty from 1 billion to just over 3 billion persons (Edward 2006). Using the World Bank's own disputed measures of poverty reduction in the liberalised globalisation era, we would not reduce by half those living below this ethical poverty line until 2209 (Woodward 2007). That would still leave 1.5 billion people living below it, and those rising above it would still experience life expectancies 10–15 years below that enjoyed by persons in high-income countries. There are also problems with some of Goal 8's targets: the open global trading system it advocates has not been of much benefit to the world's poor; developing world debts should not be made 'sustainable' (meaning at a level they can afford to repay) but in many cases cancelled outright; and most of the gains in access to essential drugs has arisen from citizen advocacy and legal actions against, and not in cooperation with, pharmaceutical companies.

These problems with the MDGs are neither insurmountable nor necessarily cause to dismiss them for their normative importance. As past experiences with national health promotion goals and targets in many countries suggest, the MDGs can be used to hold political processes accountable for their efforts. They should not, however, become ossified planning guideposts, under which communities and nations are held narrowly accountable for meeting quantifiable targets that cannot even be verified.

Pathology of instrumentalism

A deeper issue than the problematic nature of the MDGs is how the relation between health and development is seen. Until recently, development, invariably taken to mean economic growth, was viewed as preceding gains in health. Rich world aid and trade policy, when not in its own self-interest, is aimed at encouraging growth with health as a virtuous spin-off. A newer economic health/development 'story', however, posits that investing in health yields substantial economic returns (Global Forum for Health Research 2004; Commission on Macroeconomics and Health 2001). Health is no longer seen simply as a consequence of economic growth, but as one of its engines. While politically compelling this instrumental reasoning raises three concerns.

First, it increasingly silos health funding into vertical disease-based programmes for which there are targets achievable in a short time-period. Cost-effectiveness measures are applied and results-based management dominates accountability systems (see Box 6.1). These requirements are not conducive to health promotion's concerns with underlying social determinants of health or with building sustainable public health systems, aid transfers for which have fallen in recent years to support a doubling in funds for the 'securitised' HIV risk (OECD DAC online statistics 2007). Such requirements also imply that the causes and consequences of health inequities are technical problems divorced from the political and economic decisions that partly create them.

Second, the health-as-investment rationale disproportionately rewards those countries with the 'right' set of economic policies – the dominant neo-liberal model of growth through market liberalisation and global integration. They are under constant pressure to do the 'right' thing, a pressure that often extends to multilateral or bilateral trade negotiations ('if you accept our trade terms, we'll give you more aid'). There is also overlap with the national security discourse. Several countries now tie their aid disbursements to a recipient's stance on the 'war on terror'. Over 60 per cent of aid increases between 2001–04 went to Afghanistan, Iraq and mineral-rich conflict-riddled Democratic Republic of the Congo, which together account for less than 3 per cent of the developing world's poor (World Bank 2006). Most of the trumpeted aid increase in 2005 came as debt reduction for Iraq and Nigeria, the latter an oil-rich nation of increasing interest to Western countries. Once removed, aid levels actually decreased over the previous year (OECD DAC 2006), and fell yet again in 2007.

Box 6.1   Global public-private partnerships: For better, for worse?

Since the early 1990s there has been a multitude of initiatives that bring together state, market and civil society actors, often referred to as global public-private partnerships (GPPPs). In health these include the Global Alliance for Vaccine Initiative (GAVI), Global Fund to Fight AIDS, Tuberculosis and Malaria (GFATM), and Global Alliance for Improved Nutrition (GAIN). One of the key innovations of GPPPs has been to involve for-profit organisations directly in decision-making, the appropriateness of which has been questioned. Many of the GPPPs are disease-focussed or, in the case of GAIN, narrowly targeted to vitamin and mineral food supplementation. Analyses of GPPPs to date raise concerns about their vertical approach, longer-term sustainability, undermining of local health systems and fragmenting of global health governance. There are also concerns about potential conflicts of interest between the need to tackle issues such as poverty and inequality through fundamental structural change and the vested interests of private sector 'partners' in the existing economic order, since the governance of resource mobilisation and allocation has remained firmly under the control of major donors. These programmes, by offering substantially higher salaries to health workers, also contribute to an internal 'brain drain' of health workers away from more comprehensive services to intervention-specific initiatives (Hanefeld et al. 2007). This weakens already fragile public health systems, including their health promotion capacities. It also worsens the already debilitating flow of health workers – often trained at public expense – from vastly under-resourced poor countries to much less needy rich ones (Packer et al. 2007). The absence of such workers is now regarded as the single greatest barrier to any ARV 'roll out' in Sub-Saharan African countries.

There are some signs of change: The Global Fund is now setting aside part of its funding to build health systems and train health workers. South Africa's Treatment Action Campaign, described in Chapter 3, showed how an initial narrow focus on HIV and treatment expanded to a broader concern with health systems and social determinants. The same occurred in Haiti, where HIV programmes fed local demands for better health care, sanitation, water and housing. Finally, in September 2007, several GPPPs, high-income country donors, and low-income country aid recipients signed an 'international health partnership' agreement to coordinate more closely with

(Continued)

Box 6.1   *(Continued)*

the national health plans of the recipient countries (Alexander 2007). This could help minimise the fragmentation of different initiatives that tax the reporting resources of many poor countries. Even so, this new partnership explicitly restricts its priorities to health-care access and 'promotion of healthy behaviours'. No reference is made to empowerment, or to the social determinants of health.

Alongside the growth in these GPPPs has been the rise of private philanthropy. The Bill and Melinda Gates Foundation is now the world's single largest health aid donor, with a budget far surpassing that of the World Health Organization. If we accept the premise that money speaks loudly in defining public discourse and policy, we now confront a future in which global health policy is being influenced by a small circle of extremely wealthy individuals and their advisors. The Gates Foundation, for example, received in late 2006 an additional \$31 billion pledge from Warren Buffett, one of the world's richest men. Buffet, who received global accolades for his donation, made his fortune through astute investments in a global 'casino capitalism' that has been responsible for multiple financial crises, deepened poverty and worsening health in many countries. Most of the people whom his charitable donations will now partially benefit were, and remain, excluded from playing the very game by which he made his wealth. Pertinent to this book's concern with underlying determinants of health one study found that 87 per cent of Buffett's investments are in companies facing allegations of environmental irresponsibility or human rights violations (Clark 2007).

Third, the confluence of technical intervention and the 'growth is good' sloganeering blinds commentary on the impossibility of many of the world's poorest countries to grow their way into better health, given only a modest boost from wealthier nations. Aid historically has been the major form of capital transfer from rich to poor for health as development purposes. The resurgence of global activism around the need for greater levels of aid spending has been accompanied by renewed critiques of aid as dependency-producing with little to show in terms of development returns over a half century of effort (Easterly 2006). Africa, which has received almost \$1 trillion in aid over the past 50 years, has failed to develop economically.

What such arguments ignore is the counterfactual: What shape might Africa now be in if no aid had been disbursed, given the reliance of many poor African countries on aid for much of its public sector spending? What might have happened if Africa had not lost as much or more in capital flight over this same period due to corruption, profit repatriation and the recycling of aid funds back to the donor country for the purchase of its goods and services? Stated polemically, aid transfers to Africa over the past half-century merely offset the plunder of the continent, often by the same donor nations (Bond 2006). Even given rightly criticised ineffective and inefficient uses of much aid spending, recent meta-analyses find that aid does increase economic growth (Taylor 2007), which other studies argue likely occurs through investments in health, education and other forms of human capital development (Commission on Macroeconomics and Health 2001). As Sachs (2007) shows, the likelihood of many poor African countries being able to raise through their own taxes sufficient revenues to fund even a fraction of the estimated minimum requirements for health is non-existent. They are decades away from being able to do so, and that is if we assume large growth rates of questionable environmental sustainability. 'Foreign aid', Sachs concludes, 'is therefore not a luxury for African health. It is a life-and-death necessity' (Sachs 2007).

Aid inadequacies

The most serious concern is that aid transfers continue to be resoundingly inadequate. Neither the health-development link increasingly prominent in rich country promises nor the white-banded celebrity-led movement to 'make poverty history' have sustained aid efforts. The most recent and authoritative estimate of what it would cost for all countries to reach the MDGs puts the price at an additional $60–$120 billion a year in aid (United Nations Millennium Project 2005). This is double of what donor countries presently give, but less than their repeatedly promised 0.7 per cent of Gross National Income (GNI) on which all but a handful of European countries have repeatedly failed to deliver. It is also a fraction of what Canada, the USA and other wealthy nations have spent on tax reductions for their rich over the past five years (see Figure 6.1). Had donor nations abided by their 0.7 per cent target when they first made it in 1975, they would have transferred $2 trillion more to developing nations over the past 30 years than they actually did (Urban Settlements Knowledge Network Final Report 2007).

Most poor countries also continue to pay more in debt servicing costs to public and private foreign creditors and to the World Bank and International Monetary Fund than they receive in aid (see Figure 6.2). Many of the debts still owed by the world's poorest countries are odious: loans knowingly made to corrupt officials, for work of no net benefit, for purposes of military repression or without the consent of the eventual

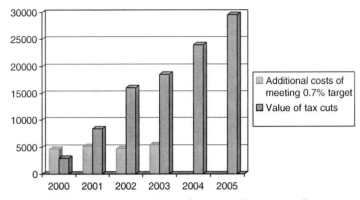

Source: OECD Development Assistance Committee, *Development Co-operation 2004 Report*, *DAC Journal 2005*;6(1)[full issue] and earlier years; Canada Department of Finance, *The Budget Plan 2003*, Table A1.9

Figure 6.1   Comparative costs, aid and tax cuts, Canada 2000–5, Millions of C$

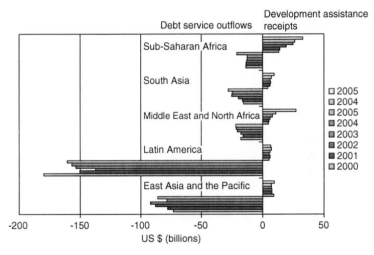

Source: World Bank, World Development Indicators (accessed March 4, 2008); Graph generated by Ted Schrecker, University of Ottawa

Figure 6.2   Worldwide, external debt service dwarfs development assistance flows

debtors; and by international law these debts should be considered uncollectible (Howse 2007). Using international legal definitions, one recent study estimates that $726 billion of the current debt of 13 developing countries is odious and should be cancelled and, further, that 10 countries should actually receive refunds of $383 billion in past payments on such debts (Mandel 2006).

Stated somewhat differently, the continent of Africa since the 1970s has borrowed $540 billion, paid back $550 billion and still owes $295 billion (United Nations Conference on Trade and Development 2004) due to accumulating interest charges. If fully repaid, the world's poorest and sickest continent would have transferred over $300 billion to the world's richest and healthiest ones. Rich world donor countries, pressured by moral outrage expressed by civil society groups from both sides of the debt equator, now offer partial debt relief to the 40 nations known as the 'Heavily Indebted Poor Countries' (HIPCs), But most of the world's poor do not live in HIPCs and most of the developing world's debt is not owed by HIPCs. This makes debt relief programmes ineffectual at a global scale. Even for those countries receiving debt relief, the amounts are only a fraction of the estimated new revenue requirements for the MDG targets. And to qualify for debt cancellation, these countries must subscribe to many of the same neoliberal policies originally imposed under structural adjustment, which added to their debt burdens in the first place.

A questionable model of development

Some of these problems are being addressed. More countries are untying their aid. Several have pledged to reach the 0.7 per cent commitment by 2015 or sooner, although considerable doubt on the strength of those promises remains. There is growing support for disbursing more aid directly to governments rather than spreading it thinly, and for an end to all forms of conditionality apart from transparency and accountability; monies go where they are intended and make a positive difference in peoples' lives. There is increasing pressure on the World Bank and IMF to remove or reduce their macroeconomic conditionalities on loans, grants and debt relief. Many Latin American and some Asian countries are now simply rejecting any new monies from these institutions partly because of recently created regional lending banks under their more direct control. These regional banks themselves are an effect of globalisation, the result of accumulating foreign reserves arising from outsourced manufacturing in Asia and from oil exports to high-income countries from Venezuela. Such distancing from the World Bank and IMF, however, remains a luxury poorer African and other Asian countries cannot afford.

As with security, health promotion activists need not dismiss the value of the development discourse. When invoking it, however, they need to recast it in at least two ways. First, the concept of development must be centred on human potentials rather than market performance, a point long argued by progressive 'new internationalists'. This requires continued scrutiny and critique of the hegemony of economic rationalism that defines neoliberal globalisation. Second, in an increasingly interdependent economic world, the transfers, now called 'aid', should not be seen as 'aid' at all but as redistributive obligations. Politically, redistribution on a global scale is no different than the financial transfers federated nations make between their component states, or that the European Union makes between its member nations: reallocating fiscal resources from its more populous or wealth-generating members to those states or nations that are less populous or poorer. Such transfers are usually made on the basis of strengthening social solidarity and maintaining social cohesion, the absence of which leads to a loss of faith in democratic governance, a rise in domestic disturbance and, ultimately, economic chaos. Even the World Bank in its 2007 *Global Economic Prospects* Report (World Bank 2007), while extolling the gains of increasingly globalised market capitalism, cautioned that the environmental damage and income inequalities that it was creating would lead increasingly to social unrest. This implies the need for solidarity-building mechanisms of global redistribution, albeit a conclusion that seems to elude the World Bank itself.

Health as global public good

The limitations of the development/aid discourse have nonetheless given rise to a third: that of global public good. Health promoters frequently invoke public or common good as shorthand to capture an ethic that places collective benefit above individual gain. In this use the term has the same evocative imprecision as 'community' (Labonté 2000). In classic economic theory, public good has a more exact meaning. It is something whose use is open to all, and whose use by one does not diminish its use by others, for example, air, water, biodiversity, peace and even – the classic example used to illustrate the concept – the order created by traffic lights.

A global public good is one whose benefits extend to all countries, people and generations. The concept is based on the premise that '[i]n today's world, globalization has brought about interdependencies that blur the distinction between domestic and external affairs. The best way to ensure one's own well-being is to be concerned about that of others' (Kaul & Faust 2001). A stable climate is one example of a global public good. Efforts to correct its inverse 'global public bad', greenhouse gas emissions, are also considered global public goods. Definitional boundaries remain vague, however, and identifying such goods remains more a matter of public policy than economic theory (Woodward & Smith

2003; Kaul & Mendoza 2003). Nonetheless, there are two axiomatic qualities of a global public good: its benefits are not confined to citizens of one nation; and, as with all public goods, it is under-provided in the market because its use by all engenders free riders, those who enjoy the good but pay nothing for it. Global public bads, in turn, are characteristically private or public decisions made in one country that have undesirable spill-over effects on people in other countries. Global public goods not only fill in for market failures in provision; they also correct for market 'successes' that create negative public externalities.

Preventing disease, not promoting health

Health, or more precisely what creates it, is considered by some, but not all, to be a global public good. There is more agreement that what prevents the global public bad of disease fits better with the concept. A reasonably short, but still plentiful, list of such goods has been suggested:

- Cure for disease
- New treatment regime for disease
- Control of air and water pollution emissions
- Uncovering basic research findings
- Monitoring disease
- Disseminating research findings
- Curbing epidemics (Sandler & Arce 2000)

Definitional differences nonetheless question the usefulness of the global public good discourse in advocacy for greater health financing. A narrow definition lends itself to more effective policy advocacy, but can lose sight of important equity and gendered dimensions. A more elastic definition that allows for numerous claims to the title of a global public good for health loses its policy relevance, and therefore its effectiveness. A recent effort by the World Health Organization concluded that a narrower definition was the better approach, emphasising three areas: the production, dissemination and use of knowledge; policy and regulatory regimes to prevent disease; and effective and accessible health systems (Woodward & Smith 2003).

There are critics of the concept: some argue that it is not accepted as an appropriate paradigm for health development (Deneulin & Townsend 2006), confusing and weaker in policy advocacy than human rights arguments. Others contend that global public goods, like the development discourse, do not sufficiently address equity in health and fail to address why inequities have arisen in the first place (Mooney & Dzator

2003). A more serious limitation is its utilitarian approach to global cooperation. As with the security discourse, its underlying premise is that shared interests are the key rationale for collective action, a perspective that reflects a particular value system in contrast with needs- or justice-based human rights or ethics.

Strategically, the discourse bridges between health as security and health as development. It suggests the importance of funding and building new multilateral institutions for the global research, regulation and services provision that will minimise the harm of 'diseases without borders'. The growth of various global disease funds, notably The Global Fund (to fight AIDS, Tuberculosis and Malaria), are good examples of this. Despite their problems these funds begin to de-couple aid from the strategic interests of specific donor nations. Fidler (2007) further argues that 'public health constitutes an *integrated public good* that benefits the state's pursuit of security, economic well being, development and respect for human dignity'. That is, arguing health as a global public good helps states to meet many of their other global health objectives, making it, by Fidler's estimate, 'a "best buy" for foreign policy'. Moreover, the underlying theoretical and empirical public good argument – that there exists profound market failures in key areas of human health and survival demanding new forms of global financial 'risk pooling' and regulation – is one that is likely to have greater traction with economists in treasury departments than any of the other global health discourses.

Other examples of global public goods for health include

- The 2005 revision of the International Health Regulations which requires WHO member states to strengthen core disease surveillance and response capacities and to report public health events to WHO.
- The Framework Convention on Tobacco Control (FCTC) which requires states parties to enact bans on tobacco advertising, marketing and promotion, implement warnings on packages and implement measures to protect exposure to second-hand smoke (see Box 6.2).

Health as commodity

Even so, the global public goods discourse must compete in treasury departments with the one outlier – health as tradable good. There is some pretence that such trade will lead to better outcomes, but the reality is that health is reduced to goods (such as drugs and new technologies) or services (private health insurance, facilities or providers), the

Box 6.2   Health promotion activism and the Framework Convention on Tobacco Control (FCTC)

The International Framework Convention on Tobacco Control (FCTC) was adopted by the World Health Assembly in May 2003 and is considered the first international health treaty or the first global healthy public policy. As of September 2006, 168 countries have signed the agreement and 139 have become state parties to it following ratification. The FCTC requires these countries to enact bans on tobacco advertising, marketing and promotion, implement warnings on packages and measures to protect exposure to second hand smoke, and 'encourages' them (in multilateral parlance, a term that conveys intent without obligation) to raise tobacco taxes and consider litigation to hold the tobacco industry liable for its wrongdoings. The FCTC is not as strong a treaty as health and civil society organisations (CSOs) wanted. Several of these CSOs participated in the negotiating forum that led to the FCTC, and continue to lobby for amendments and compliance as a 'Framework Conventional Alliance'. They are credited with maintaining pressure against the continuous efforts of countries such as Germany, Japan, and the USA, each with large tobacco industries, to weaken substantially the health provisions. Japan, whose government is a key stakeholder in its tobacco industry, played a particularly obstructionist role and successfully watered down the FCTC wording in several key sections (Assunta & Chapman 2006).

There is little doubt that trade liberalisation in tobacco increases smoking rates. World Bank research found that reduced tobacco tariffs in a number of Asian countries resulted in a 10 per cent rise in smoking rates above what it would have been without trade liberalisation. To prevent trade policy taking precedence over health protection, health organisations and WHO have urged the exclusion of tobacco from trade treaties (BMA 2002, Macan-Markar 2004). The FCTC acknowledges the link between trade and tobacco but, significantly, contains no provisions to address it. The need for continued global anti-tobacco health activism persists.

increased cross-border flow of which is designed to maximise profit, not health.

The indirect effect on health of trade treaties, though receiving less global health attention, is actually likely to have greater impact. Open borders in many low- and middle-income countries, often coerced through loan conditionalities from the World Bank and IMF, as we have seen, led to domestic economic decline and loss of public revenues for health and education. A more pervasive effect, and one experienced by most countries, is increased economic insecurity (Blouin et al. 2007). Workers and producers in the sectors that were protected from foreign competition may see their revenues decrease or their employment disappear when tariffs or regulatory barriers are removed. The negative impacts are not limited to one-time adjustments to trade reforms. Displaced workers have to move to other sectors which may lack jobs or require a different set of skills (Torres 2001). One poignant example of how this insecurity leads to negative health outcomes is the sharp rise in the suicide rate among cotton farmers in the Warangal District in Andra Pradesh, India (Sudhakumari 2002), and in Maharashtra, India (Mishra 2006). In 1991, the Indian government changed agricultural policy to encourage farmers to produce commodities for exports such as cotton. Due to the high volatility of world market prices in cotton, the absence of any domestic insurance programmes and a decline in state support for rural activities, many cotton farmers became heavily indebted and increasingly desperate.

At the same time, net job losses in rich countries due to outsourcing to lower-wage nations have not been as great as sometimes claimed, or as substantial as losses due to technology changes in production. The threat of outsourcing, however, has been used effectively by companies to exact wage and working concessions from their labour force (Martin 2007). Auto giants, Ford and General Motors, are threatening to move all of their US production factories to lower-wage countries unless their unionised workers take major pay cuts (*Guardian Weekly*, 31.08.07, p. 16). In response, auto worker unions in the USA agreed to a two-tiered wage system, where all new employees would receive starting wages less than half the previous amount (Keenan 2007). Not only does this create unhealthy inequalities in the workplace, it will put downwards pressure on all other manufacturing sector wages. Open trading in currencies also has a negative impact. Between 2005–07, Canada's dollar rose over 30 per cent in value against the US dollar. In response, according to a survey of business leaders, over 20 per cent of remaining manufacturing in Canada closed shop and moved to low-wage, fixed-currency China (Chase 2007). Most of the new jobs in Canada exist in the part-time and insecure services sector, or in that even less secure option known as 'self-employment'.

An alphabet soup of trade treaties

The World Trade Organisation (WTO) is the best-known institution overseeing global market integration through liberalisation of trade in goods, services and finance. The WTO is the successor to an earlier and more informal body known as the General Agreement on Tariffs and Trade (GATT), founded in 1947 to undo some of the protectionism among the industrialised nations that arose during the interwar period of high unemployment. Significantly, the benefits of gradual tariffs reduction in the post-War period were seen in the context of Keynesian economics and the prominent role it gave to government interventions into the economy, particularly in debt-funded countercyclical spending, that is, that governments should borrow and spend more in public works during periods of recession and high unemployment. Liberalisation under the WTO has taken place in a context of neoliberal economics which truncates the role of government in the economy, and seeks to reduce government debt and spending regardless of economic cycle (Collier 2006). Also important is that the GATT was essentially a 'gentlemen's club' of rich countries; developing nations played little role in them until the 1980s and 1990s, and there was no requirement for reciprocal trade concessions on their part.

All that changed with the birth of the WTO in 1995. As trade tariffs came down, by GATT obligations for rich nations and through structural adjustment requirements for poorer ones, trade talks focussed on expanding markets and investment opportunities for wealthier countries. This led to a new suite of treaties that covered investment, services, domestic regulations, even government procurement, many of which have potentially far-reaching health implications (see Table 6.2). For most of these, and with only limited forms of what in trade-talk is called 'special and differential treatment', all developing countries are now subject to formal rules and binding dispute settlements. The implications of these agreements were not well understood by many trade negotiators in rich countries, never mind the fewer and less prepared negotiators from poorer ones (Labonté & Sanger 2006a/b; Labonté et al. 2007). The bottom line of increased liberalisation and global market integration has been a rise in capital's share of global wealth, relative to labour's (Labonté & Schrecker 2007); and to such an extent that the World Bank recently warned of globalisation's widening wage gaps between skilled and unskilled workers, and how this might increase a call for national protectionist policies in high- and low-income countries alike (World Bank 2007).

The key health and development criticism about WTO and other trade agreements is a simple one that this book has previously noted: Equal rules for unequal players will only produce unequal results. A fair trading system is one that handicaps the rich while discriminating in favour of the poor. That was the principle that guided world trade before the

Table 6.2 WTO agreements with major public health implications

Agreement	Health Impacts
GATT 1994	Reduced tariffs in many developing countries led to job losses in 'uncompetitive' sectors, with subsequent impacts on poverty, and declines in net public revenue, decreasing the funds available for health, education, water/sanitation and other key health determinants.
AoA (Agreement on Agriculture)	Continuing export and producer subsidies by the USA, EU, Japan and Canada depress world prices and cost developing countries hundreds of millions of dollars in lost revenue which could be used to fund health, education and other health-promoting services. Subsidised food imports from wealthy countries undermine domestic growers' livelihoods. Market barriers to food products from developing countries persist and deny poorer countries trade-related earnings.
SPS (Agreement on Sanitary and Phytosanitary Measures)	Requires scientific risk assessments even when foreign goods are treated no differently than domestic goods (i.e., there is no discrimination). Such assessments may be costly and imperfect.
TBT (Technical Barriers to Trade Agreement)	Requires that any regulatory barrier to the free flow of goods be 'least trade restrictive as possible'. Many trade disputes over domestic health and safety regulations have invoked this agreement. Only one so far has clearly ruled in favour of health over trade.
GATS (General Agreement on Trade in Services)	Locks in privatisation levels in committed service sectors, several of which (health care, education, environmental services) are important to promoting public health, and are frequently prone to market failure, i.e., private provision often excludes access to the poor. Once a service sector is committed, there is no cost-free way to extend public provision of that service in the future.
TRIPS (Agreement on Trade Related Intellectual Property Rights)	Extended patent protection can limit access to essential medicines. Higher resulting cost of drugs can consume public funding otherwise useful for primary health care or investing in other health determinants.
TRIMS (Agreement on Trade Related Investment Measures)	Prohibits government's abilities to place domestic purchase requirements on foreign investment; such requirements can increase domestic employment, which can be important to improving population health.
AGP (Agreement on Government Procurement)	Limits government's abilities to use its contracts or purchases for domestic economic development, regional equity, employment equity or other social goals with strong links to better population health. While currently a plurilateral (voluntary) agreement, there is negotiating pressure to make it a binding multilateral agreement for all 150 WTO member nations.

WTO; it is one that needs re-enacting. Rich world promises to strengthen 'special and differential treatment' for poorer WTO members have so far not been honoured. Instead, developing countries are being pressured to lock-in a schedule of tariff reductions on almost all goods, removing for them the very flexibilities used by presently rich countries to become so (Chang 2002). The most recent *least* developed countries to join the WTO have actually had to make deeper liberalisation commitments than the wealthiest OECD countries, foregoing important development policy flexibilities in the process (Mehrotra 2004).

The negotiating pressure on poorer nations reveals a popular misconception about the WTO and, for that matter, the World Bank and the IMF. These institutions are often cast as the cause of the particular form of neoliberal globalisation that is producing unhealthy effects worldwide. They are not. It is true that people working within these institutions are often ideologically committed to neoliberal economics; there is a lack of transparency or democratic accountability in these institutions; and their organisational structure very much discriminates against the interests of or participation by poorer countries or civil society organisations. But these institutions are creations of governments; the source of whatever is wrong with them lies with these governments, notably the wealthier ones who were the victors in World War Two, and who dominate actual decision-making or negotiating sessions within them. This is an empowering fact for activist health promoters concerned about globalisation, since the targets for global health promoting advocacy work are simply different sectors of the same state structures that are targets for national health-promoting advocacy work.

An overpopulation of regional and bilateral trade treaties

The power behind trade treaties becomes clearer when we recognise the growing importance of bilateral and regional trade treaties. Talks have stalled at the WTO, a result of civil society activism visible as the 'Battle of Seattle' during the 1999 WTO Ministerial Meetings; developing world mobilisation within the WTO; continuing rich world undermining of the 'Doha Development Round' by demanding more 'give' by developing countries before allowing them any new 'take'. Many of the richer nations, particularly the USA and the EU, are now spending more time negotiating regional and bilateral trade treaties where it is easier to impose their will on smaller countries by virtue of their economic might. They have already gained most of what they want from the global trade deals; any more is easier to obtain through bilateral or regional deals that can then be 'ratcheted up' to the WTO level.

The North American Free Trade Agreement (NAFTA) between Mexico, the USA and Canada is one of the best-known examples of a regional trade deal. While it generated some impressive trade and investment gains for Mexico, the weakest partner, these were transitory and failed to translate into any real domestic economic growth, development, poverty reduction or health improvement (UNCTAD 2007). NAFTA also contains a controversial provision that allows private companies to directly sue national governments for potential lost profits due to public policy decisions. Examples with public health implications include Canada's retreat from plain-packaging for cigarettes, withdrawal of a ban on a potentially neurotoxic gasoline additive, a fine against a Mexican municipality for stopping creation of a toxic dump site that could pollute its source of drinking water and an attempt by an American water company to sue a Canadian province for over $10 billion in lost potential earnings from its ban on bulk water exports (Labonté & Sanger 2006a). Recent NAFTA tribunals, however, appear to be reducing rather than expanding the scope of this controversial provision.

Bilateral investment agreements (BITs) are another example of treaties with negative health outcomes. BITs began their explosive rise after the collapse of talks to create a multilateral agreement on investment (MAI) and now number over 2200 (Peterson 2004). Most BITs are intended to protect foreign investors and are often highly restrictive of performance requirements that governments might impose on such investment. Like NAFTA, they allow companies to sue directly governments over policy changes not in their favour. Many of the BIT cases now in arbitration relate to Latin American or African water concessions. Private investors are seeking to overturn government regulations on tariffs, taxes and water quality; or are seeking multimillion dollar compensation because governments cancelled their contracts due the companies' own failure to meet their obligations. Some foreign mining companies are threatening to use BITs to seek high levels of compensation from the South African government which, to rectify the historic exclusion of the Black majority from the country's economy, is changing its domestic legislation on ownership of mineral resources (Peterson 2004). BITs generally lack any reference to development goals and dispute that tribunals have erred on the side of protecting foreign investors. This effectively minimises any risks such investors face due to changing socio-political, economic or environmental conditions. Governments intervening to mitigate the health or social costs of changed conditions, or to respond to citizens' needs for better living conditions, are increasingly facing costly challenges and fines if their actions diminish the profitability of foreign investments. Of 255 investor-state lawsuits filed under BITs, over two-thirds have been in the past four years, most are from rich-world companies against developing nations and two-thirds of the cases so far heard have resulted in these countries having to make large pay-outs to these private companies (*Guardian Weekly* 31.08.07, p. 25).

Of cures and care

There are two WTO trade treaties that directly commodify health and have received the greatest health promotion attention: Agreement on Trade-Related Intellectual Property Rights (TRIPS), which extends patent protection that may limit poor countries' access to essential medicines; and General Agreement on Trade in Services (GATS), which locks-in existing health care privatisation to the benefit of elites and private companies but to the detriment of those unable to pay the costs. Some progress on amending TRIPS to allow easier access to cheaper generic drugs was made in 2003. But the rules remain cumbersome and costly, and the USA has since been pressurising its poorer trading partners to accept so-called 'TRIPS-plus' deals that take away the flexibilities they won at the WTO. The 2006 Democrat majority in both US houses of government has led to some potentially significant shifts in that country's bilateral trade policy, essentially loosening some of the TRIPS-plus language in them so that they are more WTO-equivalent and making compliance with labour rights and some environmental agreements core obligations subject to disputes and trade retaliation (ICTSD 2007). The power of big pharmaceutical multinationals to impose extended patent protection may also be diminishing, in part due to health activist pressures.

GATS is a more complex agreement combining bottom-up options and top-down requirements. The main concern is that the agreement could accelerate an already global trend in health services privatisation. GATS negotiations have ground to a halt as developing countries scrutinise more clearly its costs and benefits, since only a handful of the larger ones have service industries that might compete with those in the rich countries aggressively pushing GATS. Nonetheless, 54 WTO members, most of them developing nations, have already made commitments to liberalise some health services under GATS (see Box 6.3).

Governments may still want to experiment with commercialisation in some components of their health systems. But until governments have demonstrated their ability to regulate private investment and provision in health services in ways that enhance health equity, they should avoid making any commitments in binding trade treaties. It is not clear that

Box 6.3   Thailand's note of caution

Thailand has not made commitments in health services under the GATS but has actively participated in global trade in health services since the early 1990s, notably the promotion of private urban hospitals and health tourism. Facilitated through tax incentives to investment in private hospitals, this has enabled a rapid and substantial rise in the number of foreign patients being treated, most coming from high-income countries such as Japan, the USA, Taiwan, the UK and Australia, but also increasingly from Middle Eastern oil-rich nations. In 2001, over 1 million foreign patients were estimated to have been treated in both private and public facilities (though predominantly in the former). The government policy is to continue to increase the number of foreign patients. The resources used to service one foreigner are the same as those used to service four or five Thais. In order to address the increased demand for health professionals created by foreign patients, the Thai government in 2004 approved a policy to increase by over 10,000 the number of doctors in the following 15 years. This measure may address some of the future shortage of physicians, but does not address the immediate needs or deal with the question of how the incomes generated by medical tourism can be better harnessed to benefit the local population (Pachanee & Wibulpolprasert 2006).

The rapid growth in medical tourism, estimated at over 30 per cent annually, is not restricted to Thailand. Other countries ramping up private hospitals for private, or privately insured, overseas patients are India, Singapore, South Korea and the Philippines. Together with the flow of health workers from developing to developed countries, primarily nurses, we are witnessing the rapid creation of a global private health system for those who can afford it. The long-term implications for public health systems – which, unlike private systems, remain locked within national borders – are troubling, especially given the lack of adequate public health systems and health workers in many of the countries seeking to benefit from these private flows.

any government, anywhere in the world, has met this test. There are further political and ethical considerations associated with the GATS, underscored by the South African experience. One of the last acts of that country's apartheid regime was to commit to fully liberalise trade in health services. The post-apartheid government subsequently passed national legislation guaranteeing certain health rights by requiring needs-testing before service providers can set up shop in different parts of the country. Intended to improve equity in access, this provision violates its GATS commitments, leaving the country vulnerable to costly disputes (Sinclair 2006). Such a potential outcome leads some to call for cancelling all existing GATS commitments on health services and removing health services from the scope of its subsequent negotiations (Woodward 2005).

Health can be, and is being, commodified; but it is not a commodity. Public systems for health care arose in most developed countries because private systems proved inadequate and inequitable, a fact being rediscovered by most of the world's developing countries. For health promotion activists, the stance on this particular discourse is clear: trade treaties, which are intended to promote private commercial interests, are no place to negotiate international rules for health, health care and other health determinants, such as education and water/sanitation.

Health as human right

Indeed, there are clear conflicts between the health/commodity discourse and that of health as a human right, embodied in a number of international declarations, covenants (treaties) and plans of action. Covenants – which are legally binding on countries that ratify them – do not require states to guarantee that all people enjoy the same level of health. They do obligate states to ensure that all people enjoy the same access to goods and services essential to the enjoyment of this right. All human rights covenants contain a provision for 'progressive realisation', meaning that a country's compliance with rights obligations will vary according to its available resources to do so, but that it must, year by year, move progressively towards complete fulfilment. This obligation jars against that of WTO membership which requires commitment to progressive liberalisation of trade. To the extent that such liberalisation disadvantages poorer countries in terms of their capacities to collect and disburse public revenues or ensure equitable access to essential health services it contradicts their obligations to progressively realise human rights.

Domestic equity

A key text on the right to health is Article 12 of the International Covenant on Economic, Social and Cultural Rights (ICESCR). Article 12 proclaims 'the right of everyone to the enjoyment of the highest attainable standard of physical and mental health.' This Article, and its definitive 2000 'General Comment 14', read a little like the World Health Organization's founding document and the Ottawa Charter for Health Promotion but with a trenchant difference: it specifically obligates States Parties (those that have ratified the Covenant) to ensure provision of a number of health care and public health services, as well as equitable and affordable access to such key underlying health determinants as 'safe and potable water and adequate sanitation, an adequate supply of safe food, nutrition and housing, healthy occupational and environmental conditions, and health-related education and information, including on sexual and reproductive health' (General Comment 14 para 11). Countries' performances in doing so are reviewed periodically by the UN Human Rights Committee that oversees this Covenant.

Global responsibility

There are further international obligations. State parties to the Covenant must respect the right to health in other countries, partly by ensuring that any other international agreements they negotiate 'do not adversely impact upon the right' (General Comment 14 para 39). This is where the potential conflict between free trade and human rights enters. States Parties to the covenant must protect against infringements of this right by third parties such as corporations, using their legal or political influences. They must also fulfil this right, which for rich countries means enhanced international assistance and cooperation to poorer countries to allow their progressive realisation of this right.

The former UN Special Rapporteur on the Right to Health, Paul Hunt, whose second three-year term expired in 2008, issued several assessments on the real and potential conflicts between trade and health, focussing principally on extended intellectual property rights and their denial of access to essential medicines, health services trade and the migration of health workers from poor to rich countries. He also commented *a priori* on the human rights implications of bilateral trade agreements in negotiation i.e. the 'TRIPS-plus' requirements of US-negotiated trade deals, usually at the invitation of the developing country partner.

While Hunt's advice, and that of his successor, is non-binding, it adds substantial leverage to civil society campaigns opposed to trade deals that limit access to health care and other essential goods or services. This includes a 2006 global right to health campaign by dozens of civil society organisations under the broad umbrella of the People's Health Movement, now active in 40 different countries. The focus of this campaign is a 'mobilisation of action from below' through training and capacity-building sessions, documenting violations of health rights and lobbying national governments for policy change. Its most active campaign, in India, has conducted a number of people's tribunals where evidence of lack of access to health care and its damaging effects have combined with lobbying and court actions to hold the government accountable to its domestic and international legal obligations to maintain health services (http://www.phmovement.org/en/campaigns/righttohealth). A key premise of its activist work is to build the capacities of local organisations to monitor violations of the right to health.

Such popular mobilisations within countries have so far proved to be the only means of achieving policy change under the right to health. Apart from 'naming and shaming' at a global level, international human rights treaties lack enforcement courts. Despite the rhetorical support for human rights offered by the world's most powerful nations, no single dispute panel at the WTO has yet to consider a human rights argument in its deliberations (Harrison 2007); yet the WTO's rules have largely been set by these same 'rights-talking' governments. Scores of countries, however, have adopted all or parts of the Covenant and the right to health within their constitution. As such, the right becomes domestically judiciable, and has been used successfully in numerous campaigns (see Box 6.4).

Efforts to advance human rights as the guiding frame for twenty-first-century global governance are growing. All UN bodies are now obliged to apply a human-rights based approach, although how this should be done and what this means for each UN agency still remains unclear. The key features nonetheless are consonant with health promotion: participation, empowerment and universality. Like any discourse advancing the possibility of global justice, rights-based arguments are easily dismissed by the realist ideology common to many governments and media commentators as romanticism, a waste of energy or, worse, diverting attention from the real work of growing economies or fighting the war on terror.

Some activist scholars and civil society organisations, in turn, argue against the present emphasis on human rights, which are *individual* and not *collective* rights, for their lack of class analysis. This diverts energies away from a deeper critique of, and efforts to mobilise against, the appropriation of capital by global elites and the ongoing commodification of most aspects of life. Rights scholars themselves sometime express concern over potential competition between different rights: Does the right to security of person, for example, require a government to allow private health systems to compete with public ones so that those with the

Box 6.4 When health activism meets the law

The human right to health requires the provision of essential medicines as a core duty that cannot be traded for private property interests or domestic economic growth. This has long placed human rights and the TRIPS agreement on a collision course, although the combined power of collective mobilisations and legal activism appears to be eroding the corporate claims to intellectual property rights. Legal scholars talk of life cycle in which legal rights become social norms, moving from norm emergence, to norm acceptance and 'cascade', to norm internalisation where what was once contentious becomes taken-for-granted and no longer a matter of public debate.

Lisa Forman (2007), an expert on TRIPS and the right to health, argues that the Treatment Action Campaign became a precipitating event the led to a 'cascade' with a sharp upsurge at the UN in international statements on treatment as a human right and articulations of state obligations on ARV. The same year saw the WTO issue its Declaration on TRIPS and Public Health. A second case in South Africa bypassed the courts, and went to that country's Competition Commission, where activists successfully argued that the high prices for ARVs levied by two big drug companies violated regulations against excessive pricing and South Africa's guarantee of the 'right to life'. A third South African case forced the government to supply ARVs to HIV+ prisoners (Singh et al. 2007). These rhetorical and legal victories were matched by considerable ARV price shifts, from over $15,000/year per person to as low as $150/year. New global funding mechanisms were also created; and in five years, access to ARV in Sub-Saharan Africa has increased from under 1 per cent to current levels of 28 per cent (Labonté et al. 2007).

Even countries where the right to health has not been formally written into its domestic legislation have been found liable to obligations under Article 12 of the ICESCR. In Argentina, people affected by haemorrhagic fever successfully argued before the courts that the country's ratification of the ICESCR obligated it to finance treatment and prevention of the epidemic disease. Argentina's government countered that it didn't have the money; the courts said, 'find it, because you are responsible'. A similar ruling was made against the Ecuadorian government's decision to suspend an HIV programme. In India, the High Court in 2007 upheld a compulsory license not for

(Continued)

Box 6.4   *(Continued)*

an ARV, but for a patented cancer medicine, thus allowing production of cheaper generics. Thailand similarly has approved compulsory licenses for several patented ARVs and for drugs used to treat heart disease. In both cases the patent holding pharmaceutical companies have exacted some economic revenge by withdrawing other drugs from their markets or withholding research and development investments; and have threatened challenges before the WTO. But only governments can initiate a challenge at the WTO, and the home countries of these drug multinationals have indicated that they have no intent to do so.

ability to pay can avoid wait-times for public care that could pose a risk to life (Mathews 2007)? Given the slow global dominance of Western liberalism with its individualisation over the more communitarian ethos of many developing countries, this is a realistic concern. It is also leading some human rights activists to urge prioritisation among rights, giving more weight to those which, while still applied to individuals, obligates states to act in ways that benefit larger collectives (as in the right to health) or to meet the needs of the most disadvantaged and vulnerable. Others are urging the importance of building upon General Comment 14 to create a full-blown collective right to public health (Meier 2007). But it would still take a wilful naïveté to assume that the existence of legally binding state obligations under unenforceable human rights treaties is sufficient in itself.

Whether or not 'rights-talk' proves to be a sustainable countervailing discourse to our still dominating neoliberalism is unknown. At the same time, human rights are 'the most globalized political value of our times' (Austin 2001), representing the most widely shared language of opposition to devaluation of health that results from the globalisation-driven spread of markets. For 'health as human right' reframes, at a basic and ethically important level, each of the other four discourses:

- Security becomes human-centred rather than nation-centred.
- Debt cancellation and development assistance become legal obligations and not intermittent charity.
- Global public goods for health similarly become binding requirements.
- And trade is subordinated as a means to the right to health (or development more broadly); it is never an end in itself.

The health imperative of redistribution

Global health is the new challenge for a 20-year mature health promotion, and a just globalisation is its new prerequisite. How should this challenge and prerequisite be framed? The assumption underlying any examination of discourses is that these linguistic constructions set the boundaries of problem-definition and intervention. In that sense, each global health discourse examined has limitations but all, apart from the commodification discourse, have something strategic to offer.

Security gives global health interventions greater traction across a range of political classes than a rights-based argument alone. To the extent that this strengthens a base of public health expansion; securitisation of health may be a prerequisite to its eventual de-securitisation (Fidler 2007). But vigilance is needed to avoid national security from trumping human security.

Development remains the invitation to global governance debates. It provides a seat at the table. Risks inherent in its 'investing in health' instrumentalism can be tempered by continuously reminding decision makers to distinguish 'which one is the objective (human development) and which one the tool (economic growth)' (Global Forum for Health Research 2004). The accountability advocacy of international NGOs continues to pressure rich nations to move beyond the inadequate patchwork of broken aid promises to a global system of taxation and redistribution.

Global public goods provides a language by which economists of one market persuasion can convince economists of another that there is a sound rationale for a system of shared global financing and regulation.

Human rights, though weak in global enforcement, has advocacy traction and legal potential within national boundaries. Such rights do not resolve embedded tensions between the individual and the collective, an issue to which human rights experts are now attending.

This resolution requires firm ethical reasoning, presently lacking in the legalistic nature of human rights treaties (Ruger 2006). This need, in turn, has created scholarly momentum to articulate more rigorous argument for a *global health ethic*. Competitors for such an ethic range from Rawls' liberal theory of assistive duties based on 'burdened societies' in need (Rawls 1971) to Sen's and Nussbaum's emphases on minimum capabilities needed for people 'to lead lives they have reason to value' (Sen 1999; Nussbaum 2000), to Pogge's more recent arguments for a new ethic of 'relational justice' (Pogge 2002). The latter offers the most compelling moral case for what other analysts argue is the urgent necessity for a global entrenchment of rights, regulations and redistribution (Deacon et al. 2005). Pogge bases his reasoning on evidence that economic institutions operating on an international scale have been complicit in creating many of the conditions that lead to ill health, notably the 'radical inequality' of persisting poverty. Persons involved in upholding these institutions are thus implicated in creating subsequent ill health, even though they may be half-way around the world (hence the 'relational' nature of justice) (Pogge 2004). Globalisation, as we have come to know it, is not a natural or inevitable fact but a series of deliberate decisions that disproportionately favour some over others. Alternatives to the global order – in the form of regulation, redistribution and the institutions required to manage them – are technically feasible and would allow human rights obligations and health equity to be better fulfilled. On this basis, Pogge concludes, the current global order is morally unjust and indefensible.

Health promotion's grandest challenge: Revalorising redistribution

Relational justice implicates all of us in the struggles to make the world fairer and healthier. Two approaches to this in current vogue are 'ethical consumerism' and increased wealthy philanthropy. Ethical consumerism means purchasing goods that are produced under reasonable work conditions and with as light an environmental touch as feasible. But consumption in itself has never made distribution equitable. Even its 'fair trade' global movement, while commendable, usually offers only marginally better returns for poorer producers in poor countries and fails to deal with the environmental and economic limitations of reliance on primary commodity exports. Neither has philanthropy ever made distribution equitable. Charity is not a substitute for justice. Progressive taxation, popular mobilisations and the scrappy world of public policymaking are what created the Western world's most equitable system of governance: the post-War welfare state. As much as health promoters complain of the rules-bound rigidities of its bureaucracies, the welfare state is the best system humans have so far created to allocate resources on the basis of principle rather than nepotism or power. The problem is that economic globalisation is challenging the welfare state's survival or delivering it stillborn in virtually all of the world's countries. If capital is global, then so must be systems for its taxation and redistribution. Several systems of global taxation have been proposed, of arms sales, carbon emissions and financial transactions to name a few. One is already operational: a tax on airline fuel along with creation of a new organization (UNITAID), also known as the International Drug Purchasing Facility, to finance essential medicines and health systems in poor countries. There is a new 'Leading Group' of nations comprising Brazil, France, Indonesia, Norway, Senegal, South Africa and Thailand, exploring other forms of 'solidarity levies for development'.

Another important step would be closure of offshore tax havens that allow multinational enterprises and wealthy individuals to shelter their income from national tax regimes. A recent study by the Global Tax Justice Network (Tax Justice Network 2005) estimated that $11.5 trillion of high-income individuals sit in such accounts, representing $255 billion in lost annual tax revenue. This amount is more than enough to fill the MDG funding gap, and is roughly equal to what detailed UN estimates calculate must be spent annually to stabilise and return greenhouse gas emissions to their 1990 level by 2030 (*Guardian Weekly* 07.09.07, p. 4). No estimates of corporate profits in such havens exists, although annual profits from US-based companies held offshore soared from $88 billion in 1999 to $149 billion in 2002 (Tax Justice Network 2007). Between the two, high-income evaders and corporate avoiders, there would be enough recaptured and fairly taxed capital to substantially reduce the worst of the world's health problems and their causes and to finance an avoidance of climate disaster.

Despite being tarnished by over two decades of unbridled market greed, redistribution remains health promotion's most important policy goal and, arguably, global health discourse. Even a small amount of redistribution is far more efficient in reducing poverty than is economic growth (Woodward & Simms 2006). Redistribution is ethically defensible since by relational justice we are all implicated in how globalisation and market-driven politics is affecting the widening chasms of wealth and health inequalities. Sustainability demands redistribution, since the growth to lift people out of poverty would almost certainly destroy the environmental resources needed for survival.

There is a cost to redistribution. To meet the ethical poverty line of $3/day, a 30 per cent tax on consumption that exceeded the US median level would be required. This would affect about 6 per cent of the world's population, but up to half of those living in rich countries. This means less bankable income or fewer purchases for most of us reading this book. But there is an almost folkloric abundance of evidence telling us that happiness has not risen with rich world per capita income over the past half century. Nor does health improve much with rising income past a surprisingly modest threshold, whereas stress and disease do rise with income inequality.

Simply put: in the rich world, enough is already too much. In the poor world, too little is not enough. The scales need rebalancing. That is the moral quest of this millennium. Will health promotion be able to rise to it and play its part?

7
Glocalisation: Health Promotion's Next Grand Challenge?

> Certain things cannot be achieved, but this is not a reason to give up seeking them.
>
> > Mário Quintana, Brazilian poet.
> > (Becker et al. 2007)

> [T]oday no place is constituted wholly by local or global factors. At the same time glocal spaces . . . have tremendous potential as a base for new and transformative politics and identities.
>
> > (Harcourt & Escobar 2002)

This final chapter discusses competing ideas about how to improve health equity at both a local and global scale. It begins by revisiting the story of the two women factory workers in Bangladesh and Pakistan in Chapter 5, and how individual choices by those of us in the rich world are necessary, but insufficient local, strategies. It then discusses three approaches to empowering the local, globally: relocalising the economy, democratising global governance, and overhauling the very bases of economic practices. It concludes with some thoughts on what this means for health promoters committed to an empowering practice.

Saying no is necessary but not sufficient

We started our examination of globalisation's effects on health with the depressing tale of two women workers caught between globalisation's promises of modernity and financial independence, and its reality of production conditions that rivalled the worst of Europe's headlong rush into industrialisation two centuries earlier. We ended with a hint of optimism based on renewed international efforts to establish core labour rights in these countries.

In an ironic twist, countries that are more open to international trade, including many low-income nations such as Bangladesh, actually report fewer violations of core labour rights than do closed countries (Neumayer & De Soysa 2005a/b). No one is sure why, although scrutiny by NGOs, attention by trade unions in countries where its workers lost their employment from outsourcing and occasional consumer boycotts may all play some role in this outcome. It is harder for gross violations of human rights to go unnoticed in an increasingly Internet-linked world; this is perhaps globalisation's most health promoting effect to date. That open countries have better labour rights than those who remain economically closed does not, however, mean that their workers necessarily benefit from these rights. Indeed, as the authors of the study on trade openness and labour rights themselves conclude, 'it is entirely possible . . . perhaps even likely, that globalisation boosts the bargaining power of capital at the expense of labour, which would put downward pressure on outcome-related labour standards such as wages, working times and other employment conditions' (Neumayer & De Soysa 2005a). In other words: it is one thing to have a right *de jure* (in law) and quite another to have it *de facto* (in fact).

There are at least two reasons for this. The first has to do with the extent to which trade openness in many countries has increased the informal nature of employment. Women working on piece-rates from their home or men selling second-hand clothing in local markets do not benefit from formal labour rights, with a few exceptions (see Box 7.1). The second has to do with 'the bargaining power of capital', in this instance Wal-Mart, now the largest corporation in human history. Wal-Mart and, to compete, all its competitors no longer shop the world to find the least expensive goods for their stores. They create bidding wars amongst factories to produce at the prices they dictate, reversing the historic capitalist bargaining between producers (those who make) and retailers (those who sell). Under these constraints, having the right to organise and to bargain collectively for better working conditions is meaningless to production workers. Even in its retail operations, Wal-Mart is notoriously anti-union, closing any store where workers have managed to organise successfully. It was also recently found guilty of not compensating many of its retail workers forced to work overtime (Joyce 2006). But as long as people shop there, the global power imbalances that Wal-Mart, its copycat competitors and the ethos of 'cheap consumerism' have created will keep the poor and marginalised of the developing world trapped in the personal pathologies of a 'healthy' global economy.

Box 7.1 The Self-employed Women's Association (SEWA)

In Ahmedabad, India, there are around 100,000 street vendors, forming a sizeable proportion of the informal employment sector in the city. They sell fruit, vegetables, flowers, fish, clothes, vessels, toys, footwear, and many other items for daily and household use. Most vendors have been selling in the city's markets and streets for generations. Like other poor self-employed women, the vegetable sellers of Ahmedabad live in poor parts of the city. They start work at dawn, buying their wares from merchants in the wholesale markets. They frequently need to borrow money, incurring very high rates of interest, and routinely face harassment and eviction from their vending sites by local authorities. The Self-Employed Women's Association (SEWA), a union of almost one million workers, is a striking example of collective action by these women and others like them, to challenge and change these conditions. To strengthen control over their livelihoods, vegetable sellers and growers (all SEWA members) linked together to set up their own wholesale vegetable shop, cutting out exploitative middlemen. As a result, both growers and sellers have seen improved incomes through better prices for their produce. SEWA also organises child care, running centres for infants and young children, and campaigns at the state and national level for child care as an entitlement for all women workers. Further, SEWA members are improving their living conditions through slum upgrading programmes to provide basic infrastructure such as water and sanitation. This happens in partnerships with government, people's organisations and the corporate sector.

In order to solve the problem of access to credit, the SEWA Bank provides small loans and banking facilities to poor self-employed women, such as the vegetable sellers, avoiding the huge interest rates demanded by private loan agents. The Bank is owned by its members, and its policies are formulated by an elected Board of women workers. In times of health crisis, poor families not only lose work and income, but often also have to sell assets to secure the wherewithal to pay for treatment: poor informal sector workers and their families are pushed further into the cycle of poverty and indebtedness. With SEWA, however, when the vegetable sellers or their family members fall ill, collectively organised health insurance can be used to pay for health-care costs. SEWA has started an integrated insurance scheme for women in times of crisis. Frequently harassed

(Continued)

Box 7.1   *(Continued)*

by local authorities, the vegetable sellers campaigned with SEWA to strengthen their status through formal recognition in the form of licences and identity cards, and representation on the urban Boards that govern market activities and urban development. That campaign, started within Gujarat, subsequently went all the way to the India Supreme Court, and inspired international attention and alliances. SEWA web site: http://www.sewa.org/services/bank.asp

Source: WHO Commission on Social Determinants of Health, *Achieving Health Equity: from root causes to fair outcomes*. Geneva: World Health Organization, 2007.

The localised health-promoting response: just say no. We can exercise personal empowerment in the choices we make by assessing their relative impacts on empowerment (and environment) more globally. Otherwise we simply gain in our health and power by displacing diseases and powerlessness to other, less seen corners of the world.

But individual choices are insufficient. Health promoters have argued this insufficiency with respect to environmental determinants for some time: it is far more effective and efficient to regulate and subsidise costs for energy retro-fitting of private residences than to rely on hundreds of millions of individual consumer choices, especially when the initial retro-fitting costs may be unaffordable for many. The same applies to how we govern our economies. The issue is whether we can (or should) relocalise our economies, democratise their globalisation or rebuild our entire economic practices in policy-possible ways.

Relocalising the economy

The second of our two gardening stories with which the book opened was framed around the future-survival need to source our food locally. The 'carbon footprint' of food has become the latest environmental front line, whether it pertains to reducing Western societies' carbon-intensive red meat diet (and the globalisation of this diet to such populous nations as China) or seeking to restrict the flow of long-distance produce.

Consuming locally inevitably raises the issue of trading-off short-term poverty alleviation for the world's poorest for longer-term environmental sustainability, which at this point is enjoyed most by the world's richest. One UK organisation recently proposed a ban on organic food imports from poor countries because of the air miles involved in their shipping. This would have devastated tens of thousands of poor small farmers in Kenya, Ethiopia, Uganda and Tanzania, where producing organic produce for export, notably cut flowers, herbs, essential oils and cotton, has become the major source of agriculture-led economic growth (Hartley 2007). On the one hand, as a Kenyan delegate to an international health conference complained, 'growing flowers to send to Europe, is that any way to develop our country?' (Canadian Conference on International Health 2007). On the other hand, as a Kenyan Kikuyu farmer pleaded, 'a ban on export markets will be the death for us.' In the end, the UK organisation compromised by putting off the decision to a later date (Vidal 2007a).

Not that calculating environmental costs are easy to make. New Zealand lamb shipped to the UK exhausts only 1520 pounds/ton (including its airfreight), compared to the UK's domestic lambs expelling 6280 pounds/ton (Wente 2007). The reason is that New Zealand lamb free-ranges on clover fields while UK lamb relies upon carbon-heavy animal feed. Similarly, some studies find that the carbon footprint of African flowers shipped to Europe is less than that of flowers grown locally due to less use of pesticides, fertilizers, heating and machinery (Hartley 2007).

Consider, too, that many of the world's poorest countries in Africa are not net food-exporters, but net food-importers. Without buying food grown in other countries people would starve. Only part of this is due to population growth exceeding the supply of arable land. Another is the legacy of the nineteenth century 'white man's burden', which divided Africa among the European colonisers in such a way that many of the newly minted nations lacked then, and now, sufficient land, water, coastal access and other natural resources to be either food or, more broadly, economically self-sufficient. Lurking in the background is the power of the global food transnational companies, many based in the USA. These companies, through their influence on the US government, succeeded in pushing through a WTO Agreement on Agriculture that, with its array of delays and subsidy boxes, is still advantaging high-income country corporate farmers at the cost of low-income country household producers. In the telling words of the US Agriculture Secretary at the start of negotiations on the Agreement, the 'idea that developing countries should feed themselves is an anachronism . . . they could better ensure their food security by relying on US agricultural products' (Bello 2002).

Behind this complexity is an even more profound problem: the 'inexorable decline' noted by the United Nations Environmental Programme in the planet's water, land, air, plant and animal and fish stocks. This decline has led to global food shortages, a rapid drop in global food reserves and a rise in retail food prices that is placing the cost beyond the reach of poorer groups in countries throughout the world (Vidal 2007b). One of globalising drivers behind this: the recent, rapid and massive conversion of food-productive land into cane and maize crops for use as ethanol, a 'biofuel' that is helping high-income countries reduce their dependency on foreign-controlled and declining oil reserves. Increasingly food-scarce regions around the world (from India, Africa and Brazil to the USA) are committed to ramping up substantially biofuel production in the coming years. At the same time, conservative estimates place the number of environmental refugees seeking food and water beyond their borders at 1.8 *billion* by 2025 (Glenn & Gordon 2007).

It is the apparent health-suicidal tendencies of such trends that have led some to campaign urgently for a dramatic relocalising of our economies. Colin Hines' book, *Localization: A Global Manifesto* (2007) is one of the more popular, yet carefully reasoned, arguments for the active rejection of economic globalisation. The 'local' could, for many industries, be the nation; though for environmental goods such as food, Hines argues for regions that do not exceed the circulation of local papers. His premise is that economic policy should invert its present bias favouring liberalised global trade and instead favour

- Safeguarding nation and regional economies against imports of goods and services that can be produced locally;
- Site-here-to-sell-here rules for industry;
- Localising money flows to rebuild the economies of communities;
- Local competition policies to ensure high-quality goods and services;
- The introduction of resource and other taxes to help pay for such a fundamental and expensive transition, and to guide it in such a way that adequately protects the environment;
- Fostering democratic involvement in both the local economic and political systems;
- A redirection of trade and aid, such that it is geared to help the rebuilding of local economies, rather than international competitiveness (Hines 2007, p. viii).

Hines' arguments are similar to many other globalisation critics and activist organisations. His rejections of free trade tenets and the economic mantra of international competitiveness in favour of more robust local economies are buttressed by scores of useful policy suggestions for rewriting our present global rules. The one major weakness with his argument is that it privileges the nation state as the largest boundary for the local. Nations, or even regions within nations, would be empowered to discriminate against foreign imports in favour of domestic producers – the very protectionism that others have argued partly spurred Europe's two great wars in the last century (Nye Jr. 2002; Bello 2007). There is also the problem of domestic producers being no less monopolistic, predatory or exploitative than transnational firms, though this could be rectified through strong, democratic regulation of the private sector. But there is a nagging global question: *does it promote health equity?*

Does it promote health equity?

Despite the environmental rationale for relocalising the economy, replacing an open-trading system with a protectionist one that favours local production will not solve the short-term dilemmas facing poorer countries and health promotion's quest for greater global health equity. Returning to the issue of food and whether it is better or worse to 'grow one's own': agriculture-led export growth has been aptly described as a 'dead-end' for poorer countries' long-term economic development. It is; and it often does little to promote equity or sustainable agriculture unless it is carefully monitored and regulated to do so. But agriculture-led export remains important for a period of time in order for poorer countries to earn the foreign currencies they need to purchase the technologies they require to develop their domestic manufacturing, or to leapfrog directly into high technology services (Glenn & Gordon 2007). Even if a nation can produce its own food in more sustainable ways, for a rich country to shut down market access to all poorer countries' food exports is too blunt an instrument and one that can aggravate, rather than alleviate, global wealth inequalities. The localising manifesto to redirect economies to become nationally self-sufficient, without concomitant efforts to redistribute financial and material resources globally, condemns smaller, poorer countries to remain the world's lowly paid gardeners and woodcutters.

Instead, there are both environmental and equity goals to be achieved through better managed systems of global trade – a 'glocalising' of the economy. This differs from 'localising' it, as it recognises the need to render local what can be localised while democratising what remains globally necessary for local survival. As Walden Bello, one of the developing world's more prominent activist-academics and founder of the NGO Focus on the Global South, points out in his provocatively titled book *Deglobalization*, what is needed is a 'double movement of "deglobalization" of the national economy and the construction of a "pluralist system of global economic governance"' (Bello 2002). 'Deglobalization', Bello emphasises, 'is not about withdrawing from the international economy' (2002). Rather, it is a deliberate reorienting of national economies from their emphasis on production for export to production for the local market. In that it parallels the main arguments put forward by Hines, but with a less insistent approach to localisation *per se*. Key measures to 'deglobalize' include

- Building up domestic savings to avoid a reliance on foreign investors and markets for development finance,
- Undertaking reforms for income and land redistribution to create a more vibrant internal market,
- Placing equity ahead of growth in national development strategies to reduce environmental disequilibrium,
- Making economic decisions a matter of public debate rather than private market choice,
- Strengthening civil society monitoring of the private sector and the state and
- Creating new production linkages between community-run cooperatives, the local private sector and state enterprises with minimal involvement of transnational corporations.

But this 're-empowerment of the local and the national', Bello acknowledges, 'can only succeed if it takes place within an alternative system of global economic governance' (Bello 2002). What does such an alternative pluralist system look like? For Bello, the answer is simple: one in which the power of the 'three sisters' of globalisation (the World Bank, IMF and WTO) is weakened and that of others, such as the ILO and UN agencies charged with health and human development, strengthened. He writes: 'It is in a . . . more fluid, less structured, more pluralistic world, with multiple checks and balances, that the nations and communities of the South – and the North – will be able to carve out the space to develop based on their values, their rhythms, and the strategies of their choice' (Bello 2002).

This may be true, but more policy precision on what a more pluralistic or democratised system of global governance is also needed.

Democratising the global economy

George Monbiot, like Hines and Bello, a 'public intellectual' who has written extensively and critically of globalisation's present course, posits that the problem is not that we have too much globalisation but that we have too little. In his book, *The Age of Consent* (Monbiot 2003), he summarises an oft-claimed flaw with globalisation-as-we-know-it: borders no longer restrict (at least very much) the movement of capital, goods and elites (Bauman's 'tourists' described in Chapter 5) but are raised for unwanted labour (the 'vagabonds') and mark the terminus of democratic politics. We have globalised the economy without globalising an effective governance system of regulatory and redistributive checks and balances. Monbiot, while sharing Hines' criticisms of globalisation, sketches a competing 'manifesto' to localism urging, among other reforms:

- Creating a World Representative Parliament (WRP), established by a founding treaty among nations, with elected representative based on population. The WRP would not be a direct governance voice, but a moral voice overseeing the myriad of existing global actors (transnational corporations) and governance institutions (the IMF, the WTO, the World Bank, the multiple UN agencies).
- Democratising the UN by replacing the 'one nation, one vote' system with a population-weighted vote system, capturing the power now vested in the undemocratic UN Security Council.
- Replacing 'free trade' with 'fair trade' rules that institutionalise the principle of greater development equity for poorer nations.
- Establishing an International Clearing Union (ICU), originally proposed by the influential twentieth century economist John Maynard Keynes, but rejected by the USA in the post-World War Two 'Bretton Woods Conference' that created today's global governance institutions. The ICU would function to prevent trade deficits and international debt accumulation, thus stabilising global trade.

These ideas, like those advanced by Hines and Bello, have a powerful normative ring to them. Elections to the WPR, for example, would allow more local concerns to be expressed directly within global forums and about globalisation processes. Some critics were quick to dismiss Monbiot's alternative 'manifesto': Could we ever expect such powerful nations as the USA and rising India and China to agree to creation of a world parliament when they won't even agree to participate in the International Criminal Court? Would the rich nations who control the voting at the World Bank and IMF ever give up the powers they have over these institutions? In one sense the critics are right: we almost need the form of global democracy Monbiot is writing about in order to create it; in which case it would no longer be necessary. But we must also be mindful of

Quintana's aphoristic reminder that having no idea (as yet) on how such reforms might be achieved is no reason to abandon them. Sometimes referred to as 'international cosmopolitanism', the ideas in Monbiot's manifesto have serious academic and political provenance in efforts to increasingly 'legalise the international' by establishing democratic regulations at the supranational level that correspond to those existing within the world's democracies.

As Chapter 4's discussion of the policy process hinted, there are also ways to take incremental steps towards achieving such ends, pushing the policy frame beyond its present boundary but not so far that the canvass of possibility rips apart. In some ways this prodding of policy choices within the limits of social democracy was the remit for the Globalisation Knowledge Network, a group of academic and NGO activist researchers working alongside the World Health Organization's Commission on Social Determinants of Health. The Commission, comprising 20 former heads of states, ministers and senior academics, and chaired by the eminent social epidemiologist Sir Michael Marmot, was charged to examine how governments and people could improve health equity (a concept we explored in Chapter 1) by affecting the determinants of health (which we discussed in Chapter 2). The Network's task was to comb the worldwide evidence base for how globalisation functioned as a 'determinant of health determinants' and what are the policy implications arising from such a review (Labonté et al. 2007). Many of the Network's findings informed the evidence reviewed in the previous two chapters. Here we elaborate on three only: the need to restrain global trade, to reinvent global governance and to reconfine capital.

Restraining trade

Regarding liberalisation, the Network emphasised the importance of health ministries and NGOs participating more fully in national discussions shaping countries' negotiating positions in current and future trade agreements. National health and development goals should be given priority over trade and growth. Rich country pressures on developing countries to 'lock-in' and agree to a formula to steadily reduce their tariffs should cease until these countries show evidence of developing broader and more equitable tax bases to offset the loss of tariff revenues. There should be sufficient flexibility in any tariffs reduction formula to allow countries to raise and lower these border taxes over time to meet their domestic development goals. Intellectual property rights should be removed from the WTO and returned to the World Intellectual Property Organisation, where disputes are settled through negotiation rather than through trade sanctions. As we argued in Chapter 6, governments should not commit to liberalise (commercialise) trade in health and other essential services until they have experience regulating commercial provision in ways that do not undermine equity. Pressure from health activists in Canada, as one example of health-promoting advocacy in the globalisation arena, led that country to declare that it would not liberalise trade in any of its health, education or social service sectors.

Some international NGOs have been pushing to have trade agreements incorporate 'social clauses' – essentially using the enforcement rules of trade treaties to pressure governments to honour their environmental, human and labour rights obligations. Sound in principle, social clauses may be risky in practice. Developing countries argue that they could become a form of 'back door protectionism' by which richer countries can close their borders to imports from poorer ones less able to implement these obligations. An alternative option is to alter the process by which trade disputes are resolved. Most disputes originate from rich countries against each other, or against poorer ones. These disputes are settled by closed panels of trade policy experts. These experts generally do not consider health, human rights or development goals, only the narrow interpretation of trade rules. While WTO agreements include a few weakly worded clauses that allow exceptions to trade rules for health, environment or national security purposes, dispute panels have almost always interpreted these to give trade the benefit of the doubt. So far human rights obligations have never been considered in their deliberations. A simple way to rectify this would be to create a parallel panel comprising health, human rights and development experts that would determine if a country's failure to comply with a trade rule was necessary for it to meet its human rights obligations or development goals. The latter would include not only the Millennium Development Goals (MDGs) (Chapter 6), but also those associated with the 'right to development' declared by the United Nations in 1986 (the USA was the only country to vote against this Declaration). This would allow civil society groups within countries to pressure their own governments to act on such obligations; it would not, as with social clauses, surrender more national sovereignty to trade treaty organisations such as the WTO. Instead, and following Bello's advice, it would weaken rather than strengthen the role of the WTO in global governance, something most international NGOs and many UN agencies agree is necessary. It would lead to global ridicule of, and other forms of pressure against, any country that insisted on enforcing a successful trade dispute that only came at the cost of denying another country its abilities to meet internationally agreed upon human rights and development goals.

Another important health aspect of global trade is the 'nutrition transition' taking place in many low- and middle-income countries. Diets based on local foods are being transformed into dependence on imported processed foods, creating obesogenic food environments and increasing the prevalence of chronic disease. The evidence linking nutrition transition to trade, though not yet conclusive, is highly suggestive. The growth of transnational supermarkets has further led to changes in food availability, accessibility, price and, through marketing, desirability. This has shifted demand for home-produced foods to dependence on store-bought processed foods. Global regulation of food trade is considered important for two reasons: improving domestic food security and decreasing the health problems of over/under malnutrition. Many health activists are now calling for negotiations of a framework convention related to food trade, using the Framework Convention on Tobacco Control as a potential model. The challenge will be confronting countries such as the USA, which intervened to 'water down' an earlier WHO strategy document on diet, physical activity and health in order to protect its transnational food companies (Lee et al. 2007). But health promoters played an important role in the years of mobilising and advocacy that eventually brought tobacco under stronger regulatory control; there is no reason they cannot do the same with food security and global food regulation.

Reinventing global governance

Global governance is not the same as global government. The latter, though potentially incubated by Monbiot's suggestion of a World Representative Parliament, would replicate the authority that nation states currently exercise over their citizens. This is unforeseeable in any near term. Global governance involves governments but extends to the messy amalgam of 'stakeholders' and organised social actors – non-governmental, private, institutional – and their efforts to individually or collectively influence power and decision-making at the international level. There is 'thick governance' in some sectors, such as in global rule-setting and enforcement bodies like the WTO and its member nations; and 'thin governance' in many others, notably the health, rights and social sectors.

Many of the key institutions involved in global governance that affect health have woefully inadequate systems to ensure participation, transparency and accountability. Representation on the Executive Boards of the IMF and the World Bank, for example, substantially reflects the weighted votes of the members. Developed countries that account for 20 per cent of IMF members and 15 per cent of the world's population have a substantial majority of votes in both institutions. Developing countries, by contrast, are seriously under-represented relative both to their share of Fund and Bank membership and to their share of world population. Despite recent efforts to engage with a broader range of stakeholders, improve public information systems and provide fuller reporting of activities by many of these institutions, the transparency of key decision-making processes in both institutions remains inadequate. As Chapter 6 noted, their influence, and certainly that of the IMF, may be on the wane. The Fund's loan portfolio, and hence the weight its pro-liberalisation economic policies carry, has shrunk from $105 billion in 2003 to just $17 billion in 2007 (Weisbrot 2007). Only the world's poorest countries are still captured by its tutelage. The reason many others have been released, however, bears its own health risks: the luck, or curse, of sitting on and exploiting oil reserves or other scarce natural resources, often with little regard to the environmental or human health effects.

The WTO, while nominally more democratic (one country, one vote, though negotiating decisions are assumed by consensus if no country protests), also does not do well on 'good governance' criteria of participation, transparency and accountability (Blagescu & Lloyd 2006). This is primarily because in practice most substantive discussion takes place outside formal structures through a complex series of meetings, such as 'mini-ministerials', to which only the most powerful countries are invited. Closed negotiations are the preferred mode, with decisions often made without full approval by low- and middle-income countries. For example, at the 1996 Singapore Ministerial meeting of the WTO, involving all 150 nation members, only 30 were invited to the informal meeting where the major decisions were made. The remaining countries were asked to accept these decisions as a *fait accompli* on the last night of the negotiations (Jawara & Kwa 2003). For many observers the actual governance of the WTO defaults to 'relative market size' as the 'primary source of bargaining power' (Karns & Mingst 2004). This leads some to urge a complete scrapping of the WTO. Others believe that this would weaken the potential collective bargaining power of poorer nations within the WTO, leaving them vulnerable to bilateral trade pressures from more powerful countries. At minimum, the reach of trade obligations into the policy space of governments can be shrunk, while that of international organisation working for health and social goals can be expanded and strengthened. This strengthening can extend to their formal roles within the WTO; the WHO, for example, presently has an observer role only on just two of the WTO's many governing committees.

This expansion and strengthening, however, is not cost-free. One of the major weaknesses in the current UN system of agencies is that their core budgets have been frozen for the past decade. They have become increasingly reliant on countries willing to give them special project funding to perform their work. This makes UN agencies more beholden to donor countries (that is, the rich countries) than to the consensus goals arrived at by all member nations through the UN General Assembly or, in the case of the World Health Organization, the annual World Health Assembly. It robs these agencies of the political independence they need and makes them less likely to provide policy advice or undertake programming that might run counter to the interests of the wealthier donor countries. The WHO in particular has fallen behind the World Bank and, more recently, the huge swell of private health philanthropy in being able to influence global health policies. Once again, the USA has been the major force trimming the UN system's capacities. Until the bureaucracies of global governance – which is one way to consider the role played by UN agencies – are less constrained in their work, global governance will continue to be the privilege of the powerful, such as the Group of 8 Nations (the G8, comprising the USA, UK, Germany, France, Russia, Italy, Japan and Canada, and now with more regular invitational participation by China, India, Brazil, Mexico and South Africa) (Labonté et al. 2004).

Reconfining capital

One of the important tasks of any reformed system of global governance is limiting the global free flow of capital. As Chapter 5 noted, daily betting on short-term currency fluctuations is huge and continues to risk fiscal crises throughout the world which inevitably hurts the health of the poorest. The countries that weather these crises best are precisely those that retain restrictions on the inward/outward flow of money. As Chapter 6 pointed out, liberalisation of financial markets has also aided rich individuals and corporations in their ability to park much of their wealth or profits in small tax-haven countries. At the same time, the conventional policy advice from both the World Bank and the IMF – to say nothing of the power of private financiers the world over – has been for countries to lower their taxes to attract investors. Closing tax havens or issuing companies and wealthy individuals with global tax identity numbers in order to fairly tax them for public goods are both technically feasible remedies. So, too, is imposing a 'Tobin tax' on all currency exchanges, named for the Nobel economics laureate, James Tobin, who first proposed it.

This tax would be low enough that most travellers, who also exchange currencies, would scarcely notice it, but large enough to discourage currency gamblers. Some countries, such as Brazil, have already instituted such a tax, hypothecating it for public health services. France and Belgium also have currency taxes. More recent proposals include a 'Spahn tax', named for a German economist who argued for a two-tiered currency tax system: a very low Tobin tax for normal times and a much higher one when currency exchanges became volatile and potentially destabilising. If stock markets suspend trading when swings in share prices and exchange volumes become too wild to allow panicky traders to 'cool down', the same should apply to trade in currencies. There is also support growing among some 53 nations belonging to a recently formed (2006) 'Leading Group on Solidarity Levies to Fund Development' to use currency taxes to fund global health and development projects. If this Group sustains its momentum, it successfully begins the longer-term project of creating a global taxation/redistribution structure that Chapter 6 argued was essential for promoting global health equity.

The limits of global governance?

Democratising global governance nonetheless presumes the emergence of shared goals; therein lays its political weakness. Ideas still matter. In an essay on the 'new global politics of poverty', Alain Noël write that 'ideas that catch fire tend to be anchored in conceptions of justice that matter to social actors', noting that the main political reforms of the past century have not been implemented for instrumental reasons but from the organised and moral force of progressive social movements (Noël 2006). But Bello offers another important caution to the idea that global governance, however democratised, provides the better option to localisation:

> [I]t is . . . questionable that, even if one could conceive of a globalization that takes place in a socially equitable framework, this would, in fact, be desirable. Do people really want to be part of a functionally integrated global economy where the barriers between the national and the international have disappeared? . . . Indeed, the backlash against globalization stems not only from the inequalities and poverty it has created but also the sense of people that they have lost all semblance of control over the economy to impersonal international forces.
>
> (Bello 2007)

One could quibble that digital technologies have already psychologically blurred national borders in many peoples' minds, while also creating international links that make 'community' and the empowerment one experiences through social groups transnational, and not merely translocal. But the more profound question is whether global capitalism can (or should) be saved. As Bello continues:

> [N]eoliberal globalization is not a new stage of capitalism but a desperate and unsuccessful effort to overcome the crises of over-accumulation, over-production, and stagnation that have overtaken the central capitalist economies since the mid-seventies. By breaking the social democratic capital-labor compromise of the post-World War II period and eliminating national barriers to trade and investment, neoliberal economic policies sought to reverse the long-term squeeze on growth and profitability. This 'escape to the global' has taken place against a backdrop of a broader conflict-ridden process marked by renewed inter-imperialist competition among the central capitalist powers, the rise of new capitalist centers, environmental destabilization, heightened exploitation of the South . . . and rising resistance all around.
>
> (Bello 2007)

Whether or not we accept Bello's analysis, tinkering with global governance might best be seen as opening a door to demands for a more radical rethink of how we could structure our economic relations in ways that promoted health, ended poverty and saved the planet. This is not to abandon the quest for global governance. It is to recognise that the most important goals for health and survival may not necessarily be shared; and that the current structures of our global institutions and how they condition or constrain economic practices is in need of a very fundamental overhaul.

Globalising the economy as if poverty, health and the environment mattered

In such a far-ranging overhaul, what steps might be taken that embody the ideals of equity and sustainability while also accounting for the reality of political feasibility?

Firstly, the critique of globalisation's current economic shortcomings needs to be sustained. Politicians of many political persuasions find it easy to agree with those presently benefiting from globalisation's deepened and enlarged markets that all that is needed are 'transitional safety nets . . . to help the adjustment to dislocation' and that enable people 'to take advantage [of globalisation] and roll with it rather than oppose it' (Bergsten 2000). On the one hand, there is evidence that, even in the stiff face of international competition, some Asian countries have been able to extend and deepen their social protection policies (Labonté et al. 2007). Yet an unregulated global market makes it 'more difficult to reconcile the demands of social responsibility with the demands of profitability' (Bello 2002). Thus, on the other hand, even such bastions of Nordic global solidarity as Denmark and Finland are now developing globalisation policies that 'centre entirely on the success and competitiveness of the[ir] "own" nation' (Kosonen 2007). Only within a context of continuous interrogation and critique of globalisation and national responses to it can a sufficient 'glocal' space for consideration of alternatives be created.

But, beyond critique, a health-promoting global activism must also provide a roadmap of where we want to go, and how we might get there. David Woodward (2007), an economist formerly with the UK-based *new economics foundation* and a member of the Globalisation Knowledge Network, has given these issues considerable thought. He suggests that there are three major tasks our global economy must be restructured to achieve:

- Provide the means ('capabilities' or capacities) for fulfilment of the right to health.
- Eradicate poverty, not just at the $1/day level, but at the 'ethical' $3/day level.
- Control climate change and natural resource depletion.

The first is dependent on the other two; and persisting poverty and environmental degradation both stem from the same root of a gross misdistribution in global wealth and power. Neither of the two current approaches to economic development, Woodward argues, can resolve both problems simultaneously.

The first approach, the neoliberal model of globalisation of which this book has been most critical, is grossly less efficient in reducing poverty that is redistribution, is increasing rather than reducing inequalities and allows most of the benefits of growth to be captured by a small number of people. These people must consume vastly greater amounts of goods and services in order for the poverty-reducing effects of growth to 'trickle down'. This is patently unfair and unsustainable. The second approach, embodying many of the reforms for global governance discussed earlier in this chapter, would reconstruct global trade and finance rules in ways that allowed today's poorer countries to industrialise or develop in the same way as today's wealthy nations, by subsidising their export-led growth and/or restricting imports to protect and promote domestic companies. This approach might create more equity between nations, but it still relies upon the rich within these countries getting richer and consuming more goods and services in order for the wealth to 'trickle down' to their poorer neighbours.

Woodward argues that economic policy must now be designed to meet all three goals (health, poverty eradication and environmental sustainability) at the same time. Such policies are likely best enacted locally, with national and global policies functioning to enable this. To reduce poverty, governments can support microcredit and income generation schemes; labour-intensive public works programmes that give priority to the infrastructure needs of the poor; public procurement designed to benefit small and medium-sized local enterprises; small farmers; strengthened social safety nets; and, as needed, can direct cash transfers. The underlying premise of these policies is that priority would go to increasing poor people's production of local goods and services that, in turn, are needed most by poorer households. The demand for these goods and services would increase as poverty rates themselves fall. The intent is to break the economy's growth dependence on increased, but unnecessary, consumption by the rich, in favour of increased and necessary consumption by the poor.

To reduce growth's carbon footprint, international agreements are needed to 'roll-out' microrenewable technologies in all parts of the poor world. The cost of this would be covered, in part, through various forms of international taxation on present global trade/travel. There is growing consensus among many environmental economists that technologies for radically carbon-reduced economic growth already exist. What does not exist is the political commitment by the world's governments to pool wealth to fund their rapid deployment – which is where a global health argument framed in the discourse of global public good holds strategic appeal. The increasing pace of climate change may itself begin to force such a commitment that environmental activism alone has so far failed to mobilise. Consistent with other findings from the Globalisation Knowledge Network, Woodward calls for escalating taxes on luxury consumption of natural resources. Water for essential household consumption (a so-called minimum 'lifeline') would be free with the cost rising progressively with use. Water for swimming pools, bottling soft drinks or keeping golf courses green in desert climates would cost dearly.

Woodward's proposals also, and more controversially, call for trad-able carbon emission permits, around which there is less civil society consensus owing to the likelihood that this could lead to wealthier countries simply buying their excess consumption/emission at the longer-term expense of poorer ones. Woodward's proposals address this in part by calling for allocation of an equal carbon ration to each per-son to be held, in part, by their governments. Companies would need to purchase carbon permits from governments to carry out their busi-ness, passing on the cost to consumers and thereby allowing market 'supply/demand' pricing to work for environmental ends. Governments would also have another source of revenue for spending in pro-poor development ways. Households would receive remaining allocations, which poorer households under-consuming could sell to richer house-holds over-consuming. This process would eventually balance out as poorer households consumed more to the average, the above-average consumption of richer households became too costly.

Globally, agreement on universal tariffs shared equally by exporters of tropical products would stop the downward spiral in their price, benefit-ing economically poorer countries even while reducing demand for these products. Developing countries dependent on export of minerals and fuels could organise collectively to create 'bidding up' rights to these resources by transnational companies, rather than the present bilateral 'bidding down' that characterises such exchange. Such a 'cartelisation' worked for the Organisation of Oil-Exporting Countries (OPEC). It could also work for those countries now exporting coltan, copper, phosphate or any other global commodity. This would, of course, require 'South-South' or regional economic agreements between low- and middle-income countries; but such agreements are now on the rise. Examples are the Southern African Development Cone, Mercosur (an economic union agreement involving several South American countries) and the Chiang Mai Initiative, under which several Asian countries will pool their foreign currency holdings to create their own stabilisation fund independent of the Western, high-income dominated IMF.

These 'do-able' ideas do not preclude a wholesale overhaul of global governance. The system established in 1944, which predates climate change and was agreed upon when most of today's low-income coun-tries were still colonies, does not and cannot meet the needs of the twenty-first century. Woodward's suggestions, along with others described in this chapter, establish the goals and policy baseline for what a renewed global governance system would need to achieve. How we mobilise the public and political support necessary to create such a system is another matter, although many of the 'local' health promotion strategies described in earlier chapters are as relevant to global transformation as they are to neighbourhood change.

What can health promoters do?

The ideas presented in chapters 4, 5, and 6 might also seem overwhelming to the majority of those working in health promotion. Health promotion remains rooted in localities and continues to struggle to up its ante to the national level, much less the global. Most health promoters are engaged in programmes involving face-to-face encounters with citizens, not in efforts to tip the minds of global policymakers. The question remains: how can they more effectively 'glocalise' their work? While some of the answers to this question have been embedded throughout this book, we summarise a few below.

First, health promoters should recognise that this task is not simply about their professional lives. It is also about their lives as citizens. Actions here span several sectors:

1. Environmental: travel less, eat less carbon-intensive diets, consume less, live more locally, prepare for more climate change/ecological refugees
2. Economic: share the wealth – stand up for the virtues of fair taxation, corporate regulation, local production/consumption cycles whenever possible, and national foreign policies that aim at increasing global equity rather than mercantile competitiveness
3. Social: combat the potential for local racism as the planetary movements of people increase (whether fuelled by their desire to partake of the rich world's opportunities increasingly on global offer, or for political, economic or ecological necessity)

Second, these actions can extend to our professional lives. Do not stop the local empowerment. Paul Farmer, a physician and international social justice advocate working primarily in the poorest communities of the poor nation of Haiti, points out that 'genuine change', by which he means framing economic and social development around the principle of health as a human right, 'will be most often rooted in small communities of poor people' (Farmer 2003). Much of the knowledge of globalisation's present pathologies and some of the means to correct them gestated first in the popular struggles of poorer communities around control over land, water, housing, income, health care, education and other basic rights. We saw in Chapters 3 and 6 how a national struggle for access to essential medicines (the Treatment Action Campaign) precipitated significant changes in global public and private policies. It continues to deepen: recent generosity on the part of many multinational pharmaceutical companies in financing research into treatments for 'neglected diseases' (diseases that affect the hundreds of millions of people living in the tropics who cannot afford to pay for medicine) is as much a response to their global shaming over the South African court case as any moral enlightenment. What becomes important in all of our localised work, then, is finding ways to link empowerment struggles in one community with those in other localities around the world. The global economic constraints affecting local empowerment are becoming universally more similar, even if they are of differing intensities depending on the baseline wealth of a community. Recognising both the opportunities and necessity to build global solidarity from the work of local mobilisations, a number of civil society organisations are now premised almost exclusively on what could be called a 'glocalising' approach to health promotion (see Box 7.2).

Third, we need to attend carefully to growing xenophobia and racism. This is perhaps the most perfidious and difficult externality of globalisation's dislocations to combat. Analyses of the causes of inequalities lend themselves to reasoned debate. Once these inequalities become constructed as a function of race or ethnicity (as in, 'these migrants are taking my job') they submerge to an irrational location that is much harder to penetrate by those who seek fairness and more easy to manipulate by those who seek power by the old rule of 'divide and conquer'. Robert Putnam, famous for popularising the concept of 'social capital', has recently written how societies experiencing growth in their ethnic diversity show a decline in both 'bonding' (within group) and 'bridging' (between group) forms of social capital. Stated bluntly, trust between people declines (Bunting 2007). Importantly, Putnam argues for historical context. Many countries have successfully experienced large waves of migration and ethnic diversity in the past, not without initial tensions and not with periods of extreme religiosity on the part of new arrivals. Marketing tolerance and deliberately building links within and between émigré populations and native-born citizens are the healthy prescriptions. Exaggerating or stereotyping differences are not. In our experience, some of health promotion's most empowering local projects and trenchant health policy critiques in recent decades have been diffusing tensions between ethno-cultural groups by supporting those marginalised by their ethnicities while

Box 7.2   Glocalising health activism

The People's Health Movement (PHM) is a global network of health activists. As one example of its advocacy, the PHM launched a campaign in 2006 to strengthen the right to health with a focus on defending the right to health care. The campaign looks at what measures are needed to tackle human rights violations in the context of a broader analysis of power and social inequalities. It seeks social transformations indispensable to resolving such inequalities as they affect health. As such, the campaign focusses on changing national and global health sector reform policies that affect access to health care by the poor, the disadvantaged and the marginalised. It also seeks to put in place mechanisms to effectively redistribute resources. PHM activists have documented violations of the right to health and planned joint actions with claim holders (citizens) and duty bearers (states) to stop these violations. Capacity building of PHM cadres and partners in civil society, responsible for calling duty bearers to account is seen as indispensable in this process of social mobilisation and empowerment. PHM (as of November 2007) has also carried out over 30 country assessments of the status of the right to health care (www.phm.org). One of the key purposes of the PHM has been to give a voice to those currently excluded from global forums, and to diversify the views represented within them as a means of improving the governance of global health.

The Association for the Taxation of Financial Transaction for the Aid of Citizens (ATTAC) is another global advocacy group founded in France to support the Tobin and Spahn taxes on currency transactions. But there is another side to progressive global taxation, and that is preventing capital from gaining further 'rights' in our globalised economy. ATTAC, which now has branches in 40 countries, is credited by many with contributing to France's decision to withdraw from OECD talks on a proposed Multilateral Agreement on Investment (MAI), leading to the collapse of the talks (Waters 2004). The Organisation for Economic Co-operation and Development (OECD) is a network of the world's originally 20, and now 30, wealthiest nations. It had proposed an investment treaty that would have allowed foreign private investors to move their money in and out of countries without restriction; to invest in almost all economic, social and natural resource sectors preventing nations from regulating foreign owner

(Continued)

Box 7.2   *(Continued)*

ship for domestic development purposes; and to sue nations if future government regulations led in any way to a loss in their potential profits. The successful campaign against the MAI included local mobilising efforts by advocacy groups in several other OECD countries, notably Canada. It marked the political birth of the global justice movement. While the MAI is now history, wealthy countries (the EU, the USA) continue to push for a multilateral investment agreement at the WTO in clear contradiction with the aims of the 1986 Declaration on the Right to Development (Ghosh 2005). Monitoring, vigilance, local mobilisation and global advocacy: struggles for global equity require that all four be unflagging.

building common cause across ethnic divides. This is locally empowering work with global resonance.

Fourth, most of the globalising practices that negatively affect health equity are products of individual nation's decisions. Even the WTO is simply a 'club of nations'; problems in its governance – for example, that business lobby groups are far more likely to be involved in formal ministerial meetings than are public interest NGOs – are due to the will of its (generally more powerful) member states. Reforming globalisation's more toxic policies or rules cannot be separated from changing the globalisation politics of national governments. To that end, health promoters (at least some) can become more active through their professional organisations or other civil society groups to pressure their national governments to adopt global policy positions that enhance, rather than imperil, health equity. Some countries have begun already to do that. Norway, for example, is mobilising international support to increase and streamline funding to poorer countries to help them meet the health-specific MDGs. It also is attempting to create greater 'coherence' in its foreign policy and in at least two ways. It is presently withholding part of its contribution to the World Bank's International Development Association (which makes loans to low-income countries) because the Bank's conditionalities on such loans still constrain too much the policy space of countries receiving such loans (Bretton Woods Project 2008b). The Norwegian government elected in 2005 also stated that its own trade negotiating position would ensure 'that the WTO rules [do] not deprive poor countries of the management right and means that have been important in developing our own society into a welfare society' (Norwegian Labour Party 2005). This differs markedly from the mercantilist negotiating positions of most other high-income countries. Canada's 2004 International Policy Review, for example, variously claims that 'much of the world's population is essentially powerless, either victims of stalled development or citizens of states too weak to affect the global agenda' (which acknowledges, albeit in patronising tones, the global asymmetry in power and wealth); but that 'Canada is in a race with many countries . . . one we cannot afford to lose' (which undermines the previous claim by promoting a 'beggar my neighbour' approach to global trade and commerce). A study of Canadian policy-leaders similarly found that their commitment for Canada to altruistically 'do the right thing' in terms of health, development and aid coexisted in unresolved tension with its presumed need to retain a competitive edge in the global marketplace (Nixon 2006).

Finally, if health promoters' localising work exceeds their time-resources to become more engaged in global health efforts, they can support financially those campaigning civil society groups that continue to hold states and multilateral institutions to health equitable account. This has become a trickier endeavour in recent years, as 'charitainment' – the celebrity led, feel good approach to 'attend a free rock concert, buy a T-shirt and wear a white wrist band' to 'make poverty history' – is reframing complex issues of power and politics into catchy media slogans that fail to sustain protest momentum for the long haul of policy change. It took over 25 years of gritty, evidence-backed campaigning and raucous street protests by NGOs to finally (and only partly) obtain some measure of debt cancellation in 2005 for the world's poorest countries. The role of celebrities in aligning with global political causes should be cheered; but not when it begins to dull the analyses and policy prescriptions that have finally gained some traction in government and multilateral forums only after years of hard effort and local campaigning.

Revalorising the idea of empowerment: A closing caution

This book has made much of the concept of empowerment. What was emancipating about the term arose first from popular struggles (women's, the poor, ethno-racial and sexual minorities) to exact legal rights and entitlements from the state. Only later did it become an abused marketing slogan or, as Moore (2001) calls it, 'cheap talk' used by the World Bank and other multilateral organisations to sound politically stylish without changing their policy *status quo*. The 'cheap' part of the empowerment talk, in Moore's estimate, is the elision it makes with 'community'. Since community empowerment has been another theme running throughout this book, we want to distance ourselves from the premise that empowerment is only, ever or best experienced at that level. It is this mythology that Moore attacks in many multilateral organisations' embrace of the term. He argues that most experiences of meaningful change in the social distribution of power have arisen when groups mobilised translocally on the basis of systemic oppression: as wage workers, women, tenants, small farmers, even as slum-dwellers. Local empowerment cannot be separated from political forms of empowerment at national and international levels.

At the same time, empowerment's non-material base, the psychological experience of feeling powerful, has gained increasing prominence as an important health determinant. As inequalities in wealth and privilege increase, as they are globally, the prospects of equitable empowerment, whether material or non-material, diminish. The reason for emphasising this is that, while the health inequities arising from inequalities have both material (physical) and non-material (psychological) effects, both outcomes arise from a fundamentally *material* inequality (manifest in what Chapter 2 described as 'power-over'). Empowerment cannot be reduced only to a psychological experience (Chapter 2's description of 'power with' or 'power-from-within'). Health promotion actions to challenge relative powerlessness cannot be restricted to initiatives that bolster peoples' experiences of power, without also changing the unfair capture of global wealth and a decreasing amount of natural resources by elite groups. As the World Health Organization's Commission on Social Determinants of Health noted in its Interim Statement (2007):

> We see empowerment operating along three interconnected dimensions: material, psychosocial, and political. People need the basic material requisites for a decent life, they need to have control over their lives, and they need political voice and participation in decision-making processes. Although individuals are at the heart of empowerment, achieving a better distribution of power requires collective social action – the empowerment of nations, institutions, and communities.
>
> (p. 10)

Empowerment, despite the semantic abuses it has suffered in recent years, is an idea that still matters to health promotion. It begins with communities identifying what they need to improve and sustain their health. It progresses to the extent governments support, or can be made to support, policies that provide communities with the resources they need for local actions. It extends to broader public policies affecting the distribution of resources and power nationally, a political enterprise that rarely succeeds without the pressure exerted by translocal civil society organisations or coalitions of local groups. It stretches, now, even further, to recreating rules and systems of global governance that ensure all people have the capabilities to 'lead lives they have reason to value' (Sen 1999).

Health promoters have roles to play at every level in this process. It will not be easy, but our very survival, and not only our health, may depend upon our willingness to do so.

Bibliography

Alam, K. & Hearson, M., 2006. *Fashion victims: The true cost of cheap clothes at Primark, Asda and Tesco.* [Online]. http://www.waronwant.org. [Accessed 18 October 2006].

Alexander, D., 2007. The international health partnership. *The Lancet*, vol. 370, no. 80, pp. 3–4.

Anonymous, 2005. The eight commandments. *The Economist.* 7 July, pp. 25–8.

Asian Development Bank, 2007. Inequality in Asia: Key indicators 2007 special chapter highlights. [Online]. http://www.adb.org/Documents/Books/Key_Indicators/2007/pdf/Inequality-in-Asia-Highlights.pdf [Accessed November 2007].

Assunta , M. & Chapman, S., 2006. Health treaty dilution: A case study of Japan's influence on the language of the WHO Framework Convention on tobacco control. *Journal of Epidemiology and Community Health*, vol. 60, pp. 751–6.

Atkinson S., Ngwengweb, A., Macwan'gic, M., Ngulubed, T.J., Harphame, T. & O'Connell, A., 1999. The referral process and urban health care in sub-Saharan Africa: The case of Lusaka, Zambia. *Social Science & Medicine*, vol. 49, pp. 27–38.

Austin, W., 2001. Using the human rights paradigm in health ethics: The problems and the possibilities. *Nursing Ethics*, vol. 8, no. 3, pp. 183–95.

Baggott, R., 2000. *Public health: Policy and politics.* London: St. Martin's Press LLC.

Barder, O. & Birdsall, N., 2006. *Payments for progress: A hands-off approach to foreign aid (working paper No. 102).* Washington, DC: Center for Global Development.

Basu, S., 2003. *AIDS, empire, and public health behaviourism.* [Online.] http://www.equinetafrica.org/newsletter/index.php?issue=28 [Accessed 1 February 2005].

Baum, F., 2008. *The new public health.* Melbourne: Oxford University Press.

Baum, F. & Harris, E., 2006. Equity and the social determinants of health. *Health Promotion*, vol. 17, no. 3, pp. 163–5.

Baum, F. & Sanders, D., 1995. Can health promotion and primary health care achieve health for all without a return to their more radical agenda? *Health Promotion International*, vol. 10, no. 2, pp. 149–60.

Bauman Z., 1998. *Globalization: The human consequences.* Cambridge: Polity Press.

Becker, D., Edmundo, K.B., Guimaraes, W., Vasconcelos, M.S., Bonatto, D., Nunes, N.R. & Baptista, A.P., 2007. Network of healthy communities of Rio de Janeiro – Brazil. *International Union for Health Promotion and Education* vol. XIV, no. 2.

Bello, W., 2002. *Deglobalization: Ideas for a new world economy.* London: Zed Books.

Bello, W., 2007. The post-Washington dissensus. *Focus on Trade.* Number 132. [Online]. http://www.focusweb.org

Bergsten, C.F., 2000. *The backlash against globalization.* Speech delivered at the 2000 meeting of the Trilateral Commission, Tokyo, April 2000 (downloaded from the Internet.)

Bergsten, C.F., 2000. *The backlash against globalization.* Speech before the Trilateral Commission, Tokyo, 9 May (http://www.iie.com/TESTIMONY/fred glab.htm).

Bernier, N., 2007. Health promotion program resilience and policy trajectories: A comparison of three provinces. In M. O'Neill, et al., eds *Health promotion in Canada: Critical perspectives.* Toronto: Canadian Scholars' Press Inc.

Berridge, V., 1999. Passive smoking and its pre-history in Britian: Policy speaks to science? *Social Science and Medicine,* vol. 49, pp. 1183–96.

Besley, T. & Kudamatsu, M., 2006. Health and Democracy. *American Economic Review,* vol. 96, pp. 313–56.

Birdsall, N., 2006. *The world is not flat: Inequality and injustice in our global economy (WIDER Annual Lecture 2005).* Helsinki: World Institute for Development Economics Research.

Bjaras, G., Haglund, B.J.A. & Rifkin, S., 1991. A new approach to community participation assessment. *Health Promotion International,* vol. 6, no. 3, pp. 199–206.

Blagescu, M. & Lloyd, R., 2006. *2006 Global Accountability Report: Holding power to account.* London: One World Trust.

Blouin, C., Bhushan, A., Murphy, S. & Warren, B., 2007. *Trade liberalisation,* Background Paper for the Globalization Knowledge Network, World Health Organization Comission on Social Determinants of Health, [Online] http://www.globalhealthequity.ca/projects/proj_WHO/index.shtml

BMA., 2002. *Tobacco under the microscope: The doctor's manifesto for global tobacco control.* London: BMA Tobacco Control Resource Centre.

Bond, P., 2006. The dispossession of African wealth at the cost of African health. *International Journal of Health Services,* vol. 37, no. 1, pp. 171–92.

Boseley, S., 2006. Herceptin costs 'put other patients at risk'. *Guardian Weekly.* 1–7 December, p. 8.

Boulle, J. & Avafia, T., 2005. *Treatment Action Campaign (TAC) Evaluation.* [Online] http://www.tac.org.za/Documents/FinalTACEvaluation-AfaviaAndBoulle-20050701.pdf

Bratt, J.H., Weaver, M., Foreit, J., De Vargas, T. & Janowitz, B., 2002. The impact of price changes on demand for family planning and reproductive health services in Ecuador. *Health Policy and Planning,* vol. 17, no. 3, pp. 281–7.

Brehm, J. & Rahn, W., 1997. Individual-level evidence for the causes and consequences of social capital. *American Journal of Political Science,* vol. 41, pp. 999–1023.

Breman, A. & Shelton, C., 2001. *Structural adjustment and health: A literature review of the debate, its role-players and presented empirical evidence (Working Paper WG6: 6).* Geneva: WHO Commission on Macroeconomics and Health.

Bretton Woods Project, 2008a. *IFC and health 'unsubstantiated claims'.* 1 February [Online] http://www.brettonwoodsproject.org/art-559967 [Accessed 6 February 2008].

Bretton Woods Project, 2008b. *Donor contributions to IDA up record amount Norway, civil society not satisfied.* 1 February [Online] http://www.brettonwoodsproject.org/art-559964 [Accessed 6 February 2008].

Brock, K. & McGee, R., 2004. *Mapping trade policy: Understanding the challenges of civil society participation, Working paper 225.* [Online] Brighton, Sussex: Institute for Development Studies. http://www.ids.ac.uk/ids/bookshop/wp/wp225.pdf [Accessed 1 February 2005].

Brown, E.R., 1979. *Rockefeller medicine men: Medicine and capitalism in America.* Berkeley: University of California Press.

Brown, E.R. & Margo, G.E., 1978. Health education: Can the reformers be reformed? *International Journal of Health Services*, vol. 8, no. 1, pp. 3–26.

Bryant, T., 2006. Politics, public policy and population health. In Raphael, D., Bryant, T., & Rioux, M., eds *Staying alive: Critical perspectives on health, illness, and health care*. Toronto: Canadian Scholars' Press.

Buchanan, D., 2000. *An ethic for health promotion: Rethinking the sources of human well-being*. New York: Oxford University Press.

Bunting, M., 2007. Immigration is bad for society, but only until a new solidarity is forged. *The Guardian*. June 18.

Burris, S., 1997. The invisibility of public health: Population-level measures in a politics of market individualism. *American Journal of Public Health*, vol. 87, pp. 1607–10.

Cage S., 2007. *Roche says Tamiflu® capacity outstrips demand*. [Online]. Reuters. 26 April. http://news.yahoo.com/s/nm/20070426/bs_nm/roche_tamiflu_dc_2;_ylt= AlIFMs9BpfF_2oRyjo3U7d2Tvyli. [Accessed 3 May 2007].

Cameron D. & Stein, J.G., 2000. *Globalization triumphant or globalization in retreat: Implications for Canada*. [Online]. Ottawa, Department of Justice, Canada Research and Statistics Division, (rp02-6e). http://canada.justice.gc.ca/en/ps/rs/ rep/RP2002-6.pdf [Accessed 1 February 2005].

Canada Department of Finance, 2003. *The Budget Plan 2003*. Ottawa: Department of Finance, Table A1.19.

Canadian Conference on International Health, 2007. Personal communication, Ronald Labonté.

Canak W., 1989. *Lost promises: Debt, austerity, and development in Latin America*. Boulder: Westview Press.

Carapetis, J.R., Johnston, F., Nadjamerrek, J. & Kairupan, J., 1995. Skin sores in Aboriginal children. *Journal of Paediatrics and Child Health*, vol. 31, p. 563. Letter to Editor.

Carey, P., 2000. Community health and empowerment. In J. Kerr, ed. *Community health promotion. Challenges for practice*. London: Bailliere Tindall.

Cha, A.E., 2007. Lobbyists move into China. *Guardian Weekly*, 12 October, p. 16.

Chang, H.J., 2002. *Kicking away the ladder: Development strategy in historical perspective*. London: Anthem Press.

Chase, S., 2007. Loonie spurs factory exodus. *The Globe and Mail Report on Business*. 16 October, p. B7.

Chen, L., Fukuda-Parr, S. & Seidenticker, E. (eds) 2004a, *Human Insecurity in a Global World*. Boston: Harvard University Press.

Chen, L., Leaning, J. & Narashimhan, V. (eds) 2004b, *Global Challenges for Human Security*. Boston: Harvard University Press.

Chen, S., & Ravallion, M., 2004. How have the world's poorest fared since the early 1980s? *The World Bank Research Observer*, vol. 19, pp. 141–69.

China Labor Watch. 2007. Investigations on toy suppliers in China: Workers are still suffering. [Online] http://www.chinalaborwatch.org/EightToy%20820071 %20Final%20edit1.pdf [Accessed 23 August 2007].

Chomik, T., 2007. *Lessons learned from Canadian experiences with intersectoral action to address the social determinants of health: A summary report*. Prepared for the Public Health Agency of Canada: Chomik Consulting & Research Ltd.

Clark, A., 2007. Sage gets a Buffetting. *Guardian Weekly*, 11 May, p. 18.

Cobham A., 2002. Capital Account Liberalization and Poverty. *Global Social Policy*, vol. 2, no. 2, pp. 163–88.

Coburn, D., 2000. Income inequality, social cohesion and the health status of populations: The role of neo-liberalism. *Social Science & Medicine*, vol. 51, no. 1, pp. 135–46.

Coburn, D. & Poland, B., 1996. The CIAR vision of the determinants of health. *Canadian Journal of Public Health*, vol. 87, no. 5, pp. 308–10.

Collier, P., 2006. Why the WTO is deadlocked: And what can be done about it. *The World Economy*, vol. 29, pp. 1423–49.

Collins, C. & Green, A., 1994. Decentralization and primary health care: Some negative implications for developing countries. *International Journal of Health Services*, vol. 24, no. 3, pp. 459–75.

Commission for Africa, 2005. *Our common interest: Report of the Commission for Africa*. London: Commission for Africa.

Commission on Macroeconomics and Health, 2001. Macroeconomics and health: investing in health for economic development. [Online]. Geneva: World Health Organization http://www.cid.harvard.edu/cidcmh/CMHReport.pdf [Accessed 21 February 2005].

Commission on Social Determinants of Health (CSDH), 2007. *Achieving health equity: From root causes to fair outcomes*. Interim Statement of CSDH Geneva: World Health Organisation. http://www.who.int/social_determinants/resources/interim_statement/en/index.html accessed 1st February 2008.

Confederation of British Industry (CBI), 2006. *Transforming local services*. London: Confederation of British Industry.

Cornia, G.A., Rosignoli, S. & Tiberti, L., 2007. *Globalization and health: Impact pathways and recent evidence*. Background Paper for the Globalization Knowledge Network, World Health Organization Comission on Social Determinants of Health, [Online] http://www.globalhealthequity.ca/projects/proj_WHO/index.shtml

Coupland, R., 2007. 'Security, insecurity and health', *Bulletin of the World Health Organization*, vol. 85, no. 3, pp. 181–4.

Cueto M., 2004. The origins of primary health care and selective primary health care. *American Journal of Public Health*, vol. 94, pp. 1864–74.

Daly, H. & Cobb, J., 1989. *For the Common Good*. Boston: Beacon Press.

De Savigny, D., Kasale, H., Mbuya, C. & Reid, G., 2005. *Fixing health systems*. Ottawa: International Development Research Centre.

De Vogli, R. & Birbeck, G.L., 2005. Potential impact of adjustment policies on vulnerability of women and children to HIV/AIDS in sub-Saharan Africa. *Journal of Health Population and Nutrition*, vol. 23, pp. 105–20.

Deacon, B., Ilva, M., Koivusalo, M., Ollila, E. & Stubbs, P., 2005. *Copenhagen Social Summit ten years on: The need for effective social policies nationally, regionally and globally (GASPP Policy Brief No. 6)*. Helsinki: Globalism and Social Policy Programme, STAKES. [Online]. http://gaspp.stakes.fi/NR/rdonlyres/4F9C6B91-94FD-4042-B781-3DB7BB9D7496/0/policybrief6.pdf.

Deaton A., 2001. *Health, inequality, and economic development:CMH working paper series WG1:3*. Geneva: World Health Organisation, Commission on Macroeconomics and Health. [Online]. http://www.cmhealth.org/docs/wg1_paper3.pdf [Accessed 1 February 2005].

Deaton A., 2004. Measuring poverty in a growing world (or measuring gowth in a poor world). Princeton: Research Program in Development Studies, [Online].

http://www.wws.princeton.edu/%7Erpds/downloads/deaton_measuring poverty_204.pdf [Accessed 1 February 2005].

Deaton A., 2006. Global patterns of income and health. *WIDER Angle*. vol. 2, pp. 1–3.

Deneulin, S. & Townsend, N., 2006. Public goods, global public goods and the common good. [Online]. University of Bath: ESRC Research Group on Wellbeing in Developing Countries. http://www.welldev.org.uk/research/workingpaperpdf/wed18.pdf [Accessed 18 October 2006].

Diamond, J., 1997. *Guns, germs and steel: The fates of human societies*. New York: W.W. Norton.

Diamond, J., 2005. *Collapse*. USA: Viking Books.

Diderichsen, F., Evans, T. & Whitehead, M., 2001. The social basis of disparities in health. In M. Whitehead et al., eds, *Challenging inequities in health: From ethics to action*. New York: Oxford University Press.

Dollar, D., 2001. *Globalization, inequality, and poverty since 1980*. [Online]. Washington, DC, World Bank. http://econ.worldbank.org/files/2944_globalization-inequality-and-poverty.pdf [Accessed 1 February 2005].

Dollar, D., 2002. Global economic integration and global inequality. In D. Gruen, T. O'Brien, & J. Lawson eds, *Globalisation, living standards and inequality: Recent progress and continuing challenges, proceedings of a conference held in Sydney, 27–28 May 2002*. Australia: Canberra: Reserve Bank of Australia. http://www.rba.gov.au/PublicationsAndResearch/Conferences/2002/.

Dollar, D. & Kraay A., 2002. Growth is good for the poor. Working paper no. 2587 [Online]. Washington, DC: World Bank. http://www.worldbank.org/research/growth/pdfiles/growthgoodforpoor.pdf [Accessed 1 February 2005].

Dupéré, S., Riddle, V., Carroll, S., O'Neill, M., Rootman, I. & Pederson, A., 2007. Conclusion: The rhizome and the tree. In M. O'Neill et al. eds *Health promotion in Canada: Critical perspectives*, 2nd edn, Toronto: Canadian Scholars' Press Inc.

Durning, A., 1989. Mobilizing at the grassroots. In L. Brown et al. (eds). *State of the World*. New York: Norton.

Durodié, B., 2005. Inclusion versus experimentation. *Critical Review of International Social and Political Philosophy*, vol. 8, no. 3, pp. 359–62.

Easterly, W., 2002. *Inequality does cause underdevelopment: New evidence. Working Paper No. 1*.[Online]. Washington, DC: Center for Global Development, Institute for International Economics. http://www.undp.org/povertycentre/publications/distribution/Easterly-InequalityDoesCauseUnderdev-CGDEV-Jun02.pdf [Accessed 1 February 2005].

Easterly, W., 2006. *The white man's burden: Why the west's efforts to aid the rest have done so much ill and so little good*. New York: Penguin Press.

Edward, P., 2006. The ethical poverty line: A moral quantification of absolute poverty *Third World Quarterly*, vol. 27, no. 2, pp. 377–93.

Edwards, M., Howard, C. & Miller, R., 2001. *Social policy, public policy: From problem to practice*. Sydney: Allen & Unwin.

Elfstrom, 2006. Commentary on Chinese Labor Law [Online]. http://www.china laborwatch.org/2006%20Editorials/10-12-2006%20labor%20contract%20law.htm [Accessed 23 August 2007.]

Employment Conditions Knowledge Network (EMCONET), 2007 Final Report. [Online]. http://www.who.int/social_determinants/resources/articles/emconet_

who_report.pdf Prepared for the World Health Organization's Commission on Social Determinants of Health.

Endresen, K. & von Kotze, A., 2005. Living while being alive: Education and learning in the Treatment Action Campaign. *International Journal of Lifelong Education*, vol. 24, pp. 431–41.

Evans, P., 2005. Neoliberalism as a political opportunity: Constraint and innovation in contemporary development strategy. In K. Gallagher ed., *Putting development first: The importance of policy space in the WTO and IFIs*. London: Zed Books pp. 195–215.

Eyerman, R. & Jamison, A., 1991. *Social movements: A cognitive approach*. Cambridge: Polity Press.

Farmer, P., 2003. *Pathologies of power: Health, human rights and the new war on the poor*. Berkeley: University of California Press.

Fidler, D., 2002. *Global health governance: Overview of the role of international law in protecting and promoting global public health: WHO Global Health Governance Discussion paper no. 3*. Geneva: World Health Organization.

Fidler, D., 2007. Health as foreign policy harnessing globalization for health. *Health Promotion International*, vol 21, no. S1, pp. 51–8, Oxford University Press.

Forman, L., 2007. Trade rules, intellectual property and the right to health. *Ethics and International Affairs*, vol. 21, no. 3, pp. 3–37.

Foucault, M., 1980. Power/Knowledge: Selected interviews and other writings. In C. Gordon ed. New York: Pantheon.

Freeman, J., 1983. On the origins of social movements and a model for analyzing the strategic options of social movement organizations. In J. Freeman ed. *Social movements of the 60s and 70s*. New York: Longman.

Freire, P., 1968. *Pedagogy of the Oppressed*. New York: Seabury Press.

Freire, P., 1973. *Education for Critical Consciousness*. New York: The Seabury Press.

Freire, P. & Macedo, D., 1987. *Literacy: Reading the word and the world*. Massachusetts: Bergin and Harvey.

Freudenberg, N., 1978. Shaping the future of health education: From behaviour change to social change. *Health Education Monographs*, vol. 6, pp. 372–7.

Friedmann, S. & Motiar, S., 2005. A rewarding engagement? The treatment action campaign and the politics of HIV/AIDS. *Politics & Society*, vol. 33, pp. 511–65.

Gangolli, L.V., Duggal, R. & Shukla, A., eds 2005. *Review of Health Care in India*. Mumbai: CEHAT.

Gasher, M., Hayes, M.V., Ross, I., Hackett, R.A., Gutstein, D. & Dunn, J.R., 2007. Spreading the news: Social determinants of health reportage in Canadian daily newspapers, *Canadian Journal of Communication*, vol. 32, pp. 557–74.

Gauld, R., 2006. Health policy and the health system. In R. Miller's ed., *New Zealand Government and Politics*. Auckland: Oxford University Press, pp. 525–35.

George, S., 2004. *Another World is Possible If . . .* London: Verso.

Ghosh, J., 2005. *The economic and social effects of financial liberalization: A primer for developing countries*. New York: United Nations DESA Working Paper Series.

Gibbon, M., 1999. *Meetings with meaning: Health dynamics in rural Nepal*, unpublished PhD thesis. London: South Bank University.

Gibbon, M., Labonté, R. & Laverack, G., 2002. Evaluating community capacity. *Health and Social Care in the Community*, vol. 10, no. 6, pp. 485–91.

Glenday, G., 2006. *Toward fiscally feasible and efficient trade liberalization*. Durham: Duke Center for Internal Development, Duke University.

Glenn, J. & Gordon, T., 2007. *2007: The State of the Future*. New York: The Millennium Project, World Federation of UN Agencies.

Global Forum for Health Research (GFHR), 2004. *The 10/90 report on health research, 2003–2004*. [Online].Geneva.http://www.globalforumhealth.org/pages/index.asp [Accessed 1 February 2005].

Global Social Policy Forum, 2001. A North-South dialogue on the prospects for a socially progressive globalization. *Global Social Policy*, vol. 1, no. 2, pp. 147–62.

Goodman, R.M., Speers, M.A., McLeroy, K., Fawcett, S., Kegler, M., Parker, E., Smith, S.R., Sterling, T.D. & Wallerstein, N., 1998. Identifying and defining the dimensions of community capacity to provide a basis for measurement. *Health Education & Behavior*, vol. 25, no. 3, pp. 258–78.

Gough, I., 2001. Globalization and regional welfare regimes: The east Asian case. *Global Social Policy*, vol. 1, no. 2, pp. 163–90.

Gray, B., 1989. *Collaborating: Finding common ground for multiparty problems*. San Francisco: Jossey-Bass.

Green, L.W. & Kreuter, M.W., 1991. *Health promotion planning. An educational and environmental approach*. Toronto: Mayfield Publishing Company.

Green, L.W. & Kreuter, M.W., 2005. *Health program planning: An educational and ecological approach* (4th edn). Boston, Toronto: McGraw-Hill Higher Education.

Griffith-Jones, S. & Stallings, B., 1995. New global financial trends: Implications for development. In B. Stallings ed., *Global change, regional response: The new international context of development*. Cambridge: Cambridge University Press.

Grunberg, I., 1998. Double jeopardy: Globalization, liberalization and the fiscal squeeze. *World Development*, vol. 26, no. 4, pp. 591–605.

Gyebi, J., Brykczynska, G. & Lister G., 2002. *Globalisation: Economics and women's health*. London: Partnership for Global Health. http://www.ukglobalhealth.org/content/Text/Globalisation_New_version.doc [Accessed 1 February 2005].

Haas, P.M., 1992. Introduction: Epistemic communities and international policy coordination. *International Organization*, 46, pp. 1–35.

Habermas, J., 1984. *The theory of communicative action: Volume 1*. London: Heinemann.

Hall, A., 2007. Social policies in the World Bank: Paradigms and challenges. *Global Social Policy*, vol. 7, no. 2, pp. 151–75.

Halperin, D.T. & Epstein, H., 2004. Concurrent sexual partnerships help to explain Africa's high HIV prevalence: implications for prevention. *The Lancet*, 364, pp. 4–6.

Hanefeld, J., Spicer, N., Brugha, R. & Walt, G., 2007. *How have global health initiatives impacted on health equity?* Prepared for the Health Systems Knowledge Network of the World Health Organization's Commission on Social Determinants of Health.

Harcourt, W. & Escobar, A., 2002. Women and the politics of place. *Development*, vol. 45, no. 1, pp. 7–14.

Harrison, J., 2007. *The human rights impact of the World Trade Organisation*. Geneva: Hart Publishing.

Hartley, A., 2007. Climate change versus poverty. *The Guardian Weekly*, 31 August.

Haynes, A.W. & Singh, R.N., 1993. Helping families in developing countries: A model based on family empowerment and social justice. *Social Development Issues*, vol. 15, no. 1, pp. 27–37.

Hayward, B.M., 2006. *Public participation, in New Zealand government and politics.* Auckland: Oxford University Press.

Hearson, M. & Morser, A., 2007. *Let's Clean up Fashion: 2007 Update.* Produced by Labour Behind the Label and War on Want. [Online]. http://www.waronwant.org

Held D., 2004. *Globalisation: The dangers and the answers.* http://www.opendemocracy.net/debates/article.jsp?id=6&debateId=27&articleId=1918 [Accessed 1 February 2005].

Helsinki Process: The Responsibility to Protect, 2001. *International Commission on Intervention and State Sovereignty*, p. 11.

Heymann, J. & Kidman, R., 2007. Creating a healthier version of globalization. *Global Social Policy*, vol. 7, no. 2, pp. 139–43.

Hines, C., 2007. *Localization: A Global Manifesto.* London: Earthscan. (New edition, first published 2000.)

Hopkins, S., 2006. Economic stability and health status: Evidence from east Asia before and after the 1990s economic crisis. *Health Policy*, vol. 75, pp. 347–57.

Howse, R., 2007. *The concept of odious debt in public international law, UNCTAD Discussion Paper 185.* Geneva: UNCTAD.

Infant Baby Formula Action Network (IBFAN) [Online]. http://www.babymilk action.org/ [Accessed 21 August 2007].

Institute for Strategy and Health Policy. 2000. *Vietnam national behavior change communication strategy on population, reproductive health/family planning 2001–2005.* Vietnam: The National Committee for Population and Family Planning.

International Confederation of Free Trade Unions (ICFTU), 2003. *Export processing zones – symbols of exploitation and a development dead-end.* Brussels: ICFTU. http://www.icftu.org/www/pdf/wtoepzreport2003-en.pdf [Accessed 1 February 2005].

ICTSD, 2007. Clouds loom over US trade policy, despite successful re-negotiation of FTAs. *Bridges Weekly Trade News Digest*, vol. 11, no. 24.

International Labour Organisation, 1998. *Labor and social issues related to export processing zones.* [Online]. Geneva: ILO. http://www.ilo.org/public/english/dialogue/govlab/legrel/tc/epz/reports/epzrepor_w61/index.htm [Accessed 1 February 2005].

International Labour Organisation, 2007. *Database of international labour standards.* [Online]. Geneva, ILO. http://www.ilo.org/ilolex/english/docs/declworld.htm

International Monetary Fund (IMF), 2004. *Does the IMF always prescribe fiscal austerity? Are targets too high? Transcript of an IMF book forum.* Washington, DC: International Monetary Fund. http://www.imf.org/external/np/tr/2004/tr040608.htm [Accessed 1 February 2005].

Isreal, B.A., Checkoway, B., Schultz, A. & Zimmerman, M., 1994. Health education and community empowerment: Conceptualizing and measuring perceptions of individual, organisational and community control. *Health Education Quarterly*, 21 (2), pp. 149–70.

Jackson, T., Mitchell, S. & Wright, M., 1989. The Community Development Continuum. *Community Health Studies*, vol. 8, no. 1, pp. 66–73.

Jawara, F. & Kwa, E., 2003. *Behind the scenes at the WTO: The real world of international trade negotiations.* London: Zed Books.

Jeter J., 2002. The dumping ground: As Zambia courts western markets, used goods arrive at a heavy price. *Washington Post*, 22 April.

Jones, A. & Laverack, G., 2003. *Building Capable Communities within a Sustainable Livelihoods Approach: Experiences from Central Asia*. [Online]. http://www.livelihoods.org/lessons/Central Asia & Eastern Europe/SLLPC. 1.9.2003.

Jones, L. & Sidell, M., eds 1997. *The challenge of promoting health: Exploration and action*. London: MacMillan Press Ltd.

Jordan, T., 2002. *Activism! Direct action, hacktivism and the future of society*. London: Reaktion Books Ltd.

Joyce, A., 2006. Wal-Mart workers win wage suit. *Washington Post*, 13 October, p. D02.

Junne, G.C.A., 2001. International organizations in a period of globalization: new (problems of) legitimacy. In J.M. Coicaud et al., eds *The legitimacy of international organizations*. Tokyo: United Nations University Press, pp. 189–220.

Kabeer, N. & Mahmud, S., 2004a. Globalization, gender and poverty: Bangladeshi women workers in export and local markets. *Journal of International Development*, vol. 16, no. 1, pp. 93–109.

Kabeer, N. & Mahmud, S., 2004b. Rags, riches and women workers: Export-oriented garment manufacturing in Bangladesh. In M. Carr, ed. *Chains of fortune: Linking women producers and workers with global markets*. London: Commonwealth Secretariat, pp. 133–64.

Kahn, J. & Yardley, J., 2007. As China roars, pollution reaches deadly extremes. *New York Times*, 26 August.

Karns, M. & Mingst, K., 2004. *International organizations: The politics and processes of global governance*. Colorado: Lynne Rienner Publishers, Inc.

Kaul, I. & Faust, M., 2001. Global public goods for health: A framework for analysis and action. *Bulletin of the World Health Organization*, vol. 79, no. 9, pp. 869–74.

Kaul, I. & Mendoza, R., 2003. Advancing the concept of public goods. In I. Kaul et al., *Providing global public goods: Managing globalization*. New York: Oxford University Press for the United Nations Development Programme, pp. 78–111.

Keenan, G., 2007. Parts maker riles CAW with two-tier wage plan. *The Globe and Mail Report on Business*, 19 Oct., p. B3.

Kernaghan, Charles (Statement of), 2007. Director of the National Labor Committee, Before the Subcommittee on Interstate Commerce, Trade and Tourism, Committee on Commerce, Science and Transportation, 14 February. http://www.nlcnet.org/admin/media/document/Legislation/CK_testimony070214.pdf [Accessed 22 August].

Khoon, C.C., 2006. What's new in the 'Arusha Statement' on new frontiers of social policy. *Global Social Policy*, vol. 6, no. 3, pp. 265–9.

Knippenberg R., Alihonou, E., Soucat, A., Oyegbite, K., Calivis, M,. Hopwood, I., Niimi, R., Diallo, M.P., Conde, M. & Ofosu-Amaah, S., 1997. Implementation of the Bamako Initiative: Strategies in Benin and Guniea. *International Journal of Health Planning and Management*, vol. 12, no. 1, pp. 29–47.

Knoke, D., 1988. *Organizing for collective action: The political economies of associations*. New York: Walter de Gruyter, Inc.

Kosonen, P., 2007. Reports on globalization: The global social dimension vs national competitiveness. *Global Social Policy*, vol. 7, no. 2, pp. 230–6.

Krugman, P., 1995. Growing world trade: Causes and consequences. *Brookings Papers on Economic Activity*, pp. 327–77.

Kuyek, J. & Labonté, R., 1995. *From power-over to power-with: Transforming professional practice*. Saskatoon: Prairie Region Health Promotion Research Centre.

Labonté, R., 1990. Empowerment: Notes on professional and community dimensions. *Canadian Review of Social Policy*, vol. 26, pp. 64–75.

Labonté, R., 1991a. Econology: Integrating health and environment. *Health Promotion International*, vol. 6, no. 1, pp. 49–65.

Labonté, R., 1991b. Principles for sustainable development decision-making. *Health Promotion International*, vol. 6, no. 2, pp. 147–56.

Labonté, R., 1993a. *Health promotion and empowerment: Practice frameworks.* Toronto: Centre for Health Promotion/Participation.

Labonté, R., 1993b. Partnerships and participation in community health. *Canadian Journal of Public Health*, vol. 84, no. 4, pp. 237–40.

Labonté, R., 1994a. Death of program, birth of metaphor. In A. Pederson et al. eds *Health Promotion in Canada*. Toronto: WB Saunders.

Labonté, R., 1994b. Health promotion and empowerment: Reflections on professional practice. *Health Education Quarterly*, vol. 21, no. 2, pp. 253–68.

Labonté, R., 1996. *Community development in the public health sector: The possibilities of an empowering relationship between state and civil society.* Toronto: York University. Unpublished PhD dissertation.

Labonté, R., 1997. *Power, participation and partnerships.* Melbourne: VicHealth Foundation.

Labonté, R., 1998. *A community development approach to health promotion: A background paper on practice tensions, strategic models and accountability requirements for health authority work on the broad determinants of health.* Edinburgh: Health Education Board for Scotland.

Labonté, R., 2000. Health promotion and the common good: Towards a politics of practice. In D. Callahan ed., *Promoting healthy behaviour: How much freedom? Whose responsibility?* Georgetown University Press.

Labonté, R., 2003. *How our programs affect population health determinants: A workbook for better planning and accountability.* Manitoba and Saskatchewan Region: Health Canada.

Labonté, R., 2006. *A morbid compulsion: Understanding addiction through the prism of population health. Policy Responses to Alcohol, Drug and Gambling Issues.* [Online]. Australia: http://www.nceta.flinders.edu.au/events/documents/RonLabonte-Morbidcompulsionpaper.pdf

Labonté, R., Blouin, C., Chopra, M., Lee, K., Packer, C., Rowson, M., Schrecker, T. & Woodward, D., 2007. *Towards health-equitable globalisation: Rights, regulation and redistribution.* Final Report of the Globalization Knowledge Network, World Health Organization Comission on Social Determinants of Health, [Online] http://www.globalhealthequity.ca/electronic%20library/GKN%20Final%20Jan%208%202008.pdf

Labonté, R. & Edwards, R., 1995. *Equity in action: Supporting the public in public policy.* Centre for Health Promotion/Participaction.

Labonté, R., Jackson, S. & Chirrey, S., 1998. *Population health and health system restructuring: Has our knowledge of social and environmental determinants of health made a difference?* A report prepared for the Synthesis and Dissemination Unit, Health Promotion and Programs Branch, Health Canada.

Labonté, R. & Laverack, G., 2001. Capacity building in health promotion: For whom? and for what purpose? *Critical Public Health*, vol. 11, no. 2, pp. 111–27.

Labonté, R. & Penfold, S., 1981. *Health promotion philosophy: From victim-blaming to social responsibility.* Vancouver: Health Promotion Directorate.

Labonté, R. & Robertson, A., 1996. Delivering the goods, showing our stuff: The case for a constructivist paradigm for health promotion and research. *Health Education Quarterly*, vol. 23, no. 4, pp. 431–47.

Labonté, R. & Sanger, M., 2006a. A glossary of the World Trade Organization and public health: Part 2. *Journal of Epidemiology and Community Health*, vol. 61, pp. 738–44.

Labonté, R. & Sanger, M., 2006b. A glossary of the World Trade Organization and public health: Part 1. *Journal of Epidemiology and Community Health*, vol. 60, pp. 655–61.

Labonté, R. & Schrecker, T., 2007. Globalization and social determinants of health: The role of the global marketplace (part 2 of 3). *Globalization and Health*, 3. [Online]. http://www.globalizationandhealth.com/content/3/1/6.

Labonté R., Schrecker, T., Sanders, D. & Meeus, W., 2004. *Fatal indifference: The G8, Africa and global health*. Cape Town: University of Cape Town Press.

Labonté, R., Schrecker, T. & Sen Gupta, A., 2005. *Health for some: Death, disease and disparity in a globalized era*. Toronto: Centre for Social Justice.

Laverack, G., 1999. *Addressing the contradiction between discourse and practice in health promotion*, unpublished PhD thesis. Melbourne: Deakin University.

Laverack, G., 2001. An identification and interpretation of the organizational aspects of community empowerment. *Community Development Journal*, vol. 36, no. 2, pp. 40–52.

Laverack, G., 2003. Building capable communities: Experiences in a rural Fijian context. *Health Promotion International*, vol. 18, no. 2, pp. 99–106.

Laverack, G., 2004. *Health promotion practice: Power and empowerment*. London: Sage Publications.

Laverack, G., 2005. *Public health: Power, empowerment and professional practice*. Basingstoke: Palgrave Macmillan.

Laverack, G., 2006. Evaluating community capacity: Visual representation and interpretation. *Community Development Journal*, vol. 41, no. 3, pp. 266–76.

Laverack, G., 2007. *Health promotion practice: Building empowered communities*. London: Open University Press.

Lavis, J., 2002. Ideas at the margins or marginalized ideas? *Health Affairs*, vol. 21, no. 2, pp. 107–12.

Lavis J., Ross, S., Stoddart, G., Hohenadel, J., McLeod, C. & Evans, R., 2003. Do Canadian civil servants care about the health of populations? *American Journal of Public Health*, vol. 93, no. 4, pp. 658–63.

Lee, K., Koivusalo, M., Labonte, R., Ollila, E., Schrecker, T., Schuftan, C. & Woodward, D., 2007. *Globalization, global governance and the social determinants of health: A review of the linkages and agenda for action*. Background Paper for the Globalization Knowledge Network, World Health Organization Commission on Social Determinants of Health, [Online], http://www.globalhealthequity.ca/projects/proj_WHO/index.shtml

Lerner, M., 1986. *Surplus powerlessness*. Oakland: The Institute for Labour and Mental Health.

Lewis, S., 2005. *Race against time*. CBC Massey Lecture Series: House of Anansi Press.

Lindquist, E.A., 2001. *Discerning policy influence: Framework for a strategic evaluation of IDRC-supported research*. http://www.idrc.ca/uploads/user-S/10359907080discerning_policy.pdf [Accessed 24 March 2007].

Lister, J., 2007. *Globalisation and health systems change*. Background Paper for the Globalization Knowledge Network, World Health Organization Commission on Social Determinants of Health, [Online], http://www.globalhealthequity.ca/projects/proj_WHO/index.shtml

London School of Economics, 2006. *What is civil society?* www.lse.ac.uk/Depts/ccs/what_is_civil_society.htm [Accessed 22 February 2006].

Lukes, S., 1974. *Power: A radical view*. London: Macmillan.

Macan-Markar, M., 2004. Trade Accords Can Be Bad for Health. *Asian Times*.

Magnussen, L., Ehiri, J. & Jolly, P., 2004. Comprehensive versus selective primary health care: Lessons for global health policy. *Health Affairs*, vol. 23, no. 3., pp. 167–76.

Manandhar, D.S., Osrin, D., Shrestha, B.P., Mesko, N., Morrison, J., Tumbahangphe, K.M., Tamang, S., Thapa, S., Shrestha, D., Thapa, B., Shrestha, J.R., Wade, A., Borghi, J., Standing ,H,. Manandhar, M. & Costello, A.M., 2004. Effect of a participatory intervention with women's groups on birth outcomes in Nepal: Cluster-randomised controlled trial. *The Lancet*, vol. 364, pp. 970–9.

Mandel, S., 2006. *Odious lending: Debt relief as if morals mattered*. London: New Economics Foundation.

Marmot, M., 2006. *Health in an unequal world – social circumstances, biology and disease*. HARVEIAN ORATION, 18 October. [Online]. http://www.rcplondon.ac.uk/event/details.aspx?e=312

Martin, J.P., 2007. *Addressing the globalisation paradox*. OECD.

Mathews, S., 2007. Discursive alibis: Human rights, millennium development goals and poverty reduction strategy papers. *Development*, vol. 50, no. 2, pp. 76–82.

McKnight, J., 1987. Regenerating community. *Social Policy (Winter)*, pp. 54–8.

Mead, Margaret Anthropologist, [Online.] http://www.brainyquote.com/quotes/authors/m/margaret_mead.html

Mehrotra, S., 2004. Global institutions in local decision-making: The Trojan horses of the new millennium? *Global Social Policy*, vol. 4, no. 3, pp. 283–7.

Meier, B.M., 2007. Advancing health rights in a globalized world: Responding to globalization through a collective human right to public health, 35 *Journal of Law, Medicine & Ethics*, pp. 545–55.

Melucci, A., 1989. *Nomads of the present: Social movements and individual needs in contemporary society*. Philadelphia: Temple University Press.

Metzler, M., Amuyunzu-Nyamongo, M., Mukhopadhyay, A. & Salazar, L., 2007. Community interventions on social determinants of health: Focusing the evidence. In D. McQueen et al. eds *Global perspectives on heath promotion effectiveness*. New York: Springer Science + Business Media, LLC.

Milanovic, B., 2003. The two faces of globalization: Against globalization as we know it. *World Development*, vol. 31, no. 4, pp. 667–83.

Milward, B., 2000. What is structural adjustment? In G. Mohan G et al. eds *Structural adjustment: Theory, practice and impacts*. London: Routledge.

Mishra, S., 2006. Farmers' suicides in Maharashtra. *Economic and Political Weekly*, vol. 41, no. 16, pp. 1538–45.

Monbiot, G., 2003. *The age of consent: A manifesto for a new world order*. London: Perennial.

Mooney, G. & Dzator, J.A., 2003. Global public goods for health: A flawed paradigm? In R. Smith, R. Beaglehole, D. Woodward & N. Drager. eds, *Global public goods for health: Health economic and public health perspectives*. Oxford: Oxford University Press.

Moore, M., 2001. Empowerment at last? *Journal of International Development,* vol. 13, pp. 321–9.

Mouy, B. & Barr, A., 2006. The social determinants of health: Is there a role for health promotion foundations? *Health Promotion Journal of Australia,* vol. 17, no. 3, pp. 189–95.

Nah, S-H. & Osifo-Dawodu, E., 2007. *Establishing private health care facilities in developing countries: A guide for medical entrepreneurs.* Washington DC.: The International Bank for Reconstruction and Development/The World Bank.

Navarro, V., Schmitt, J. & Astudillo, J., 2004. Is globalization undermining the welfare state? The evolution of the welfare state in developed capitalist countries during the 1990s. *International Journal of Health Services,* vol. 34, no. 2, pp. 185–227.

Ndikumana, L. & Boyce J.K., 2003. Public debts and private assets: Explaining capital flight from sub-Saharan African countries. *World Development,* vol. 31, pp. 107–130.

Needham, C., Hoang, T. K., Nguyen, V. H., Le, D. C., Michael, E., Drake, L., Hall, A. & Bundy, A. P., 1998. Epidemiology of soil-transmitted nematode infections in Ha Nam Province, Vietnam. *Tropical Medicine and International Health,* vol. 3 (11), pp. 904–12.

Neilson, S., 2001. *IDRC-supported research and its influence on public policy. knowledge utilization and public policy processes: A literature review.* IDRC Evaluation Unit. [Accessed 25 March 2007] http://idrinfo.idrc.ca/archive/corpdocs/117145/litreview_e.html

Neumayer, E. & De Soysa, I., 2005a. *Globalization, women's economic rights and forced labour.* EconPapers. [Online]. http://econpapers.repec.org/scripts/redir.pl?u=http%3A%2F%2F129.3.20.41%2Feps%2Flab%2Fpapers%2F0509%2F0509011.pdf.

Neumayer, E. & De Soysa, I., 2005b. Trade openness, foreign direct investment and child labor. *World Development,* vol. 33, pp. 43–63.

Nixon, S., 2006. *Canada's international response to HIV/AIDS: A critical public health ethics inquiry.* PhD.: University of Toronto.

Noël, A., 2006. The new global politics of poverty. *Global Social Policy,* vol. 6, no. 3, pp. 304–33.

Norton, A., Conway, T. & Foster, M., 2001. *Social protection concepts and approaches: Implications for policy and practice in international development (Working Paper 143).* London: Overseas Development Institute.

Norwegian Labour Party, 2005. *The Soria Moria Declaration on international policy, chapter 2: International policy.* Oslo: Norwegian Labour Party. [Online]. http://www.dna.no/index.gan?id=47619&subid=0.

Nussbaum, M., 2000. *Women and human development: The capabilities approach.* Cambridge: Cambridge University Press.

Nye Jr., J.S., 2002. *The paradox of American power: Why the world's only superpower can't do it alone.* Oxford: Oxford University Press.

O'Brien R., 2002. Organizational politics, multilateral economic organizations and social policy. *Global Social Policy,* vol. 2, no. 2, pp. 141–62.

O'Neill, M. & Stirling, A., 2007. The promotion of health or health promotion? In M. O'Neill et al. eds *Health promotion in Canada: Critical perspectives.* 2nd edition. Toronto: Canadian Scholars' Press Inc, Toronto.

OECD Development Assistance Committee, 2005. Development Co-operation 2004 Report, *DAC Journal,* 6 (1).

OECD Development Assistance Committee, 2006. *Final ODA data for 2005*. [Online]. http://www.oecd.org/dataoecd/52/18/37790990.pdf

OECD-DAC. *Development database on aid activities: CRS online*. [on-line] http://www.oecd.org/document/0/0,2340,en_2649_34447_37679488_1_1_1_1,00.html (Accessed May 6, 2007).

Offe, C., 1984. *Contradictions of the welfare state*. Boston: MIT Press.

Office of the High Commissioner for Human Rights, 1996. *8 General Comment No. 25: The right to participate in public affairs, voting rights and the right of equal access to public service (Art. 25)*. Geneva: United Nations Human Rights Commission.

Olson, M., 1965. *The logic of collective action: Public goods and the theory of groups*. Boston: Harvard University Press.

Pachanee, C.A. & Wibulpolprasert, S., 2006. Incoherent policies on universal coverage of health insurance and promotion of international trade in health services in Thailand. *Health Policy and Planning*, vol. 21, pp. 310–18.

Packer, C., Labonté, R. & Spitzer, D., 2007. *Globalisation and health worker migration*. Background Paper for the Globalization Knowledge Network, World Health Organization Commission on Social Determinants of Health, [Online] http://www.globalhealthequity.ca/projects/proj_WHO/index.shtml

Pan-American Health Organisation International Conference on Health Promotion, 1992. Bogotá, Colombia.

Parkinson, J., 2006. *Direct democracy in New Zealand government and politics*. Auckland: Oxford University Press.

Peart, A. & Szoeke, C., 1998. Recreational water use in remote Indigenous communities. *Cooperative Research Centre for Water Quality and Treatment*. Unpublished.

Pederson, A., O'Neill, M. & Rootman, I., eds, 1994. *Health promotion in Canada*. Toronto: WB Saunders.

Perkins, J., 2006. *Confessions of an economic hit man*. London: Ebury Press.

Perry, P. & Webster, A., 1999. *New Zealand politics at the turn of the Millennium*. Auckland: Alpha Publications.

Peterson, L.E., 2004. *Bilateral investment treaties and development policy-making*. Winnipeg: International Institute for Sustainable Development.

Pindar, L., 2007. The federal role in health promotion: Under the radar. In M. O'Neill et al. eds, *Health promotion in Canada: Critical perspectives*, 2nd edition. Toronto: Canadian Scholars' Press Inc.

Pogge, T., 2002. *World Poverty and Human Rights*. Polity, Cambridge.

Pogge, T., 2004. Relational Conceptions of Justice: Responsibilities for Health Outcomes. In S. Anand et al (eds) *Public Health, Ethics and Equity*. Clarendon Press, Oxford.

Pogge, T., 2008. Growth and inequality: Understanding recent trends and political choices. *Dissent*, Winter 2008, http://www.dissentmagazine.org/article/?article=990.

Pokhrel, S. & Sauerborn, R., 2004. Household decision-making on child health care in developing countries: The case of Nepal. *Health Policy and Planning*, vol. 19, no. 4, pp. 218–33.

Porter, C., 2006. Ottawa to Bangkok: Changing health promotion discourse. *Health Promotion International*, vol. 22, no. 1, pp. 72–9.

Przeworski, A., Bardhan, P., Bresser Pereira, L.C., Bruszt, L., Choi, J. J. & Comisso, E. T., 1995. *Sustainable democracy*. Cambridge: Cambridge University Press.

Public Health Agency of Canada, 2007. *Crossing sectors: Experiences in intersectoral action, public policy and health.* Her Majesty the Queen in Right of Canada, represented by the Minister of Health.

Raphael, D. & Bryant, T., 2006. Maintaining population health in a period of welfare state decline: Political economy as the missing dimension in health promotion theory and practice. *International Union for Health Promotion and Education.* vol. XIII, no. 4 , pp. 236–42.

Ravallion, M., 2006. Looking beyond averages in the trade and poverty debate. *World Development,* vol. 34, pp. 1374–92.

Rawls, J., 1971. *A Theory of Justice.* Harvard University Press, Cambridge.

Reddy, S.G. & Minoiu, C., 2005. *Has world poverty really fallen during the 1990s?* Prepared for WIDER Jubilee Conference on the Future of Development Economics. New York: Department of Economics, Columbia University [Online]. http://www.columbia.edu/~sr793/sensitivityanalysis.pdf.

Reddy, S.G. & Pogge, T.W., 2005. *How not to count the poor, version 6.2.* New York: Columbia University [Online] http://www.socialanalysis.org.

Rifkin, S., 2003. A framework linking community empowerment and health equity: It is a matter of choice. *Journal of Health and Population Nutrition.* vol. 21, no. 3, p. 173.

Rifkin, S.B., Muller, F. & Bichmann, W., 1988. Primary health care: On measuring participation. *Social Science Medicine,* vol. 26, no. 9, pp. 931–40.

Ringen, K., 1979. Edwin Chadwick, the market ideology and sanitary reform: On the nature of the 19th-centruy public health movement. *International Journal of Health Services,* vol. 9, no. 1, pp. 107–20.

Rissel, C., 1994. Empowerment: The holy grail of health promotion? *Health Promotion International,* vol. 9, no. 1, pp. 39–47.

Rissel, C., Perry, C. & Finnegan, J., 1996. Toward the assessment of psychological empowerment in health promotion: Initial tests of validity and reliability. *Journal of the Royal Society of Health,* vol. 116, no. 4, pp. 211–18.

Rootman, I., Goodstadt, M., Potvin, L. & Springett, J., eds 2001. *A framework for health promotion evaluation.* Copenhagen: WHO Regional Publications, European Series.

Roughan, J.J., 1986. *Village organization for development.* Honolulu: University of Hawaii, Department of Political Science, PhD.

Ruger, J.P., 2006. Ethics and governance of global health inequalities. *Journal of Epidemiology and Community Health,* vol. 60, no. 11, pp. 998–1002.

Sachs J., 2007. *Beware False Tradeoffs* [Online.] http://www.foreignaffairs.org/special/global_health/sachs].

Sandler, T. & Arce, D., 2000. *A conceptual framework for understanding global and transnational goods for health, paper WG2:1.* Cambridge: Commission on Macroeconomics and Health. [Online]. http://www.cmhealth.org/docs/wg2_paper1.pdf (Accessed 27 May 2003).

Seedhouse, D., 1997. *Health promotion: Philosophy, prejudice and practice.* New York/Toronto: Wiley & Sons.

Seligman, M., 1975. *Helplessness: On depression, development and death.* San Francisco: W.H. Freeman.

Sen, A., 1999. *Development as freedom.* New York: Knopf.

Sen, A., 2000. Freedom's market. *The Observer,* 25 June.

Sinclair, S. 2006. *The GATS and South Africa's national health act: A cautionary tale.* Canadian Centre for Policy Alternatives, Ottawa. Available online: http://www.policyalternatives.ca/Reports/2005/11/ReportsStudies1244/

Singh, J. Amir, Govender, M. & Mills, E., 2007. Do human rights matter to health? *The Lancet,* vol. 370, no. 9586, 11 August.

Solt, F., 2004. *Economic inequality and democratic political engagement.* [Online]. Houston: Rice University. http://www.unc.edu/~fredsolt/papers/Solt2004MPSA.pdf [Accessed 1 February 2005].

Soucat, A., Levy-Bruhl, D. & De Bethune, X., 1997. Affordability, cost-effectiveness and efficiency of primary health care: The Bamako Initiative experience in Benin and Guniea. *International Journal of Health Planning and Management,* vol. 12, no. 1, pp. 81–108.

Smithies, J. & Webster, G., 1998. *Community involvement in health.* England: Ashgate Publishing Limited.

Starhawk, M.S., 1987. *Truth or dare.* New York: Harper and Row Publishers.

Starhawk, M.S., 1988. *Truth or dare: Encounters with power, authority and mystery.* San Francisco: Harper Books.

Sudhakumari, V.M., 2002. *Globalization, economic reforms and agrarian distress in India: A Study of cotton farmer's suicide in Warangal district.* Paper presented to 2002 GDN Award for Research Papers, University of Kerala, Kariacattom Campus, Thiruvananthapuram, India.

Szreter, S., 2003. Health and security in historical perspective. In L. Chen et al. eds, *Global health challenges for human security.* Cambridge: Global Equity Initiative, Asia Center, Harvard University.

Tax Justice Network, 2005. *Briefing Paper – The Price of Offshore.* http://www.taxjustice.net/cms/upload/pdf/Price_of_Offshore.pdf [Accessed 5 May 2007].

Tax Justice Network, 2007. *Closing the Floodgates.* http://www.taxjustice.net/cms/upload/pdf/Closing_the_Floodgates_-_1-FEB-2007.pdf [Accessed 5 May 2007].

Taylor, R. & Rieger, A., 1985. Medicine as social science: Rudolf Virchow on the typhus epidemic in Upper Silesia. *International Journal of Health Services,* vol. 15, no. 4, pp. 547–59.

Taylor, S., 2007. *Aid and health.* Background Paper for the Globalization Knowledge Network, World Health Organization Comission on Social Determinants of Health, [Online]. http://www.globalhealthequity.ca/projects/proj_WHO/index.shtml

Teeple, G., 2000. *Globalization and the decline of social reform: Into the 21st century,* 2nd edition. Aurora, Ontario: Garamond Press.

Tenbensel, T., 2006. *Interest groups, in New Zealand government and politics.* Auckland: Oxford University Press.

Tenbensel, T. & Davis, P., (forthcoming). Public health sciences and policy in high income countries. In R. Detels et al. eds, *Oxford Textbook of Public Health.* Oxford: Oxford University Press.

Thieren, M., 2007. Health and foreign policy in question: The case of humanitarian action. *Bulletin of the World Health Organization,* vol. 85, no. 3, pp. 218–24.

Thorbecke, E. & Nissanke, M., 2006. Introduction: The impact of globalization on the world's poor. *World Development,* vol. 34, pp. 1333–7.

Toronto Department of Public Health, 1994. *Making communities.* Toronto: Department of Public Health.

Torres, R., 2001. *Towards a socially sustainable world economy: An analysis of the social pillars of globalization.* Geneva: International Labour Office.

Transnationale Report on Roche, 2007. http://www.transnationale.org/companies/roche.php [Accessed May 1, 2007].

Trinh H.V., Luong, X.H., Hoang, T.L., Le, T.T., Nuygen, D.H., Le, D.C., Ta, H.T., Doan, T. T. & Nuygen, N.T., 1999. *KAP study on school sanitation and control of worm infection. Ministry of Health.* Thai Binh Medical College, Thai Binh, Vietnam.

Truman, D.B., 1951. *The governmental process.* New York: Alfred Knopf Press.

Tudor Hart, J., 1971. The inverse care law. *The Lancet*, i, pp. 405–12.

UN Economic and Social Council Committee on Economic, Social and Cultural Rights. *The right to the highest attainable standard of health : 11/08/2000. E/C. 12/2000/4. (General Comments)*: Substantive Issues Arising in the Implementation of the International Covenant on Economic, Social and Cultural Rights. General Comment No. 14 (2000) The right to the highest attainable standard of health (article 12 of the International Covenant on Economic, Social and Cultural Rights) http://www.fao.org/righttofood/kc/downloads/v1/docs/AH354.pdf [Accessed July 2, 1008].

UNICEF, 2001. *Effective information, education and communication (IEC) in Viet Nam: A literature review.* Hanoi: UNICEF.

UNICEF, 2007. *Child protection information sheets.* New York: United Nations Children Fund.

UNCTAD (United Nations Conference on Trade and Development), 2004. Economic development in Africa: Debt sustainability: Oasis or mirage? [Online]. New York: United Nations. http://www.unctad.org/en/docs/iteiit20048_en.pdf [Accessed 1 February 2005].

UNCTAD, 2007. *Annual Report 2006.* [Online]. http://www.unctad.org/en/docs/dom20071_en.pdf

United Nations Economic and Social Council, 2003. *Globalization and its impact on the full enjoyment of human rights.* http://hei.unige.ch/~clapham/hrdoc/docs/globalizationbsubcomfinalareport.pdf [Accessed 7 May 2007].

UN Habitat (United Nations Human Settlements Programe), 2003. *Slums of the world: The face of urban poverty in the new millennium?* Nairobi: UN Habitat. http://www.unhabitat.org/publication/slumreport.pdf [Accessed 1 February 2005].

United Nations Millennium Development Goals http://unmp.forumone.com/eng_full_report/TF1mainreportComplete-highres.pdf [Accessed 1 November 2007].

United Nations Millennium Project, 2005. *Investing in development: A practical plan to achieve the Millennium Development Goals.* London: Earthscan. http://unmp.forumone.com/eng_full_report/TF1mainreportComplete-highres.pdf [Accessed 1 February 2005].

Uphoff, N., 1991. A field methodology for participatory self-education. *Community Development Journal*, vol. 26, no. 4, pp. 271–85.

Urban Settlements Knowledge Network (USKN-KNUS), 2007. *Final Report* [Online]. http://www.who.int/social_determinants/knowledge_networks/settlements/en/

US National Intelligence Council, 2002. *The Global Infectious Disease Threat and Its Implications for the United States*, National Intelligence Estimate NIE99-17D Available online: http://www.cia.gov/cia/publications/nie/report/nie99–17d.html, [Accessed 5 August 2002].

Van Doorslaer, E., O'Donnell, O., Rannan-Eliya, R.P., Somanathan, A., Adhikari, S. R. & Garg, C. C., 2006. Effect of payments for health care on poverty estimates in 11 countries in Asia: An analysis of household survey data. *The Lancet*, vol. 368, pp. 1357–64.

Vidal, J., 2007a. *Organic label for fair trade only. The Guardian Weekly*, 2 November.
Vidal, J., 2007b. Climate change and shortages of fuel signal global food crisis. *The Guardian Weekly*, 9 November.
Wade R.H., 2002. Globalisation, poverty and income distribution: Does the liberal argument hold? In D. Gruen et al. eds *Globalisation, living standards and inequality: Recent progress and continuing challenges, proceedings of a conference held in Sydney, 27–28 May 2002.* Canberra: Reserve Bank of Australia, 37–65 http://www.rba.gov.au/PublicationsAndResearch/Conferences/2002/ [Accessed 1 February 2005].
Wade R.H., 2003. Bridging the digital divide: New route to development or new form of dependency. *Global Governance*, vol. 8, pp. 443–66.
Wadsworth, Y. & McGuiness, M., 1992. *Understanding anytime: A consumer evaluation of acute psychiatric hospitals.* Melbourne, Victoria, Australia: Victorian Mental Illness Awareness Council (VMIAC).
Wagstaff, A. Watanabe, N. & van Doorslaer, E., 2001. *Impoverishment, insurance, and health care payments.* Washington, DC: World Bank.
Wallack, L. (2005) Media advocacy: A strategy for empowering people and communities in Minkler, M. (ed.) *Community Organizing and Community Building for Health.* 2nd edition. New York: Rutgers University Press. pp. 419–32.
Wallerstein, N. & Bernstein, E., 1988. Empowerment education: Freire's ideas adapted to health education. *Health Education Quarterly*, vol. 15, no. 4, pp. 379–94.
Wallerstein, N. & Bernstein, E., 1994. Introduction to community empowerment, participatory education and health. *Health Education Quarterly*, vol. 21, no. 2, pp. 141–8.
Walsh, J.A. & Warren, K.S., 1979. Selective primary health care: An interim strategy for disease control in developing countries. *The Lancet.* Vol. 301, no. 18, pp. 967–74.
Walt, G., 1994. *Health policy: An introduction to process and power.* London: Zed Books.
Wang, C. Yi, W.K. Tao, Z.W. & Carvano, K., 1998. Photovoice as a participatory health promotion strategy. *Health Promotion International.* vol. 13, no. 1, pp. 75–86.
Wartenberg, T., 1990. *The forms of power: From domination to transformation.* Philadelphia: Temple University Press.
Waters, S., 2004. Mobilising against globalisation: ATTAC and the French intellectuals. *West European Politics*, vol. 27, pp. 854–74.
Weisbrot, M., 2007. Changes in Latin America: Consequences for human development. *International Journal of Health Services*, vol. 37, no. 3, pp. 477–500.
Weisbrot, M., Baker, D., Kraev, E. & Chen, J., 2001. *The scorecard on globalization 1980–2000: Twenty Years of diminished progress.* Centre for Economic and Policy Research. http://www.cepr.net/globalization/scorecard_on_globalization.htm [Accessed 29 September 2002].
Wente, M., 2007. No rejoicing, bringing in the sheaves. *The Globe and Mail.* 8 September.
Werner, D. & Sanders, D., 1997. *Questioning the solution: The politics of primary health care and child survival: With an in-depth critique of Oral Rehydration Therapy.* Palo Alto: Healthwrights.
Wilkinson, R.G. & Marmot, M., eds, 2003. *Social determinants of health: The solid facts.* 2nd edition. Copenhagen: WHO Regional Office for Europe.
Wood, A., 2006. *IMF macroeconomic policies and health sector budgets.* [Online]. Amsterdam: Wemos Foundation. http://www.wemos.nl/Documents/wemos_synthesis_report.pdf.

Woodward, D., 2005. The GATS and trade in health services: Implications for health care in developing countries. *Review of International Political Economy*, vol. 12, no. 3, pp. 511–34.

Woodward, D., 2007. *Towards a pro-health model of development*. Personal correspondence with R. Labonté, September–November 2007.

Woodward, D. & Simms, A., 2006. *Growth is failing the poor: The unbalanced distribution of the benefits and costs of global economic growth*. New York: United Nations Department of Economic and Social Affairs.

Woodward, D. & Smith, R., 2003. Global public goods and health: Concepts and issues. In R. Smith, R. Beaglehole, D. Woodward & N. Drager. eds, *Global public goods for health: Health economic and public health perspectives*. Oxford: Oxford University Press.

World Bank Data from Econstats, [Online.] http://www.econstats.com/wb/index_glwb.htm. Graph prepared by Ted Schrecker

World Bank, 1993. *World development report 1993: Investing in health*. Washington DC: World Bank.

World Bank, 2006. *Strengthening Mutual Accountability, Aid, Trade, and Governance*. Washington, DC: World Bank.

World Bank. *Global economic prospects 2007: Managing the next wave of globalization*. 2007. Washington, DC: World Bank.

World Commission on the Social Dimension of Globalization (WCSDG), 2004. *A fair globalization: Creating opportunities for all*. Geneva: International Labor Organization. http://www.ilo.org/public/english/wcsdg/docs/report.pdf [Accessed 1 February 2005].

World Health Organization (WHO), 1946. Preamble to the Constitution of the World Health Organization as adopted by the International Health Conference, New York, 19–22 June, 1946; signed on 22 July 1946 by the representatives of 61 States (Official Records of the World Health Organization, no. 2, p. 100) and entered into force on 7 April 1948. Geneva: World Health Organization.

World Health Organization (WHO), 1978. *Health for all: Alma-Ata declaration*. Geneva: World Health Organization.

World Health Organization (WHO), 1986. *Ottawa Charter for health promotion*. Ottawa: World Health Organisation, Health and Welfare Canada, Canadian Public Health Association.

World Health Organization (WHO), 2005. *The Bangkok Charter for Health Promotion*. Geneva: World Health Organization.

World Health Organization (WHO), 2007. *Achieving health equity: From root causes to fair outcomes*. Geneva: World Health Organization, Commission on Social Determinants of Health.

Wray, R., 2007. God and Mammon. *Guardian Weekly*, Feb 9–15, p. 26.

Wright R.A., 2004. *A short history of progress*. Toronto: House of Anansi Press.

Yeatman, A., 1998. *Activism and the policy process*. Sydney: Allen & Unwin.

Zakus, J.D.L. & Lysack, C.L., 1998. Revisiting community participation. *Health Policy and Planning*, vol. 13, no. 1, pp. 1–12.

Zimmerman, M.A., 1990. Taking aim on empowerment research: On the distinction between individual and psychological conceptions. *American Journal of Community Psychology*, vol. 18, no. 1, pp. 169–77.

Zimmerman, M.A. & Rappaport, J., 1988. Citizen participation, perceived control and psychological empowerment. *American Journal of Community Psychology*, vol. 16, no. 5, pp. 725–43.

Index